THE CARTOON HISTORY
OF THE
UNITED STATES

Also by Larry Gonick

The Cartoon History of the Universe
The Cartoon Guide to Physics (with Art Huffman)
The Cartoon Guide to the Computer
The Cartoon Guide to Genetics (with Mark Wheelis)

THE CARTOON HISTORY
OF THE
UNITED STATES

Larry Gonick

Harper Perennial

A Division of HarperCollins Publishers

FIRST HARPERPERENNIAL edition published 1991.

Library of Congress Catalog Card Number 91-55037

ISBN 0-06-273098-3

92 93 94 95 RRD 10 9 8 7 6 5

CONTENTS

ABOUT THE AUTHOR: LARRY GONICK IS THE AUTHOR OR CO-AUTHOR OF A NUMBER OF WORKS OF GRAPHIC NON-FICTION, INCLUDING **THE CARTOON GUIDE TO GENETICS, THE CARTOON GUIDE TO THE COMPUTER, THE CARTOON GUIDE TO PHYSICS,** AND **THE CARTOON HISTORY OF THE UNIVERSE.** HE LIVES WITH HIS WIFE, KIDS, AND DOG, AND COMMUTES DAILY HALF A MILE BY AUTOMOBILE...

FEELIN' GUILTY!

THE CARTOON HISTORY OF THE UNITED STATES

PART I
(1585 - 1865)

·PROLOGUE·

WHO FOUND IT?

MERICA WAS DISCOVERED SO LONG AGO THAT NO ONE CAN REMEMBER THE DETAILS...

ꓯT APPEARS TO HAVE HAPPENED ABOUT 15,000 YEARS AGO, WHEN A TRIBE OF SIBERIANS OR MONGOLIANS CROSSED A LAND BRIDGE THAT JOINED ASIA TO ALASKA AT THE TIME.

ꓔHE LAND BRIDGE SANK, AND THE VISITORS STAYED...

THIS SURE BEATS SIBERIA!

SOME 2000 YEARS AGO, A
CHINESE SHIP DROPPED ANCHOR
OFF SOUTHERN CALIFORNIA —
LITERALLY "DROPPED": THE
ANCHOR IS STILL THERE...

OOP!

VISIT GREENLAND! BUY INTO GREENLAND!

IN A.D 985 THE VIKING **ERIC THE RED** LANDED ON A GLACIAL BLOCK HE PROMOTED AS "GREENLAND." HIS SON **LEIF ERICSSON** SAILED TO THE AMERICAN MAINLAND, NAMING IT "VINLAND." THE VINLAND COLONY FAILED, DUE TO A SHORTAGE OF "VIN."

AT LEAST IN ICELAND, YOU KNOW WHAT TO EXPECT...

THERE'S ALSO A CONFUSED, POETIC ACCOUNT OF A
POSSIBLE ATLANTIC CROSSING BY AN IRISH MONK...

THE VIKINGS WENT THAT WAY!

CHRISTOPHER COLUMBUS WAS THE MAN IN THE RIGHT PLACE AT THE RIGHT TIME. HIS "DISCOVERY" CAME IN 1492, JUST AS EUROPE WAS EMERGING FROM THE MIDDLE AGES.

FOR HUNDREDS OF YEARS, EUROPEAN CHRISTIANS HAD BEEN CRUSADING AGAINST MUSLIMS... IN THAT VERY SAME 1492, THE LAST MUSLIMS WERE EXPELLED FROM SPAIN... BUT CENTURIES OF CONTACT HAD LEFT THE SPANIARDS WITH TWO THINGS: A TASTE FOR SPICY ARAB FOOD, AND THE KNOWLEDGE THAT SPICES WERE THE MOST PROFITABLE ITEM OF COMMERCE KNOWN TO MAN !!

THE NATION THAT CONTROLS PEPPER WILL CONTROL THE WORLD!

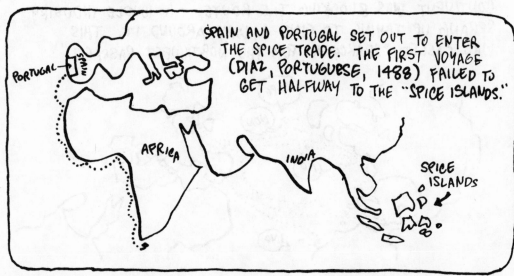

SPAIN AND PORTUGAL SET OUT TO ENTER THE SPICE TRADE. THE FIRST VOYAGE (DIAZ, PORTUGUESE, 1488) FAILED TO GET HALFWAY TO THE "SPICE ISLANDS."

PORTUGAL — SPAIN

AFRICA

INDIA

SPICE ISLANDS

SPAIN, HOPING FOR A SHORT-CUT, SPONSORED COLUMBUS, WHOSE IDEA WAS TO REACH THE EAST BY HEADING WEST.

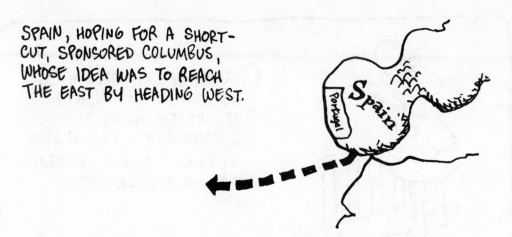

OF COURSE, HE BUMPED INTO AMERICA, ASSUMED IT WAS THE (EAST) INDIES, AND CALLED THE INHABITANTS "INDIANS."

WHEN THE TRUTH WAS REALIZED — THAT AN UNKNOWN, SPICELESS CONTINENT WAS BLOCKING THE ROUTE — A WHOLE INDUSTRY SPRANG UP TRYING TO FIND A WAY AROUND IT. THIS WAS CALLED "SEARCHING FOR THE NORTHWEST PASSAGE."

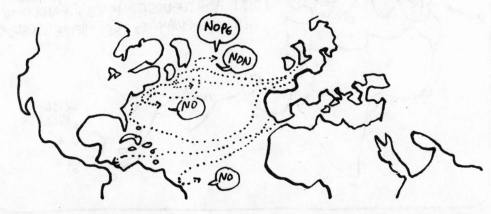

THE SPANIARDS HAD ANOTHER IDEA...
THE IDEA OF COLONIZATION... THEY
CONQUERED MOST OF CENTRAL AND
SOUTH AMERICA, LOOTED THE GOLD
OF MEXICO AND PERU, ESTABLISHED
SLAVE PLANTATIONS IN THE
CARIBBEAN, AND MADE SPAIN THE
MOST SPLENDID NATION IN EUROPE.

SPAIN'S RIVALS, ENGLAND, FRANCE, AND HOLLAND, ALL WATCHED
JEALOUSLY.

IT'S JOLLY UNFAIR!

BUT THEY WERE STILL TOO POOR, POWERLESS, OR PREOCCUPIED
TO MAKE A MOVE. IT WAS ALMOST 100 YEARS AFTER
COLUMBUS BEFORE ENGLAND PLANTED HER FIRST COLONY
IN THE NEW WORLD...

...AND THAT IS WHERE OUR STORY BEGINS...

The arriual of the Englifhemen
in Virginia.

• CHAPTER ONE •
IN WHICH ENGLAND PLANTS THIS AND THAT

IN 1585, THE FIRST ENGLISH COLONISTS ARRIVED ON ROANOKE ISLAND, VIRGINIA.

(NOW IT'S NORTH CAROLINA; THEN IT WAS VIRGINIA.)

THE COLONY WAS SUPPOSED TO BE A PROFIT·MAKING ENTERPRISE, BUT IT WAS FAR FROM OBVIOUS WHAT VIRGINIA'S SOURCE OF WEALTH WAS SUPPOSED TO BE...

ONE THING VIRGINIA DEFINITELY HAD WAS A POPULATION. IT WENT BACK AT LEAST AS FAR AS THE LAST ICE AGE, AND, AT THIS POINT, SAW NO REASON TO MAKE WAY FOR A SECOND SET OF FIRST FAMILIES...

BY 1590, THE ROANOKE COLONY HAD BECOME THE LOST COLONY.

NOTHING ELSE HAPPENED UNTIL 1602, WHEN A SEA CAPTAIN WITH THE MUSICAL NAME OF BARTHOLOMEW GOSNOLD ARRIVED, JUST AFTER DROPPING THE NAME "CAPE COD" ON NEW ENGLAND'S BIGGEST SPIT.

PREFERRING THE FRAGRANCE OF WILDFLOWERS TO THE AROMA OF DRYING CODFISH, GOSNOLD DECIDED TO ORGANIZE A SECOND EFFORT IN VIRGINIA. IN 1607, 100 COLONISTS ARRIVED, BUILT A FORT, AND CALLED IT JAMESTOWN.

DESPITE THE FORT, 2/3 OF THE SETTLERS DIED, MOSTLY OF DISEASE AND STARVATION, INCLUDING CAPT. GOSNOLD. THE REST LIVED ON HANDOUTS FROM THE "ENEMY."

AFTER THIS SECOND DISASTER, THE COLONY'S SPONSORS HAD AN ATTACK OF CONFUSION. WHAT WAS VIRGINIA GOOD FOR, ANYWAY??

LET'S LOOK ON THE BRIGHT SIDE!!

RE-EVALUATING THEIR GOALS, THEY CONSOLED THEMSELVES WITH THE THOUGHT THAT VIRGINIA WAS HELPING DISPOSE OF ENGLAND'S "SURPLUS POPULATION."

THEY QUICKLY PACKED OFF 500 MORE VOLUNTEERS, OF WHOM MORE THAN 400 PROMPTLY DIED.

INSTANT SUCCESS!

WHAT ARE THEY TRYING TO GROW HERE?

CROSSES?

10

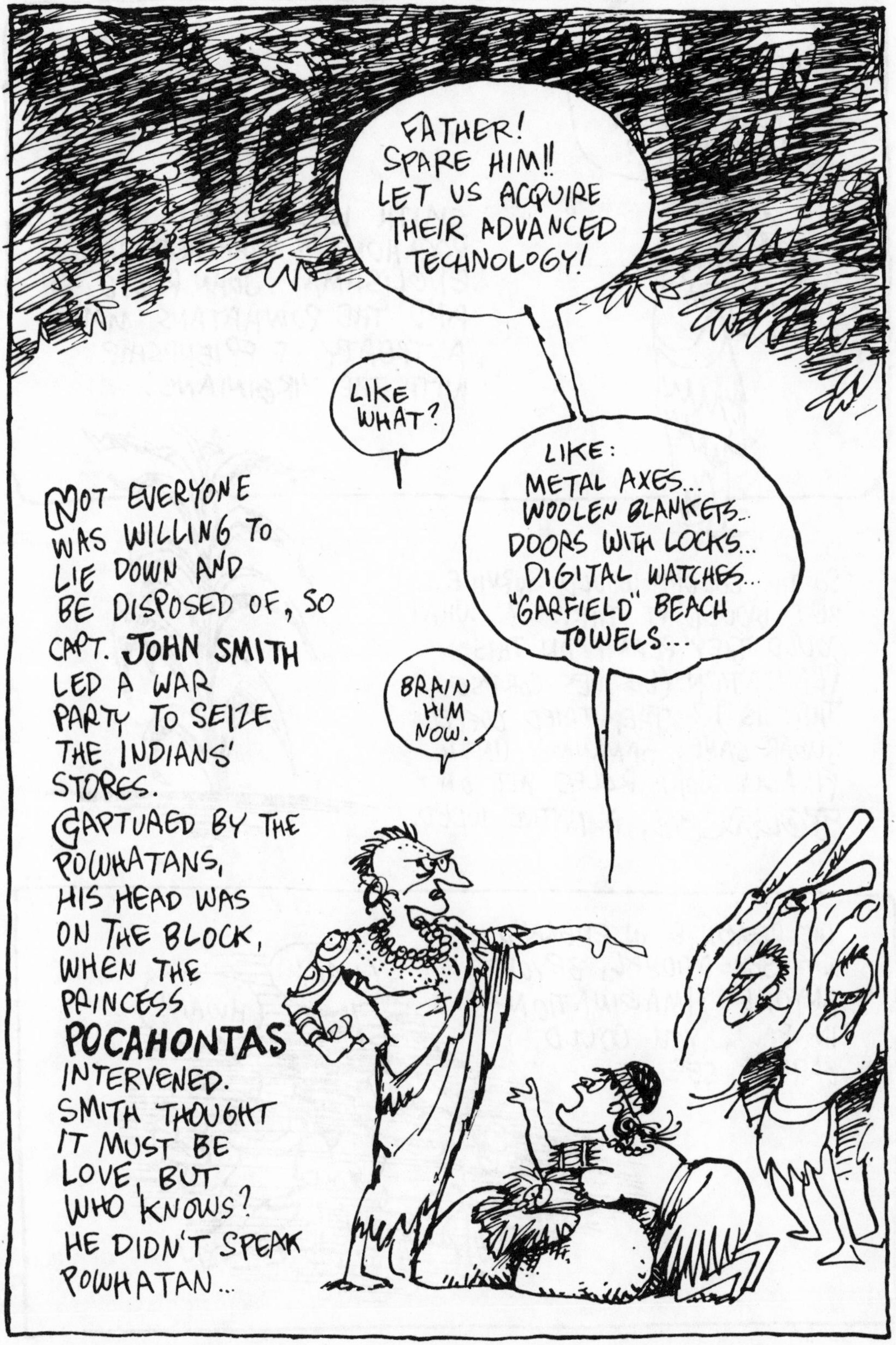
FATHER! SPARE HIM!! LET US ACQUIRE THEIR ADVANCED TECHNOLOGY!
LIKE WHAT?
LIKE: METAL AXES... WOOLEN BLANKETS... DOORS WITH LOCKS... DIGITAL WATCHES... "GARFIELD" BEACH TOWELS...
BRAIN HIM NOW.
NOT EVERYONE WAS WILLING TO LIE DOWN AND BE DISPOSED OF, SO CAPT. JOHN SMITH LED A WAR PARTY TO SEIZE THE INDIANS' STORES.
CAPTURED BY THE POWHATANS, HIS HEAD WAS ON THE BLOCK, WHEN THE PRINCESS POCAHONTAS INTERVENED. SMITH THOUGHT IT MUST BE LOVE, BUT WHO KNOWS? HE DIDN'T SPEAK POWHATAN...

STILL, HOW CAN YOU TRUST A MAN WHO CALLS HIMSELF "JOHN SMITH"?

SMITH WAS SPARED... POCAHONTAS MARRIED THE ENGLISHMAN JOHN ROLFE... AND THE POWHATANS MADE A TREATY OF FRIENDSHIP WITH THE VIRGINIANS.

SO THE COLONY WOULD SURVIVE... BUT WOULD IT THRIVE? WHAT COULD THEY PLANT ON THIS PLANTATION (BESIDES CORPSES, THAT IS)? THEY TRIED COFFEE, SUGAR CANE, BANANAS... UNTIL FINALLY JOHN ROLFE HIT ON *TOBACCO*, A NATIVE WEED.

THE RESPONSE IN ENGLAND WAS SENSATIONAL, BEYOND ANYONE'S IMAGINATION— IN FACT, YOU COULD BARELY SEE IT.

KAF!

HWAK!

THE DEMAND FOR TOBACCO WAS SO GREAT THAT VIRGINIANS BEGAN TO HAVE HOPE. TOBACCO PLANTATIONS SPROUTED EVERYWHERE, AS THE INDIANS' SACRED WEED BECAME THE COLONY'S STAPLE CROP.

NOW THEY'VE BECOME INSANELY RELIGIOUS!

THE STUFF WAS EVERYWHERE... IT DOMINATED VIRGINIA'S ECONOMY FOR CENTURIES. THROUGHOUT THE COLONIAL PERIOD, TOBACCO WAS USED AS MONEY IN VIRGINIA!

CAN YOU CHANGE A HOGSHEAD?

EVENTUALLY, ALL AMERICA BECAME ADDICTED TO SMOKING, SNIFFING, OR CHEWING. AS LATE AS 1832, AN ENGLISH VISITOR OBSERVED THAT CHEWING AND SPITTING WERE UNIVERSAL IN AMERICA.

IT'S A =PTOO= PATRIOTIC DUTY!

(EVEN TODAY THE TOBACCO INDUSTRY RECEIVES GOVERNMENT SUBSIDIES!)

IF ONLY THE DEAD COULD WORK!

THE DEMAND FOR TOBACCO ALSO CREATED A DEMAND FOR LABOR. THE INDIANS WEREN'T WILLING TO SERVE THE PEOPLE WHO WERE PLOWING UP THE HUNTING GROUNDS, AND THERE WEREN'T ENOUGH ENGLISH TO GO AROUND.

AND SO, IN 1619, THE FIRST BLACK SLAVES WERE PURCHASED.

SLAVE LABOR HAD ITS ADVANTAGES: THE SLAVE, BEING BOUND FOR LIFE, WOULD NEVER QUIT TO START HIS OR HER OWN PLANTATION... SLAVES COULD BE IMPORTED AT WILL, WHEREAS WHITES ONLY CAME TO VIRGINIA WHEN THEY WANTED TO *... SO SLAVEOWNING SPREAD.

IT'S AS ADDICTIVE AS TOBACCO!

* MORE OR LESS... SEE BELOW.

14

IRONICALLY, AMERICA'S DEMOCRATIC INSTITUTIONS BEGAN IN THE SAME YEAR AS SLAVERY. IN 1619, VIRGINIA TAXPAYERS ORGANIZED THE **HOUSE OF BURGESSES,** COLONIAL AMERICA'S FIRST ELECTED LEGISLATURE.

WHAT IS A "BURGESS"?

I DON'T KNOW WHAT IT IS, BUT I KNOW WHAT IT ISN'T...

THE ONLY ELIGIBLE VOTERS WERE WHITE, MALE LANDOWNERS.

EVEN THAT WAS TOO DEMOCRATIC FOR KING JAMES. HE DECIDED TO ABOLISH THE HOUSE OF BURGESSES, BUT DIED BEFORE MAKING THE MOVE. THE BUDDING DEMOCRACY SURVIVED, AND VIRGINIA'S BASIC WAY OF LIFE WAS ESTABLISHED.

A SLAVING, CARCINOGENIC COLONY WITH REPRESENTATIVE GOVERNMENT!

Why, YOU MAY ASK, WOULD ANY SANE PERSON LEAVE ENGLAND FOR VIRGINIA? GOOD QUESTION!! WELL, IT SEEMS THAT "MERRIE ENGLAND" WAS LOSING ITS SENSE OF HUMOR, AS LANDLORDS EVICTED FARMERS BY THE THOUSANDS, FORCING THEM TO FACE SOME VERY TOUGH CHOICES...

THERE AREN'T ANY JOBS IN THE CITY...

IF YOU GO TOO FAR INTO DEBT, IT'S JAIL FOR SURE!

I'M TOO PROUD TO BEG...

SO I STOLE A LOAF OF BREAD AND WAS SENTENCED TO DEATH...

THEN THEY OFFERED ME A CHOICE BETWEEN HANGING AND VIRGINIA...

I CHOSE HANGING.

I'D RATHER BE IN HELL IN TWO MINUTES THAN VIRGINIA IN 30 DAYS!

TRULY, WE ARE BLEST WITH A BENEVOLENT GOVERNMENT!

ON TOP OF THIS, THE CHURCH OF ENGLAND WAS **ESTABLISHED**— MEANING TAX-SUPPORTED AND GOVERNMENT-REGULATED. ITS MINISTERS WERE LICENSED, AND THEIR SALARIES WERE PAID BY THE STATE.

ALL OTHER CHURCHES WERE BANNED BY LAW.

THAT MAKES SENSE! HOW CAN MORE THAN ONE RELIGION BE TRUE?

HOW ABOUT

LESS THAN

ONE?

EVEN SO, ALL MANNER OF UNLICENSED CHURCHES SPRANG UP: BAPTISTS, QUAKERS, PRESBYTERIANS, FIFTH MONARCHISTS, THE BROTHERHOOD OF LOVE... THESE WERE THE PROTEST MOVEMENTS OF THE EARLY 1600'S.

WE DON'T HAVE RADIO STATIONS OR NEWSPAPERS, ONLY PULPITS!

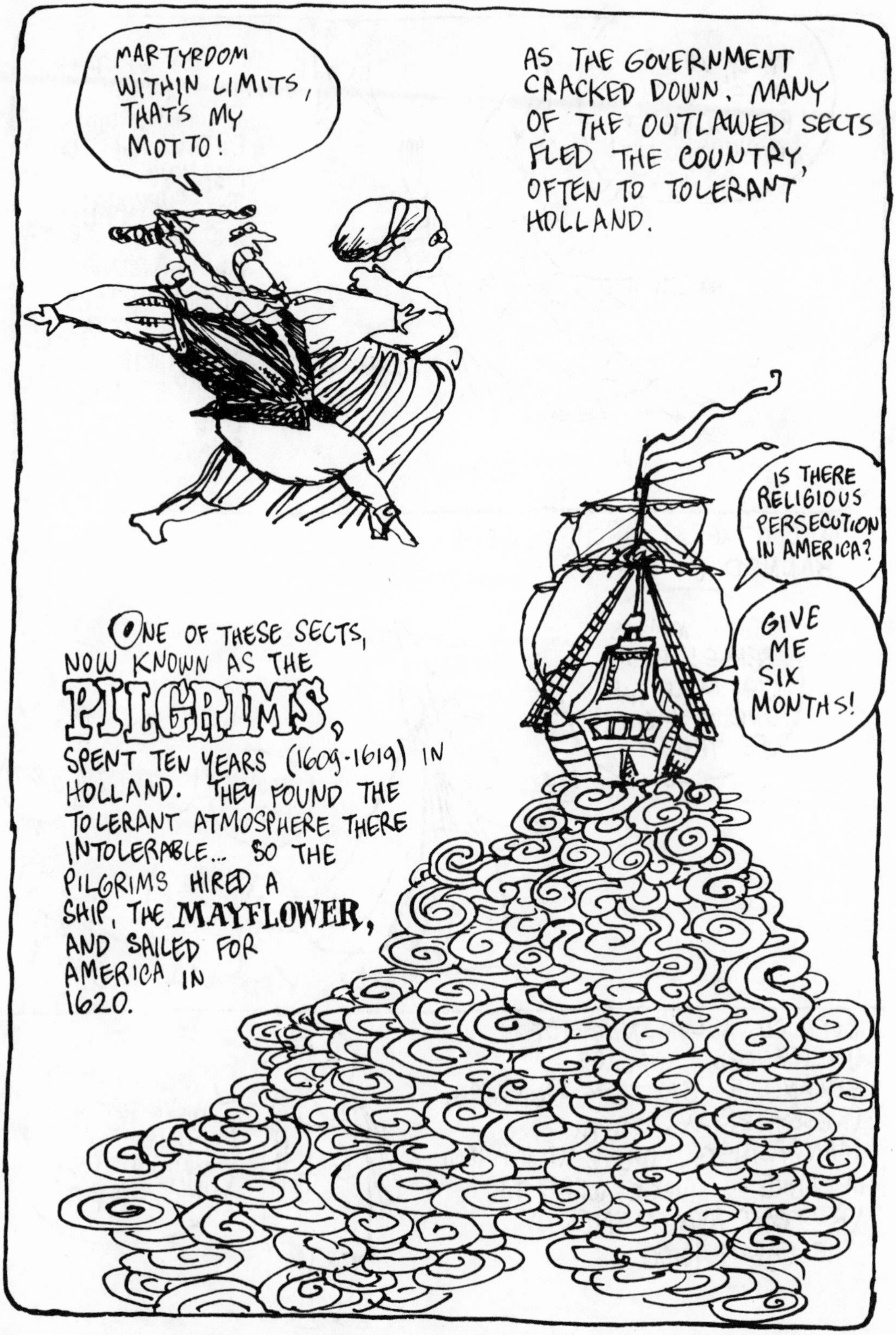
MARTYRDOM WITHIN LIMITS, THAT'S MY MOTTO!
AS THE GOVERNMENT CRACKED DOWN, MANY OF THE OUTLAWED SECTS FLED THE COUNTRY, OFTEN TO TOLERANT HOLLAND.
ONE OF THESE SECTS, NOW KNOWN AS THE PILGRIMS, SPENT TEN YEARS (1609-1619) IN HOLLAND. THEY FOUND THE TOLERANT ATMOSPHERE THERE INTOLERABLE... SO THE PILGRIMS HIRED A SHIP, THE MAYFLOWER, AND SAILED FOR AMERICA IN 1620.
IS THERE RELIGIOUS PERSECUTION IN AMERICA?
GIVE ME SIX MONTHS!

WHILE STILL ON SHIPBOARD, THE COLONISTS SIGNED THE

MAYFLOWER COMPACT,

A WRITTEN AGREEMENT TO ABIDE BY THE RULES OF THE COLONY.

THE COMPACT'S HISTORICAL SIGNIFICANCE IS IN WHAT IT IMPLIED:

THAT A GOVERNMENT DEPENDS ON THE CONSENT OF THE GOVERNED — A RADICAL CONCEPT IN 1620.

WHAT HAPPENED TO THE DIVINE RIGHT OF KINGS?

LANDING IN MASSACHUSETTS, THE PILGRIMS IMMEDIATELY FOUND THEMSELVES TRIPLY BLESSED:

FIRST, THE AREA HAD JUST BEEN DEPOPULATED BY PLAGUE: THERE WAS NO ONE TO FIGHT.

?

SECOND, ONLY HALF THE COLONISTS DIED THE FIRST WINTER.

IN VIRGINIA, THAT'D BE A POPULATION EXPLOSION...

THIRD, THE AMAZING SQUANTO: A LOCAL PATUXENT, SQUANTO HAD BEEN KIDNAPPED TO ENGLAND IN 1616, MISSED THE PLAGUE, AND RETURNED IN 1619. HE SPOKE FLUENT ENGLISH.

FORSOOTH, WHAT'S HAPPENIN'?

THANKS MAINLY TO SQUANTO'S FARMING TIPS, THE PILGRIMS REAPED A BUMPER CROP IN 1622. THEY CELEBRATED WITH THE FIRST THANKSGIVING, INVITING THE INDIANS TO SHARE THE FEAST.

OR, FROM OUR POINT OF VIEW, THE *LAST* THANKSGIVING!

WHEN...

OOG!

AND FROM OUR POINT OF VIEW?

DESPITE THE FRIENDLY ATMOSPHERE, THE PILGRIMS TRIED TO KEEP THE INDIANS IN AWE. FOR EXAMPLE, THEY HINTED THAT THEY COULD BRING BACK THE PLAGUE, IF NECESSARY.

THE ENDE JUSTIFIETH THE MEANS...

20

BUT IT APPEARED THAT THE PILGRIMS JUST COULDN'T GET AWAY FROM IT ALL! IN 1626 A WILD MAN NAMED **THOMAS MORTON** SET UP SHOP NEARBY AT "MERRYMOUNT" (A NAME WITH DEFINITE GYNECOLOGICAL OVERTONES IN THOSE DAYS), AND HOISTED A MAYPOLE.

A PAGAN ABOMINATION!

PLYMOUTH'S PINT-SIZED CAPTAIN **MYLES STANDISH** MADE A SPECIAL TRIP TO TEAR IT DOWN...

* * * * * * * * * * * * * * * * * * *

OTHER NEIGHBORS IN THOSE QUAINT DAYS INCLUDED VARIOUS FISHERMEN UP IN NEW HAMPSHIRE AND MAINE, SAMUEL MAVERICK, ANCESTOR OF TEXANS, AND WILLIAM BLAXTON OF SHAWMUT, WHO TRAINED A BULL TO RIDE, BECAUSE HE'D FORGOTTEN TO BRING A HORSE...

EE-HAW!

IN 1630 CAME THE DELUGE: 1000 PURITANS, WITH CATTLE, HORSES, SEED, TOOLS, AND BIBLES, LANDED NEAR MODERN BOSTON AND FOUNDED THE COLONY OF *MASSACHUSETTS BAY.*

THE PURITANS ARE COMING!

WHATEVER THEY ARE!

A **PURITAN** WAS SOMEONE TRYING TO "PURIFY" THE ESTABLISHED CHURCH FROM WITHIN (WHEREAS THE PILGRIMS WERE "SEPARATISTS," WHO HAD SPLIT AWAY COMPLETELY).

THE DIFFERENCE BETWEEN A PURITAN AND A SEPARATIST? ABOUT £2000 A YEAR!

THE PURITANS INCLUDED MANY RICH FAMILIES— WHILE SEPARATISTS GENERALLY HAD LESS TO LOSE.

22

Whatever their differences, Puritans and Pilgrims agreed: in their colonies, the laws would be based on Old Testament laws: no work on the Sabbath, an ear for an ear, death to witches, that sort of thing.

ABSOLUTELY NO JIVE!!

THE MASSACHUSETTS MEN SHARPENED THEIR EAR SNIPS, KICKED OUT THOMAS MORTON, FOUNDED HARVARD, SWALLOWED MAINE AND NEW HAMPSHIRE, AND DECLARED ALL NEW ENGLAND A **PURITAN COMMONWEALTH.** IT HAD A TAX-SUPPORTED CHURCH WITH LICENSED MINISTERS, AND NO OTHER CHURCHES WERE ALLOWED!!

IS THERE ANOTHER WAY?

23

SUDDENLY IT BECAME A TREND TO ESCAPE RELIGIOUS PERSECUTION BY FOUNDING AN AMERICAN COLONY.

IT'S CHIC!

LORD BALTIMORE MADE MARYLAND A CATHOLIC HAVEN IN 1634.

ROGER WILLIAMS FLED FROM RELIGIOUS PERSECUTION IN BOSTON (!) TO FOUND RHODE ISLAND IN 1635. WILLIAMS BELIEVED IN COMPLETE SEPARATION OF CHURCH AND STATE, AND RHODE ISLAND BECAME A HAVEN OF RELIGIOUS FREEDOM.

JEWS? YOU'D LET IN JEWS?

JEWS AND TURKS!

IN FACT, OF THE BUNCH OF COLONIES FOUNDED IN THE 1630'S, ONLY CONNECTICUT, IN 1636, WASN'T FORMED WITH THE EXPRESS PURPOSE OF GETTING OUT FROM UNDER SOMEBODY'S THUMB.

◁○ CHAPTER 2 ○▷
NEW COLONIES AND BABY CHICKENS

AS YOU MAY HAVE NOTICED, THE FIRST AMERICAN COLONIES WERE NOT EXACTLY CONCEIVED IN LIBERTY. TWO OF THEM WERE RIGIDLY PURITAN, WHILE THE OTHER WAS ESSENTIALLY A COMMERCIAL VENTURE, AT FIRST.

FREEDOM OF THE PRESS? THE CIDER PRESS, MAYBE!

. . . .

SO WHERE DO WE FIRST HEAR ABOUT THE "LIBERTIES OF ENGLISHMEN"?

THE ANSWER SEEMS TO BE —

WHEN THE RELIGIOUS FRICTION BETWEEN PURITANS AND ESTABLISHMENT EXPLODED INTO THE **ENGLISH CIVIL WAR** (1642 - 1648).

FREEDOM OF THE PRESS, FREEDOM OF WORSHIP, A VOTE FOR "THE POOREST HE" — TOO BAD IT WASN'T THE OFFICIAL PURITAN PROGRAM.

THESE WERE THE DEMANDS OF A SMALL GROUP OF ANTI-ESTABLISHMENT AGITATORS, THE **LEVELLERS.**

"FREEBORN JOHN" LILBURNE, LEVELLER IDEA MAN ←

THE LEVELLERS SPREAD THE WORD... AND SOON THEIR SLOGANS WERE ON THE LIPS — AND PETITIONS — OF THE PURITAN ARMY'S RANK AND FILE, THE "ROUNDHEADS."

IT MADE PERFECT SENSE — WHAT ELSE SHOULD THEY FIGHT FOR?

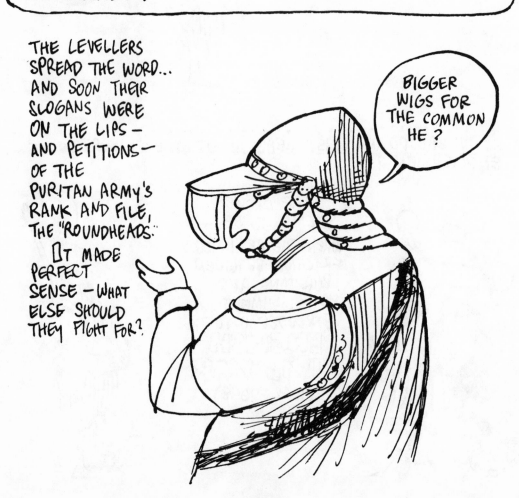

BIGGER WIGS FOR THE COMMON HE?

TOO MANY KOOKS SPOIL THE BROTH!

SECRET LEVELLER PRESSES CRANKED OUT PROPAGANDA... LEVELLER AGITATORS STIRRED UP THE ARMY...

IT WAS TOO MUCH FOR THE PURITAN LEADERS...

THEY SMASHED THE LEVELLER ORGANIZATION AND SENT THE TROOPS TO IRELAND.

'BYE!

PETITION

BUT FRESH IDEAS ARE LIKE BABY CHICKENS: HARD TO PUT BACK IN THE SHELL, ONCE THEY'VE HATCHED.

ACTUALLY, FRESH IDEAS USUALLY LIVE A LOT LONGER THAN BABY CHICKENS...

BUT BACK TO THE CIVIL WAR: THE ROUNDHEADS DEFEATED THE CAVALIERS, AND IN 1649 THEY REMOVED KING CHARLES' HEAD.

HE WASN'T DETACHED ENOUGH!

AS MASSACHUSETTS CHEERED, HORDES OF NOBLEMEN SCURRIED TO VIRGINIA FOR SAFETY. (IT'S STILL KNOWN AS "THE CAVALIER STATE.")

HM! I THOUGHT THAT MEANT MY DEVIL-MAY-CARE ATTITUDE!

IN 1654, SOME DISGUSTED DEMOCRATS LEFT VIRGINIA TO FOUND THEIR OWN COLONY— NORTH CAROLINA.

GIVE ME *LEVELLER* GROUND!

THEN, IN 1660, ENGLAND'S PURITAN EXPERIMENT COLLAPSED. THE THRONE WAS RESTORED TO CHARLES II, WHILE PURITAN REFUGEES FLED TO BOSTON.

WATCH OUT! WIGS ARE MAKING A COMEBACK!

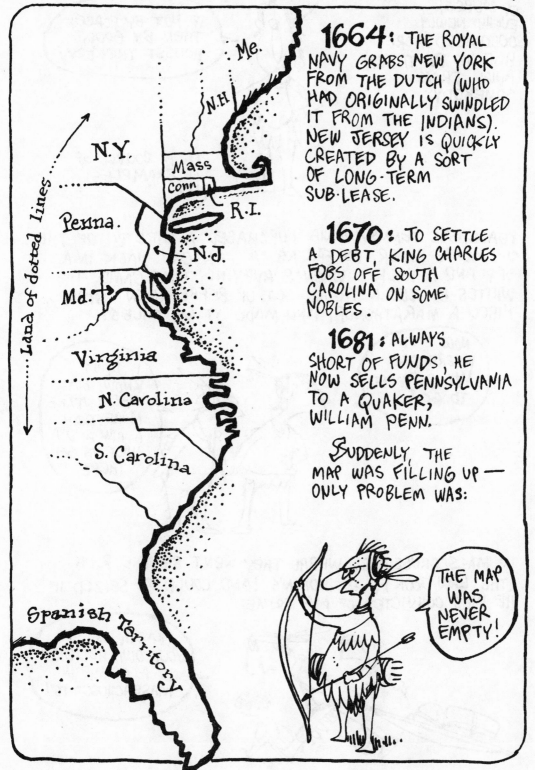

1664: THE ROYAL NAVY GRABS NEW YORK FROM THE DUTCH (WHO HAD ORIGINALLY SWINDLED IT FROM THE INDIANS). NEW JERSEY IS QUICKLY CREATED BY A SORT OF LONG-TERM SUB-LEASE.

1670: TO SETTLE A DEBT, KING CHARLES FOBS OFF SOUTH CAROLINA ON SOME NOBLES.

1681: ALWAYS SHORT OF FUNDS, HE NOW SELLS PENNSYLVANIA TO A QUAKER, WILLIAM PENN.

SUDDENLY, THE MAP WAS FILLING UP — ONLY PROBLEM WAS:

THE MAP WAS NEVER EMPTY!

Me.

N.H.

N.Y.

Mass

Conn

R.I.

Penna.

N.J.

Land of dotted lines

Md.

Virginia

N. Carolina

S. Carolina

Spanish Territory

OF COURSE, EVERY NEWLY COLONIZED ACRE HAD TO BE TAKEN AWAY FROM SOMEBODY.

IF NOT BY FORCE, THEN BY GOOD, HONEST TRICKERY!

A COUPLE OF EXAMPLES:

PEACEABLE PENNSYLVANIA PURCHASED A STRETCH OF THE DELAWARE RIVER, AS FAR AS "A MAN CAN WALK IN A DAY AND A HALF." WHEN SURVEYING TIME CAME, THE WHITES BLAZED A TRAIL, SET UP REFRESHMENT STANDS, HIRED A MARATHONER, AND MADE IT 64 MILES!

NOW WHERE ARE **WE** SUPPOSED TO GO?

I DON'T KNOW, BUT IT'LL TAKE MORE THAN A DAY AND A HALF TO GET THERE..

IN MASSACHUSETTS, WHERE THEY WENT BY THE BOOK (THE LAW BOOK), AN INDIAN'S LAND COULD BE SEIZED IF HE WAS CONVICTED OF ANY CRIME.

PRACTICING YOUR OWN RELIGION IS A CRIME IN MASSACHUSETTS!

IN **1676** THE COLONIES EXPERIENCED SEVERE GROWING PAINS.

THEY GROW, WE HAVE THE PAIN!

"PHILIP'S WAR":

IN MASSACHUSETTS, THE NARRAGANSETT **METACOMET** ("KING PHILIP") LED A GUERRILLA WAR AGAINST THE WHITES. THIS RESULTED IN THE NEAR-EXTERMINATION OF THE NARRAGANSETTS.

METACOMET'S HEAD BECAME A MUSEUM PIECE AT PLYMOUTH.

BACON'S REVOLT:

IN VIRGINIA, A CIVIL WAR ERUPTED WHEN GOV. BERKELEY TRIED TO STOP FARMERS FROM "REMOVING" INDIANS. THE INFURIATED FARMERS BURNED JAMESTOWN.

THEY WANT SLAVES ON INDIAN LAND IN THE NAME OF DEMOCRACY! MIND-BOGGLING!

BACK IN ENGLAND, THE VIRGINIA UPROAR SOUNDED LIKE REVOLUTION— AND THIS WAS 1676, A HUNDRED YEARS AHEAD OF SCHEDULE!

AND VIRGINIA'S ONE OF MY BETTER PROPERTIES!

CHARLES II

MASSACHUSETTS, MEANWHILE, WAS CHRONICALLY DISOBEDIENT. THE BAY COLONY HARBORED THE KILLERS OF CHARLES I, BARRED THE KING'S CHURCH, AND IGNORED THE KING'S TAXES AND REGULATIONS. WHAT WAS A KING TO DO? COLONIES WERE SUPPOSED TO BE LOYAL AND PROFITABLE!!

THESE ROBES ARE EXPENSIVE!

THE KING DISSOLVED THE MASS. GOVERNMENT AND SENT OVER A ROYAL GOVERNOR, WHO WAS QUICKLY JAILED BY THE BOSTON MOB.

MAKE THAT THE "LEGENDARY BOSTON MOB"!

NEVERTHELESS, THE CROWN KEPT THE COLONY, OPENED AN ANGLICAN CHURCH, AND ENDED THE PURITAN MONOPOLY IN MASSACHUSETTS FOREVER.

THIS IS THE DEVIL'S WORK!

IN THIS CLIMATE OF MORAL DEGENERATION, THE PEOPLE BEGAN SEEING WITCHES AT WORK... THE SALEM WITCHCRAFT TRIALS SENT 20 HUMANS AND TWO DOGS TO THEIR DEATHS, BEFORE THINGS CALMED DOWN.

THERE. NOW I FEEL BETTER!

...WHICH BRINGS US TO THE YEAR

1700

(AT LAST! WHEW!)

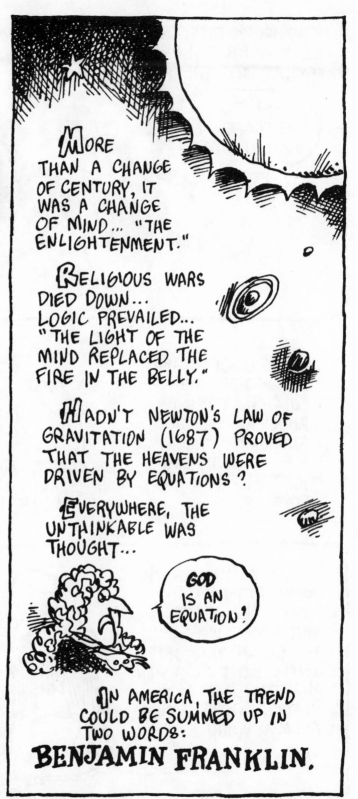

MORE THAN A CHANGE OF CENTURY, IT WAS A CHANGE OF MIND... "THE ENLIGHTENMENT."

RELIGIOUS WARS DIED DOWN... LOGIC PREVAILED... "THE LIGHT OF THE MIND REPLACED THE FIRE IN THE BELLY."

HADN'T NEWTON'S LAW OF GRAVITATION (1687) PROVED THAT THE HEAVENS WERE DRIVEN BY EQUATIONS?

EVERYWHERE, THE UNTHINKABLE WAS THOUGHT...

GOD IS AN EQUATION?

IN AMERICA, THE TREND COULD BE SUMMED UP IN TWO WORDS: BENJAMIN FRANKLIN.

BORN IN BOSTON IN 1706, FRANKLIN GREW UP WITH THE NEW CENTURY.

FOR STARTERS, HE HORRIFIED HIS PURITAN PARENTS BY BECOMING A **DEIST**, WHICH MEANT THAT HE BELIEVED IN A SORT OF ABSTRACT GOD, NOT A BEARDED JEHOVAH IN THE SKY.

ON HIS OWN WORDS:

"**S**INCE THERE IS IN ALL MEN SOMETHING LIKE A NATURAL PRINCIPLE WHICH ENCLINES THEM TO DEVOTION OR THE WORSHIP OF SOME UNSEEN POWER... THEREFORE, I THINK IT SEEMS REQUIRED OF ME, AND MY DUTY AS A MAN, TO PAY DIVINE REGARDS TO **SOMETHING**."

AND: ⬇

"**A**S TO JESUS OF NAZARETH,... I HAVE SOME DOUBTS OF HIS DIVINITY, THO' IT IS A QUESTION I DO NOT DOGMATIZE UPON... I SEE NO HARM, HOWEVER, IN ITS BEING BELIEVED, IF THAT BELIEF HAS THE GOOD CONSEQUENCE, AS IT PROBABLY HAS, OF MAKING HIS DOCTRINES MORE RESPECTED AND BETTER OBSERVED."

"DOUBTS"? "NO HARM"? "IF"? "PROBABLY"? PERFORATE HIS TONGUE!

FRANKLIN BROKE INTO PRINT AS A TEENAGER, LAMPOONING MINISTERS IN THE PAGES OF THE **NEW ENGLAND COURANT**, AMERICA'S FIRST "UNDERGROUND" NEWSPAPER (1722).

EEK AND EVIL!

BANNED IN BOSTON, BENJAMIN MOVED TO THE FREER AIR OF PHILADELPHIA IN 1723.

THERE HE WENT INTO THE PRINTING BUSINESS. (PRINTSHOPS WERE POPPING UP EVERYWHERE, AS THE COLONIAL POPULATION WAS NOW BIG ENOUGH TO SUPPORT THEM.)

HOW FREE WAS THE PRESS? WELL, UNTIL **1733**, EVEN PRINTING THE TRUTH COULD LAND YOU IN JAIL, IF YOU INSULTED THE RIGHT PEOPLE.

ALMOST EVERYTHING ABOUT ME IS LIBELOUS!

THAT YEAR, NEW YORK PUBLISHER *PETER ZENGER* WAS ARRESTED FOR LIBELING THE COLONIAL GOVERNOR.

ZENGER'S LAWYER PERSUADED THE JURY TO SET ZENGER FREE, ON THE GROUNDS THAT TRUTH CAN'T BE LIBEL — AND A GREAT PRINCIPLE WAS BORN:

THE PRESS IS FREE, THE LAWYER ISN'T!

BUT BACK TO FRANKLIN ⟹

TO MAKE A LONG STORY SHORT, FRANKLIN GREW UP TO BECOME AMERICA'S MOST SUCCESSFUL PRINTER, RICH ENOUGH TO RETIRE FROM THE BUSINESS AT AGE 42.

IT'S THE AMERICAN WAY— OR AT LEAST, MY WAY!

HIS NEXT CAREER MOVE WAS TO BECOME AMERICA'S FIRST WORLD-CLASS SCIENTIST.

IN THE THEN-HOT FIELD OF ELECTRICITY, FRANKLIN PROVED THE FAMOUS FACT THAT LIGHTNING BOLTS ARE ELECTRIC SPARKS, AND (JUST FOR FUN) HE AND HIS FRIENDS USED TO ELECTROCUTE TURKEYS.
(I DIDN'T MAKE ANY OF THIS UP!)

IN A MORE PRACTICAL VEIN, FRANKLIN INVENTED THE LIGHTNING ROD, THE STORAGE BATTERY, AN ENERGY-EFFICIENT STOVE, AND BIFOCALS.

HE COULD DO EVERYTHING EXCEPT RELAX!!

AND AS A PUBLIC CITIZEN, HE PROMOTED A VOLUNTEER FIRE DEPARTMENT, A NON-SECTARIAN COLLEGE (LATER TO BE THE U. OF PENN.), A PHILOSOPHICAL SOCIETY, A VOLUNTEER MILITIA, PAVED ROADS, STREET SWEEPING... AND HE STILL HAD TIME TO COIN CLEVER SAYINGS — ALL BEFORE **1755**.

A PENNY SAVED IS A PENNY EARNED!

TIME IS MONEY!

EARLY TO BED AND EARLY TO RISE...

:WHEW: JUST BE GLAD YOU DON'T WORK FOR HIM!

NOW YOU HAVE SOME IDEA HOW FAR THE COLONIES HAD COME BY MID-CENTURY.

A VOTE FOR THE "POOREST HE"? STILL FAR FROM IT!

SH!

NOT TO MENTION THE "RICHEST SHE"!

FREEDOM OF RELIGION? EVEN MASSACHUSETTS HAD LOOSENED UP, WHILE RHODE ISLAND AND PENNSYLVANIA WELCOMED ALMOST EVERY SECT. FRANKLIN DONATED MONEY TO THEM ALL.

NO WONDER THEY TOLERATE ME!

FREEDOM OF THE PRESS? THEN AS NOW, AS FREE AS THE NEAREST ATTORNEY!

AT LEAST THERE IS A PRESS!

AND WHERE THERE ARE LAWYERS, YOU'RE SURE TO FIND A GOVERNMENT OF LAWS... LAWSUITS... AND PROPERTY IN HEAPS... AND THAT BRINGS US TO THE NEXT CHAPTER...

THE CLOSEST THING THE AMERICAN INDIANS HAD TO MONEY WAS **WAMPUM**: BLUE AND WHITE BEADS PAINSTAKINGLY CARVED FROM CLAMSHELLS. UNLIKE WESTERN MONEY, WAMPUM WAS VALUABLE BECAUSE IT TOOK HARD WORK TO PRODUCE, NOT BECAUSE IT WAS RARE.

ALSO, YOU CAN EAT THE MEAT!

ANOTHER DIFFERENCE WAS THAT WAMPUM BEADS WERE WOVEN INTO BELTS, WHOSE PATTERNS COULD BE MADE TO SPELL OUT MESSAGES.

WHEN TWO NATIONS MADE A TREATY, THEY INSCRIBED ITS TERMS ON SACRED WAMPUM BELTS, WHICH COULD BE USED LATER AS AN AID TO MEMORY.

SO — WHEN THE DUTCH "BOUGHT" MANHATTAN ISLAND FOR $24 WORTH OF GLASS BEADS, THEY WERE PAYING WITH COUNTERFEIT WAMPUM!

RED AND YELLOW VERY IMPRESSIVE! NOW EXPLAIN WHAT "BUY" MEANS...

·· CHAPTER 3 ··

WHEN A COLONY GROWS UP, WHAT DOES IT DO FOR A LIVING?

LET'S TAKE A COLONIAL TOUR IN THE YEAR

1755

(JUST BEFORE ALL HELL BROKE LOOSE).

START WITH THE SOUTH: GEORGIA, SOUTH CAROLINA, NORTH CAROLINA, VIRGINIA, MARYLAND, DELAWARE... THE LAND OF THE LANDED ARISTOCRACY, THE LAZY PLANTATION ON THE LAZY RIVER... THE LAND OF THE "BIG HOUSE," THE FOX HUNT, THE HORSE RACE, THE GAMBLING DEBT, THE MINT JULEP.

PLANTATION PRODUCTS INCLUDED TOBACCO, INDIGO, JUTE, AND RICE. THE WORK, OF COURSE, WAS DONE BY "SHIFTLESS" SLAVES.

42

WHEN SLAVERY WAS FIRST INTRODUCED IN THE SOUTH, IT WASN'T EXACTLY LEGAL...

WELL, IT WASN'T ILLEGAL EITHER!

THERE JUST WEREN'T ANY LAWS ON THE BOOKS, AND FOR A LONG TIME, THE SLAVE COLONIES DIDN'T BOTHER TO WRITE ANY.

THIS WAS IN THE GRAND AMERICAN TRADITION OF OPPOSITION TO GOVERNMENT REGULATION, ESPECIALLY WHEN YOU'RE DOING SOMETHING UNSPEAKABLE.

SH!

BUT THEN THE LAWYERS GOT HOLD OF THE QUESTION... THEY BEGAN A LONG, EXPENSIVE ARGUMENT ABOUT WHETHER OR NOT SLAVES WERE REAL ESTATE (!)... SO THE WHITES DECIDED IT WOULD BE CHEAPER IN THE LONG RUN TO PUT SOMETHING IN WRITING.

OTHERWISE, WE'LL ALL END UP AS SLAVES OF THE LAWYERS!

THE RESULTING "SLAVE CODES" VARIED FROM ONE COLONY TO THE NEXT, BUT THEY MOSTLY LOOKED LIKE THIS:

IT WAS ILLEGAL

FOR SLAVES TO CARRY ANY KIND OF WEAPON

FOR A BLACK TO LIFT A HAND AGAINST A WHITE, EVEN IN SELF-DEFENSE

FOR SLAVES TO MARRY

FOR SLAVES TO HAVE FUNERALS

IT WAS LEGAL

FOR A MASTER TO WORK HIS SLAVES 6 DAYS A WEEK, 15 HOURS A DAY—AND THEN MAKE THEM GROW THEIR OWN FOOD ON SUNDAYS

FOR A MASTER TO PUNISH HIS SLAVES IN ANY WAY HE WANTED, INCLUDING DEATH

MORE ?

SLAVES WEREN'T ALLOWED TO HAVE LIQUOR, OR STUDY READING.

A SLAVE HAD NO RIGHT TO A JURY TRIAL... SLAVE PRISONERS WERE DENIED HEAT IN THEIR CELLS (FOR FEAR THEY'D BURN DOWN THE JAIL).

AND "RACE MIXING" WAS ILLEGAL — WHICH ONLY PROVES THAT NOT ALL THE LAWS WERE ENFORCED 100% !

ISN'T THAT RIGHT, DAD?!

WITH THOUSANDS (LATER MILLIONS) OF SLAVES IN THEIR MIDST, THE WHITE SOUTH WAS NATURALLY NERVOUS ABOUT THE POSSIBILITY OF SLAVE REVOLTS.

HOWDY, GOV'NOR!

"FREEDOM WEARS A CAP WHICH CAN WITHOUT WORDS CALL TOGETHER ALL THOSE WHO LONG TO SHAKE OFF THE FETTERS OF SLAVERY..."

—GOV. SPOTTSWOOD OF VIRGINIA

THE FEAR WAS JUSTIFIED BY MAJOR UPRISINGS IN 1663, 1687, 1712, 1720, 1739, 1741, AND LOADS OF MINOR REVOLTS.

(ALL OF THEM WERE PUT DOWN FEROCIOUSLY.)

PERSONAL UPRISINGS — I.E., RUNAWAYS — WERE SO COMMON THAT NEWSPAPERS HAD STANDARD ILLUSTRATIONS FOR RUNAWAY SLAVE ADS.

NOW APPEARING IN A FREE PRESS!

BUT THE MAIN RESTRAINT ON SLAVE REVOLTS WAS THE FACT THAT THE SLAVES ALWAYS FORMED A MINORITY OF THE SOUTHERN POPULATION. **80%** OF SOUTHERN WHITE FAMILIES NEVER OWNED A SINGLE SLAVE !!

BLESSED ARE THE POOR, FOR THEY OUTNUMBER THE SLAVES!

THIS WAS THE OTHER SIDE OF THE OLD SOUTH: THE POOR FARMERS, BEHIND THE PLANTATIONS, UP IN THE HILLS, ON THE FRONTIER, WORKING THE SECOND-BEST SOIL, LIVING IN PLACES WITH NAMES LIKE PEEDEE, THE WAXHAWS, AND NINETY-SIX. THEY WERE THE ONES WHO FACED THE INDIANS, COPED WITH BANDITS, AND WHO ULTIMATELY WOULD FIGHT TO DEFEND THE SLAVE SYSTEM.

YEW C'N CALL IT LOCAL COLOR...

AH CALLS IT DIRT PORE!

COMPLEX PLACE, THE SOUTH...

NOW ONWARD TO THE
MIDDLE COLONIES
(PENNSYLVANIA, NEW YORK, AND NEW JERSEY). IN LATER YEARS, THESE BECAME THE "SOOT STATES"....

...BUT IN THOSE DAYS, THEY WERE NORTH AMERICA'S BREADBASKET, WHERE FREE FARMERS GREW FAR MORE PEAS, BEANS, AND GRAIN THAN THEY COULD POSSIBLY EAT.

STRANGE IDEA!

OTHER POPULAR WAYS TO MAKE MONEY THERE WERE TRADE, CONSTRUCTION, THE LAW, AND REAL ESTATE SPECULATION.

MEANING: BUYING & SELLING VERMONT!

(THAT LAST SEEMED ESPECIALLY WEIRD TO THE INDIANS, WHO THOUGHT OF THE LAND AS THE MOTHER OF US ALL...)

WHO BUYS AND SELLS HIS OWN MOTHER?

MAKE ME AN OFFER...

AND ON TO
NEW ENGLAND,
WITH ITS TIDY VILLAGES, STONY SOIL, THRIFTY INHABITANTS, AND BLUE LAWS.'

ALL WORK AND NO PLAY MAKES MORE MONEY IN A DAY!

PURITAN POLITICAL POWER MAY HAVE WANED, BUT THE PURITAN ETHIC REMAINED.

THAT'S WHY NEW ENGLANDERS NAMED THEIR CHILDREN AFTER THE PURITAN VIRTUES, SO THEY COULDN'T FORGET WHAT'S IMPORTANT IN LIFE EVEN IF THEY TRIED.

MEET MY DAUGHTERS, PRUDENCE, HOPE, HONOR, FAITH, MERCY, ASSERTIVENESS, AND BOTTOMLINE.

NEW ENGLAND'S WEALTH
WAS IN ITS FORESTS...
THE BIGGEST TREES BECAME
MASTS FOR THE ROYAL NAVY,
AND THE REST WERE
TURNED INTO SHIPS IN
BOSTON, PROVIDENCE, AND
NEWPORT.

THE WHOLE ECONOMY
REVOLVED AROUND
SHIPPING: WAREHOUSING,
BARRELMAKING, ROPE
MANUFACTURE..

⟹ BUT THE
BAY COLONY'S
BIGGEST MANUFACTURING
INDUSTRY WAS
SOMETHING ELSE
AGAIN: IT WAS THE
DISTILLATION OF —

RUM

SHOCKING!

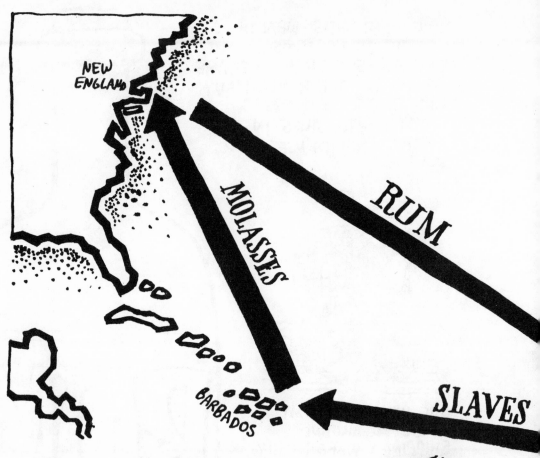

NEW ENGLAND

MOLASSES

RUM

SLAVES

BARBADOS

NOT TO WORRY... THE RUM WASN'T FOR DRINKING AT HOME...IT WAS IN REALITY ONE LEG OF THE FAMOUS

TRIANGULAR TRADE.

HERE'S THE PICTURE: THE RUM TRAVELS TO AFRICA... IS TRADED FOR SLAVES... THEY GO TO THE SUGAR PLANTATIONS OF BARBADOS... ARE TRADED (AT 1000% MARKUP) FOR MOLASSES... WHICH GOES TO NEW ENGLAND... IS DISTILLED INTO RUM...

AND ROUND AND ROUND AND ROUND AND...

THE SLAVE SHIPS WERE AN EXAMPLE OF PURITAN EFFICIENCY GONE MAD... THEY REALLY PACKED THEM IN... TRY TO IMAGINE SPENDING 40 DAYS CHAINED BELOW DECKS IN A SPACE 13 INCHES WIDE AND 18 INCHES HIGH... AND YOU HAVE THE TRIANGLE'S DREAD "MIDDLE PASSAGE."

SOME GEOMETRY LESSON!

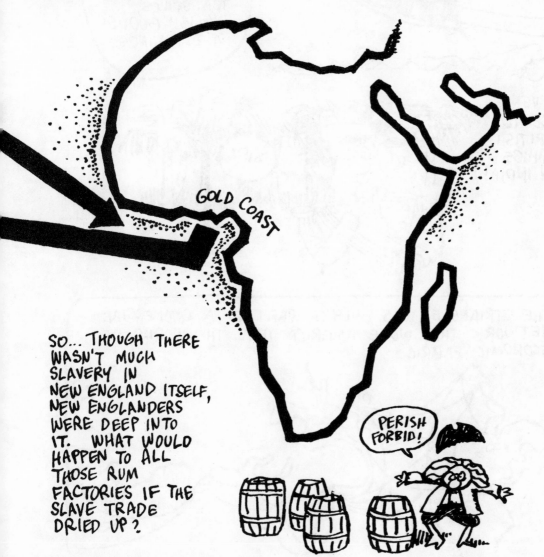

GOLD COAST

SO... THOUGH THERE WASN'T MUCH SLAVERY IN NEW ENGLAND ITSELF, NEW ENGLANDERS WERE DEEP INTO IT. WHAT WOULD HAPPEN TO ALL THOSE RUM FACTORIES IF THE SLAVE TRADE DRIED UP?

PERISH FORBID!

BOSTON "BOTTOMS" CARRIED MORE THAN JUST RUM, SLAVES, AND MOLASSES.

ALSO: BIBLES, CODFISH, BEANS, BEAVER PELTS, DEERSKINS, COWHIDE, TOBACCO, HEMP, INDIGO, TEA, SPICES, ENGLISH GOODS OF ALL KINDS..

(EVEN ICE TO BRITISH SAHIBS IN INDIA!)

SIP!

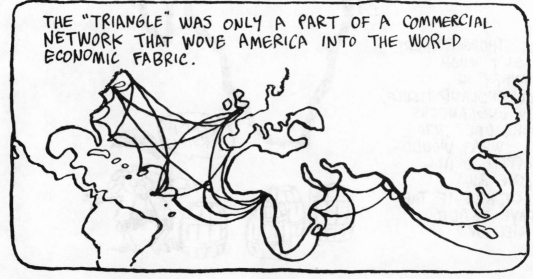

THE "TRIANGLE" WAS ONLY A PART OF A COMMERCIAL NETWORK THAT WOVE AMERICA INTO THE WORLD ECONOMIC FABRIC.

AND THE BOSTON WATERFRONT BUSTLED WITH WAREHOUSES, SHIPPING OFFICES, MARINE SUPPLY HOUSES, EXCHANGES, A CUSTOMS HOUSE (ALWAYS MYSTERIOUSLY UNDERUSED), AND TAVERNS.

WHAT'S THAT? TAVERNS?

SURE... YOU DIDN'T THINK THAT **ALL** THAT RUM LEFT TOWN?

INDEED — IT SEEMED THAT UPRIGHT, UPTIGHT BOSTON HAD DEVELOPED A RAUNCHY UNDERBELLY OF WATERFRONT WORKERS!

HM! NOR'EAST WIND TONIGHT... MUST BE TIME FOR ANOTHER RIOT...

YES... RIOTING WAS ONE OF BOSTON'S FAVORITE RECREATIONS! FOR EXAMPLE:

1737: THE "MARKET RIOTS": RIOTERS DISGUISED AS CLERGYMEN (!) DESTROYED MARKET BUILDINGS TO PROTEST GOVERNMENT REGULATION.

1747: "IMPRESSMENT RIOTS": 5000 ANTI-DRAFT PROTESTERS BURNED A BOAT IN THE GOVERNOR'S FRONT YARD.

EVERY NOV. 5: "POPE'S DAY" RIOTS... JUST TO KEEP IN PRACTICE, "NORTH ENDERS" BATTLED "SOUTH ENDERS" IN AN ANNUAL GAME OF "CAPTURE THE POPE."

THIS CONCLUDES OUR COLONIAL TOUR... BUT DON'T WORRY... THERE ARE MORE RIOTS TO COME...

THE COLONIES HAD A LOT IN COMMON: SAME LANGUAGE, SAME KING AND COUNTRY, SAME RELIGION (MORE OR LESS), SAME ENEMIES, EVEN THE SAME SLAVERY... BUT IN THOSE DAYS, BEFORE BARGAIN AIR FARES, TELEVISION, FEDERAL FUNDING, AND KENTUCKY FRIED CHICKEN, THERE WERE ALSO SOME BIG DIFFERENCES, AS THE COLONISTS SAW IT —

THE NEW ENGLANDER IS HALF MAD... HIS IDEA OF A GOOD TIME IS TO PREACH SERMONS 51 WEEKS OF THE YEAR, AND DESTROY BUILDINGS ON THE 52ND... BESIDES, HE LACKS THE REFINEMENT WHICH CAN ONLY COME FROM WIELDING ABSOLUTE POWER OVER A SERVILE CLASS...

THE SOUTHERNER'S RELIGION IS CORRUPT... HIS MORALS ARE LAX... HIS PLANTATIONS ARE CRUEL... HIS WOMEN ARE EASY... HIS LIFE IS... ¿SHUDDER¿— DEEPLY TEMPTING...

NON-PENNSYLVANIANS ARE ALL OBSESSED...

HEY, I'M JEWISH! WHERE CAN I GO BUT RHODE ISLAND?

ANY CHANCE OF UNITING ALL OF THESE? NOT IN 1755!

ZO WHAT HOPPENED?

CHAPTER 4
MIGHTY BEEFS FROM LITTLE BEAVERS GROW

On April, 1754, a Virginia militia company marched westward. Their mission: to protect English trappers and land speculators from the French competition. Their leader: the very young (22 years, 2 months), very tall (6 feet and change), and very honest (99 on a scale of 100) colonel **GEORGE WASHINGTON.**

FOR GOD AND PROPERTY VALUES!!

YOUNG GEORGE ORDERED HIS MEN TO ATTACK THE FIRST BUNCH OF FRENCH SOLDIERS THEY OUTNUMBERED, KILLING MOST, CAPTURING SOME, AND EARNING THE COLONEL A REPUTATION AS A MAN OF ACTION.

TOO BAD FRANCE AND ENGLAND WERE AT PEACE AT THE TIME...

DETAILS, DETAILS!

THE VIRGINIANS QUICKLY HEAPED UP SOME MUD WALLS AND CHRISTENED THEM "FORT NECESSITY."

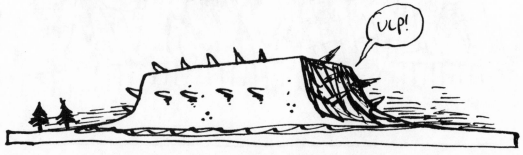

ULP!

WHEN THE REST OF THE
FRENCH ARRIVED, WASHINGTON
BARGAINED HIS PRISONERS
FOR A SAFE MARCH HOME.
THIS WON HIM A
REPUTATION AS A VERY
TOUGH NEGOTIATOR.
(HIS MEN WERE VASTLY
OUTNUMBERED.)

IF HE EVER
LEARNS THE
DIFFERENCE
BETWEEN WAR
AND PEACE, HE
WILL BE TRULY
FORMIDABLE!

THIS INCIDENT IGNITED THE

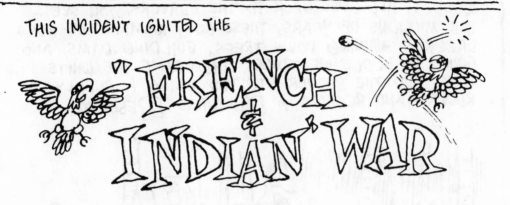

FRENCH & INDIAN WAR

(WHICH WAS A WAR OF BRITAIN AGAINST THE FRENCH AND
INDIANS, NOT A WAR OF THE FRENCH AND INDIANS
AGAINST EACH OTHER).

WHEN HOSTILITIES BROKE
OUT, WASHINGTON HOPED
FOR A MILITARY PROMOTION.
BUT BRITAIN WANTED
REGULAR ARMY OFFICERS,
NOT 22-YEAR-OLD COLONIALS,
IN COMMAND OF THE TROOPS.
DEMOTED TO MAJOR,
WASHINGTON RAN FOR THE
HOUSE OF BURGESSES,
CARRYING A GREAT
GRUDGE AGAINST LONDON.

THEY'LL
PAY FOR
THIS!

CONTENTS
ONE
GRUDGE

AT THIS POINT WE MIGHT WONDER: WHERE DID THOSE FRENCH SOLDIERS COME FROM?

FRANCE, NATURELLEMENT!

WELL, IT ALL GOES BACK TO THE BEAVERS, YOU SEE... FOR MILLIONS OF YEARS, THESE BUSY ANIMALS HAD BEEN EAGERLY GNAWING DOWN TREES, BUILDING DAMS, AND GOING TO LODGE MEETINGS. THEN CAME THE WHITE MAN, AND THE BEAVER STOPPED BEING A CUDDLY RODENT AND BECAME A *N*ATURAL *R*ESOURCE...

WE ARE SUCH STUFF AS HATS ARE MADE OF!

YES, IT GOT SO THAT EUROPEANS COULDN'T LIVE WITHOUT THEIR BEAVER HATS (NOT UNLIKE THE BEAVERS THEMSELVES).

60

STARTING IN QUEBEC IN 1608, THE FRENCH HAD BUILT A SIZEABLE AMERICAN EMPIRE BASED ON THE FUR TRADE.

BY 1754, THE BRITISH AND FRENCH EMPIRES WERE RUBBING AGAINST EACH OTHER, CAUSING A RASH ACT.

AFTER WASHINGTON'S FORAY, THE TWO POWERS DECIDED TO FIGHT IT OUT — POSSIBLY THE ONLY WAR EVER FOUGHT OVER HATS.

WHEN IT WAS OVER, IN 1763, BRITAIN HAD WON CANADA AND ITS BEAVERS, AND THE FRENCH WERE OUT OF NORTH AMERICA.

THE FRENCH AND INDIAN WAR, LIKE OTHER WARS, HAD A BEGINNING, A MIDDLE, AND AN AFTERMATH. IT DOUBLED BRITAIN'S NATIONAL DEBT AND LEFT THE COLONIAL ECONOMY IN THE DOLDRUMS (A POPULAR REST STOP FOR POST-WAR ECONOMIES).

BUT NOT TO WORRY! BRITAIN HAD A NEW (AS OF 1760), YOUNG (BORN 1738) KING, WITH PLENTY OF FRESH IDEAS AND ONLY OCCASIONAL FITS OF INSANITY: GEORGE III.

To REPLENISH THE TREASURY, THE KING'S MINISTERS DREAMED UP THE **STAMP ACT,** A TAX WHICH CAME DOWN ON THE COLONIES LIKE A FLAMENCO PERFORMANCE.

EVERY CONTRACT, NEWSPAPER, AND GOVERNMENT DOCUMENT IN THE COLONIES WAS TO CARRY A GOVERNMENT-ISSUE STAMP.

ALTHOUGH THE STAMP ACT WAS ONLY A NICKEL-AND-DIME SORT OF TAX, AMERICA COULD HARDLY AFFORD IT.

BUT THAT WASN'T THE WORST THING ABOUT THE STAMP ACT. THE WORST PART WAS THAT PARLIAMENT HAD PASSED IT WITHOUT THE CONSENT OF THE POTENTIAL TAXEES.* THIS MADE THE STAMP ACT **T**AXATION WITHOUT **R**EPRESENTATION, WHICH WOULD HAVE UPSET THE AMERICANS EVEN IF THEIR ECONOMY WASN'T DEPRESSED.

*AS PART OF AN OMNIBUS BILL, PROBABLY

THE COLONISTS, HAVING LITTLE ELSE TO DO, PROTESTED AGAINST THE STAMP ACT. THE VIRGINIA BURGESSES PASSED RINGING RESOLUTIONS (THE KIND THAT ALARM PEOPLE), INTRODUCED BY **PATRICK HENRY,** A FRESHMAN MEMBER WHO DIDN'T WANT TO LOSE HIS RIGHTS BEFORE SOPHOMORE YEAR.

MEANWHILE, THROUGHOUT THE COLONIES, CITIZENS CHANTING "LIBERTY AND PROPERTY" TOOK LIBERTIES WITH THE KING'S PROPERTY. (THESE RIOTS STARTED IN BOSTON, NATURALLY.)

THE PROTESTERS CALLED FOR A TOTAL BOYCOTT OF
ALL ENGLISH IMPORTS. FOR EXAMPLE, ANYONE FOUND
SUITED IN ENGLISH WOOLENS WOULD BE COATED IN
AMERICAN TAR AND FEATHERS.

COLONIAL WOMEN SPUN LIKE MAD — THEIR WHEELS, THAT IS —
TO KEEP THEIR FAMILIES IN HOMESPUN, AND OUT OF TAR.

HURRY UP...
I'M LATE
FOR THE
DEMONSTRATION...

JUST EXACTLY AS PLANNED, THE BOYCOTT HIT ENGLISH BUSINESS RIGHT IN THE POCKETBOOK.

SOON, THOUSANDS OF SQUEALING, WOUNDED POCKETBOOKS WERE BEGGING PARLIAMENT FOR RELIEF.

LET'S BAG IT!

IN 1766, THE STAMP ACT WAS REPEALED.

A LITTLE RIOTING IN A GOOD CAUSE ISN'T A BAD THING!

AMERICA CELEBRATED WITH BELLS, FIREWORKS, PARADES, AND REVOLUTIONARY THOUGHTS LIKE THESE!

SOMEHOW FAILING TO GET THE MESSAGE, PARLIAMENT IN 1767 PASSED A NEW TAX, THE "TOWNSHEND DUTIES," ON VARIOUS IMPORTS INTO THE COLONIES. THE HEAD CUSTOMS HOUSE WAS INTELLIGENTLY LOCATED IN BOSTON, WHERE IT WOULD BE SURE TO PROVOKE THE MOST VIOLENCE.

AFTER THE INEVITABLE RIOTS, BRITAIN SENT IN THE TROOPS, CALLED "LOBSTERBACKS" AFTER THEIR RED COATS, OR POSSIBLY THEIR CHITINOUS CARAPACES.

FACED WITH A CROWD HURLING ICEBALLS AND EPITHETS, THE SOLDIERS DISCHARGED THEIR DUTY AND THEIR WEAPONS, KILLING FIVE: THE "BOSTON MASSACRE."

THE AUTHORITIES NERVOUSLY REMOVED THE TROOPS... AND SCRAPPED THE TAXES—AGAIN. BUT THEY KEPT ONE LITTLE TAX—ON TEA—JUST TO PROVE THE POINT.

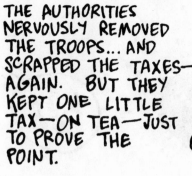

THE POINT BEING—?

THAT NO ONE CAN BOYCOTT CAFFEINE!

SO THE BOSTONIANS, DISGUISED AS INDIANS, DUMPED A SHIPLOAD OF TEA INTO THE DRINK—A TEA PARTY FOR THE FISH.

HOW ABOUT SOME MILK AND SUGAR?

AND A CUP?

HELLO AGAIN!

AS WASTING TEA WAS HIGHLY UN-BRITISH, THE REDCOATS RETURNED TO CLOSE THE PORT UNTIL THE STUFF WAS PAID FOR... AND BOSTON FELL UNUSUALLY QUIET...

THE ONLY SOUND WAS THE SCRITCH SCRITCH, SCRITCH OF A QUILL, AND THE OCCASIONAL MUFFLED CURSE AS IT BLOTTED THE PAGE... THE SOUND OF THE —

★@#$‡

COMMITTEES OF CORRESPONDENCE,

WHICH CORRESPONDED ONLY WITH EACH OTHER.

ADAMS

HANCOCK

ORIGINALLY THEY WERE CREATED BY **SAMUEL ADAMS** AND **JOHN HANCOCK.** ADAMS WAS THE BOSTON PROTEST MOVEMENT'S MASTERMIND, WHILE HANCOCK WAS ITS MASTERCHARGE ACCOUNT. "SAM ADAMS WRITES THE LETTERS AND JOHN HANCOCK PAYS THE POSTAGE," WENT THE SAYING. WHO LICKED THE ENVELOPES IS ANYBODY'S GUESS.

AT FIRST,
THE COMMITTEES
WERE ONLY IN
MASSACHUSETTS,
BUT THE IDEA
SPREAD TO
ALL THE
COLONIES.
SOON, GROUPS
OF CITIZENS
EVERYWHERE
WERE SWAPPING
REVOLUTIONARY
TIPS, LIKE
BRITAIN'S LATEST
HEINOUS DEEDS,
AND HOW TO
WASH BLOOD
OUT OF
YOUR SHIRT.

"SOAK IN COLD WATER IMMEDIATELY."

CARRIED BY PATRIOT RIDERS
LIKE **PAUL REVERE**, NEWS
OF THE TEA PARTY SPREAD
FAST — AND PROTEST
SWEPT THE COLONIES.

THE BOSTON TEA PARTY WAS
FOLLOWED BY THE GREENWICH (N.J.)
TEA PARTY, THE NEW YORK TEA
PARTY, SEVERAL CHARLESTON (S.C.)
TEA PARTIES, THE PROVIDENCE
(R.I.) TEA PARTY, THE ANNAPOLIS
TEA PARTY... SERIOUS
POLLUTION!!

AFTER SOME TIME, THE COMMITTEES OF CORRESPONDENCE DEVELOPED WRITER'S CRAMP AND DECIDED TO MEET THEIR PEN PALS FACE TO FACE IN PHILADELPHIA...

NOW I HAVE SADDLESORES, TOO!

AT A
CONTINENTAL CONGRESS.

ALL THE BIGGIES WERE THERE: PATRICK HENRY, GEORGE WASHINGTON, SAM ADAMS, HIS COUSIN JOHN ADAMS, JOHN HANCOCK, BENJAMIN FRANKLIN. IT WAS OBVIOUSLY A **H**ISTORIC **O**CCASION, AND EVERYONE WAS DEEPLY IMPRESSED, OR AT LEAST SOMEWHAT BENT OUT OF SHAPE.

AN HONOR, I'M SURE!

(ESPECIALLY THRILLED WAS BEN FRANKLIN, WHO HAD PUSHED COLONIAL UNION AS EARLY AS 1754 WITH THIS CARTOON.)

ON TOP OF EVERYTHING ELSE, HE'S A CARTOONIST?!! AWESOME!!

JOIN, or DIE.

EVERYONE'S IMPRESSED, BUT NOBODY'S SPEECHLESS!

THEY QUICKLY GOT DOWN TO BUSINESS, WHICH CONSISTED OF LOTS OF PARTIES WITH INTERESTING TALK IN THE EVENING, FOLLOWED BY INTERMINABLE SPEECHES DURING THE DAY.

BETWEEN NAPS, THEY DREW UP A **D**ECLARATION OF **R**IGHTS (TOGETHER WITH A **B**ILL OF WRONGS), A **P**ETITION OR TWO, AND AN **I**NVOICE FOR MORE TAR AND FEATHERS.

NOW WAIT A MINUTE!

FINALLY, THEY DECLARED THE CONGRESS A MOST REFRESHING EXPERIENCE AND AGREED TO DO IT AGAIN NEXT YEAR.

A COMPLETE SUCCESS!

MEANWHILE, WITH THE TROOPS STILL IN BOSTON, MASSACHUSETTS TOWNS BEGAN DRILLING THE MINUTEMEN, REVOLUTIONARIES WHO COULD BE READY TO FIGHT IN THE REVOLUTION OF A SECOND HAND.*

THE BRITISH DECIDED TO GET HOLD OF THE PATRIOTS' GUNPOWDER SUPPLY AT CONCORD, OUTSIDE BOSTON. ON THE NIGHT OF APRIL 18, 1775, THEY MARCHED.

WHA-?

THE MINUTEMEN, WARNED BY PAUL REVERE AND OTHERS, MUSTERED ON LEXINGTON GREEN. THE BRITISH OPENED FIRE; THE MINUTEMEN BOLTED; AND SAM ADAMS AND JOHN HANCOCK, AT A NEARBY HOTEL, WOKE UP. IT WAS CHAOS AT 3 A.M.

BY THE TIME THE REDCOATS REACHED CONCORD, THOUSANDS OF PATRIOT FARMERS WERE THERE TO GREET THEM. THIS TIME IT WAS THE BRITISH WHO RETREATED, MARCHING BACK TO BOSTON THROUGH A GAUNTLET OF SNIPERS.

* THIS WAS BEFORE DIGITAL WATCHES.

ADAMS AND HANCOCK HURRIED TO PHILADELPHIA AND THE
SECOND CONTINENTAL CONGRESS.

GOOD NEWS! IT'S **WAR!**

OUR GUY GETS THE INSURANCE COMPANY; YOURS GETS THE DOLLAR BILL...

BUT HOW TO GET CONGRESS TO SUPPORT A MASSACHUSETTS BATTLE? IN THE BACK ROOMS, JOHN ADAMS WORKED THE DEAL: A VIRGINIAN WOULD COMMAND THE AMERICAN ARMY, WHILE MASSACHUSETTS' OWN JOHN HANCOCK WOULD BE THE (POWERLESS) PRESIDENT OF CONGRESS.

AND SO IT WAS THAT A SOUTHERN PLANTER TOOK COMMAND OF A NEW ENGLAND ARMY...

DO MY EYES DECEIVE ME, OR DO I SEE NEGROES WITH MUSKETS?

TO WASHINGTON'S EYES, THE REVOLUTIONARY ARMY LOOKED VERY PECULIAR: RACIALLY INTEGRATED, EGALITARIAN, ITS OFFICERS ELECTED BY THE RANK AND FILE.

WASHINGTON IMMEDIATELY ORDERED:

☆ ALL BLACKS OUT OF THE ARMY

☆ NEW OFFICERS TO BE CHOSEN BY THEIR SUPERIORS

☆ A RAISE IN OFFICERS' PAY

☆ THE USE OF FLOGGING FOR DISCIPLINE

AMID THE HOWLS OF PROTEST, WASHINGTON AGREED TO LET THE BLACKS STAY, BUT REFUSED TO GIVE IN ON THE REST. SO — HALF THE ARMY WENT HOME IN DISGUST.

CHAPTER 5

IN WHICH HAPPINESS IS PURSUED, GUN IN HAND

So—it was war... on one side, a mighty empire, embracing England, Scotland, Ireland, and parts of Germany and India (although not all of them returned the embrace).

On the other—an incredible shrinking army, a self-appointed congress without the power to tax or draft, and not even a very clear idea what they were fighting for...

SOUNDS GOOD... LET'S GO WITH IT!

TOO WEAK TO WIN, CONGRESS COULD ALSO HARDLY AFFORD TO LOSE... NOT WHILE THE REWARD FOR TREASON AGAINST BRITAIN WAS AN INVITATION TO A BARBECUE — OF YOUR OWN INTESTINES.

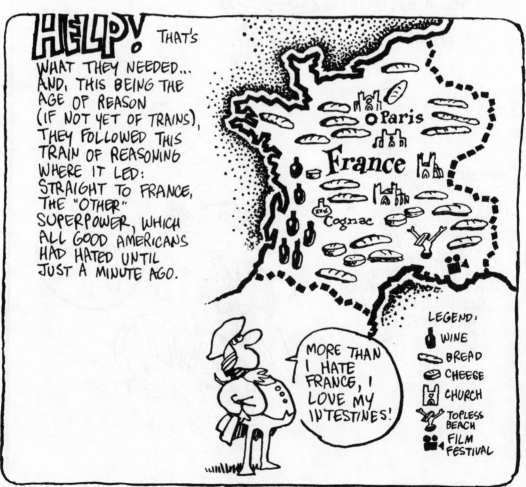

BUT—AND THIS WAS A BIG BUT— WHY SHOULD FRANCE HELP THE REBELS, IF THE REBELS' ULTIMATE GOAL WAS TO REMAIN UNITED TO GREAT BRITAIN?

UM...ER... AH... I NEVER THOUGHT OF THAT...

⇒ THAT QUESTION, AMONG OTHERS, WAS RAISED IN THE BEST-SELLING PAMPHLET **"COMMON SENSE,"** WHICH APPEARED IN EARLY 1776. IT CALLED FOR A COMPLETE BREAK WITH ENGLAND.

UP TO THAT POINT, CONGRESS HAD BEEN LOUDLY PROCLAIMING LOYALTY TO KING GEORGE... INDEPENDENCE WAS A GOAL OF ONLY THE WILDEST RADICALS... BUT "COMMON SENSE" CHANGED ALL THAT!

AS PUBLIC OPINION SWUNG AROUND, THE RADICALS SEIZED THE INITIATIVE. BY JUNE, 1776, CONGRESS HAD VOTED IN FAVOR OF INDEPENDENCE!!

IT'S COMMON SENSE!

THE TASK OF WRITING THE DECLARATION OF INDEPENDENCE FELL TO **THOMAS JEFFERSON**, A VIRGINIA CONGRESSMAN WITH A POSITIVE PASSION FOR HUMAN LIBERTY, AS LONG AS THEY WEREN'T HIS HUMANS...

GOSH!

GEE

IF PATRICK HENRY WAS THE REVOLUTION'S GREATEST ORATOR, AND SAM ADAMS THE PREMIER PROTESTER, THEN JEFFERSON WAS THE SUPREME PROSE STYLIST AND POLITICAL VISIONARY.

IS LIBERTY ANYTHING BESIDES TAX EVASION?

BEFORE JEFFERSON, THE MOVEMENT'S SLOGAN HAD BEEN "LIBERTY AND PROPERTY..."

BUT T.J. WANTED TO FOUND THE NEW NATION ON SOMETHING A LITTLE LESS CRASS...

CALL THIS "JEFFERSON'S TIME BOMB!"

THIS SUBSTITUTE SPRANG TO MIND:

"WE HOLD THESE TRUTHS TO BE SELF-EVIDENT, THAT ALL MEN ARE CREATED EQUAL, THAT THEY ARE ENDOWED BY THEIR CREATOR WITH CERTAIN UNALIENABLE RIGHTS, THAT AMONG THESE ARE LIFE, LIBERTY, AND THE PURSUIT OF HAPPINESS..."

NICE...

JEFFERSON'S WORDS WERE LESS A DESCRIPTION OF REALITY IN 1776 THAN A PROMISE FOR THE FUTURE — THAT EVENTUALLY EVERYONE WOULD GAIN EQUAL POLITICAL RIGHTS, REGARDLESS OF RACE, SEX, OR INCOME.

O, THE PROMISES OF WHITE FOLKS!

THE DECLARATION ALSO ANNOUNCED THE PEOPLE'S RIGHT TO CHOOSE ITS OWN GOVERNMENT, AN IDEA THAT HAD BEEN IN THE AIR FOR A WHILE, BUT HADN'T TOUCHED GROUND UNTIL NOW.

THE REST OF THE PAPER IS AN (INFLATED) LIST OF THE CRIMES OF KING GEORGE, WHO WAS MADE TO SOUND A BIT LIKE A

Giant life like karate practice dummy

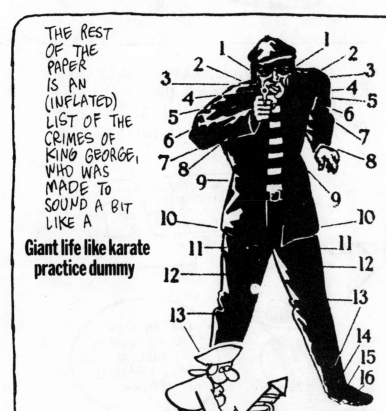

CONGRESS ACCEPTED THE DECLARATION OF INDEPENDENCE ON THE FOURTH OF JULY AND WASTED A QUANTITY OF PRECIOUS GUN-POWDER IN A FIREWORKS SHOW.

MINDFUL THAT NO NATION IS COMPLETE WITHOUT TRAPPINGS, CONGRESS QUICKLY ADOPTED A FLAG (RED, WHITE, & BLUE), AN ARMY UNIFORM (BROWN), A BIRD (BALD), ARTICLES OF CONFEDERATION (CLUMSY), AND A NAME (ALMOST AS CLUMSY AS THE ARTICLES OF CONFEDERATION):

THE UNITED STATES OF AMERICA

THIS IS A COUNTRY'S NAME?

THIS STARTED A TREND IN NATIONAL NAMES. NOW THAT AN INFINITE VARIETY OF GOVERNMENTS WAS AVAILABLE, INSTEAD OF JUST KINGDOMS, A NAME HAD TO DESCRIBE WHAT IT WAS, OR, ON OCCASION, WHAT IT WASN'T.

PEOPLE'S FEDERATED SOCIALIST REPUBLIC AND DEBATING SOCIETY OF (CONT'D NEXT SIGN)

PRETTY SOON "THE KINGDOM OF GOD" WILL BE "THE ANGELS' REPUBLIC OF HEAVEN..."

LADEN WITH THE NEW NATIONAL TRAPPINGS, BENJAMIN FRANKLIN SAILED FOR FRANCE TO NEGOTIATE FOR AID. HE WORE A BEAVER HAT TO REMIND THE FRENCH OF WHAT COULD BE THEIRS AGAIN, IF THEY PLAYED ALONG...

WHILE THE FRENCH ARISTOCRATS FELL IN LOVE WITH THE AMERICAN, THEY WERE NERVOUS ABOUT HIS GOVERNMENT. AFTER ALL, IT HAD NO KING — AN UNHEARD-OF ARRANGEMENT. FRANKLIN TRIED TO CONVINCE THEM THAT ENGLAND WAS MORE DANGEROUS THAN DEMOCRACY.

THIS PLOY SEEMED TO WORK, AND FRANCE BEGAN FUNNELING COVERT AID TO THE U.S. THROUGH DUMMY CORPORATIONS.

(90% OF U.S. GUNPOWDER CAME FROM FRANCE.)

MEANWHILE, BACK AT THE FRONT, THE WAR HAD BEGUN
WELL AND GOTTEN WORSE.
IN MARCH, 1776,
THE BRITISH, FACED
WITH WASHINGTON'S
CANNON (DRAWN THERE
FROM AFAR BY
HEROIC OXEN)* LEFT
BOSTON FOR NEW YORK
AND A PITCHED
BATTLE. THE AMERICANS,
WHO USUALLY PITCHED
NOTHING HARDER
THAN HAY, FLED IN THE
DIRECTION OF
PHILADELPHIA, GUIDED
BY THE HOWLS OF
CONGRESS.

THE FIRST — UNSUNG AND (UNTIL NOW) UNPAINTED — CROSSING
OF THE DELAWARE WAS STRICTLY IN REVERSE.

THE SECOND CROSSING WAS A SNEAK ATTACK ON CHRISTMAS
NIGHT, SURPRISING THE ENEMY WHILE THEY WERE STILL
OPENING THEIR PRESENTS. IT LOOKED SOMETHING LIKE THIS:

* THE OXEN WERE LED BY 250-LB HENRY ("OX") KNOX, WHO INSPIRED THE
ANIMALS BY RESEMBLING THEM

AS 1777 DRAGGED ON, WASHINGTON FAILED TO STOP THE BRITISH FROM TAKING PHILADELPHIA, WHILE THE BRITISH FAILED TO STOP CONGRESS FROM TAKING TO THE HILLS.

SAVE THE PAPERWORK!

CAN'T SEE A BLOODY THING!

WASHINGTON & CO. WENT OFF TO STARVE AT VALLEY FORGE, A DARK HOUR, BRIGHTENED ONLY BY BRITAIN'S INCREDIBLE DIMNESS IN NOT TAKING ADVANTAGE OF THE SITUATION.

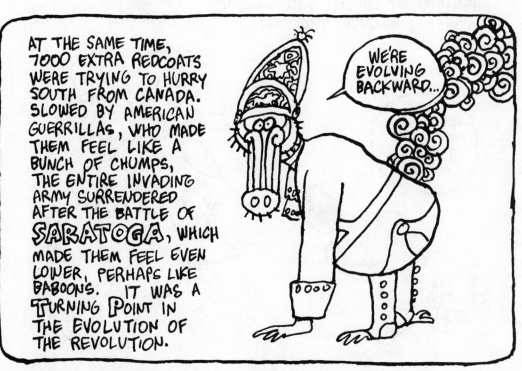

AT THE SAME TIME, 7000 EXTRA REDCOATS WERE TRYING TO HURRY SOUTH FROM CANADA. SLOWED BY AMERICAN GUERRILLAS, WHO MADE THEM FEEL LIKE A BUNCH OF CHUMPS, THE ENTIRE INVADING ARMY SURRENDERED AFTER THE BATTLE OF **SARATOGA**, WHICH MADE THEM FEEL EVEN LOWER, PERHAPS LIKE BABOONS. IT WAS A **TURNING POINT** IN THE EVOLUTION OF THE REVOLUTION.

WE'RE EVOLVING BACKWARD...

WHY A TURNING POINT? BECAUSE SARATOGA SO THRILLED KING **LOUIS** THAT HE LOST HIS HEAD AND MADE AN OPEN ALLIANCE WITH THE DANGEROUSLY DEMOCRATIC U.S.A.

I SMELL THE BLOOD OF AN ENGLISHMAN!

INSTEAD OF COVERT AID, AMERICA NOW HAD FRENCH TROOPS!

HEY, LOUIE! YOU WANT BEAVER CHAPEAU?

BY THIS POINT, A BILATERAL BATTLE HAD ESCALATED INTO A WAR WITH SIX DIFFERENT SIDES...

PATRIOTS:

WHITES & FREE BLACKS, FIRED BY DEMOCRATIC RHETORIC, FOUGHT FOR A SIMPLE GOAL:

WE WANT IT ALL!

BRITISH:

THEY ONLY WANTED TO KEEP THEIR COLONIES, BUT COULDN'T QUITE SEE SEE HOW...

TORIES:

AMERICANS LOYAL TO THE CROWN, THEY HAD ONLY WANTED PEACE & QUIET & LAW & ORDER. NOW THEY WANTED REVENGE.

SLAVES:

MASTER'S FIGHT TO GET OUT FROM UNDER ENGLAND LOOKED LIKE A GOOD OPPORTUNITY TO GET OUT FROM UNDER MASTER.

I'M GONE!

INDIANS:

MOST SIDED WITH ENGLAND, AS THEY HAD HEARD WHAT THE PATRIOTS WERE FIGHTING FOR.

BUNCHA SPECULATORS!

FRANCE:

THE FRENCH WERE TRYING TO DESTROY THE "EVIL EMPIRE," I.E., ENGLAND.

THEY HAVE NO CUISINE!!

WITH SO MANY SIDES FIGHTING IN ONE PLACE, EVENTS SQUEEZED TOGETHER: BATTLES, RIOTS, INFLATION, STRIKES, A DOG PAPERED WITH DEVALUED MONEY...

CROWDED OUT OF THE NORTH, THE WAR SPILLED SOUTHWARD, WHERE PATRIOTS FOLLOWED GENERAL NATHANIEL GREENE. GENERAL CORNWALLIS' REDCOATS ALSO FOLLOWED GREENE, TRYING HARD TO CATCH UP.

WHEN THE REGULARS HAD PASSED, TORIES AND PATRIOTS KILLED EACH OTHER IRREGULARLY... SLAVES FLED... AND PIONEERS CARRIED THE WAR WESTWARD WITH THEIR OTHER BELONGINGS.

LEGEND
STRANGE FRUIT TREE
SPILLED MINT JULEP
ESCAPED SLAVE
BRITISH   U.S.

APTER MARCHING IN LOOPS, CORNWALLIS DIZZILY RESTED AT YORKTOWN, VIRGINIA. WASHINGTON'S ARMY ($\frac{1}{2}$ FRENCH, $\frac{1}{2}$ AMERICAN) SUDDENLY APPEARED, AND THE FRENCH NAVY DELIVERED THE **COUP** WHICH IMMORTALIZED THE NAME OF ITS ADMIRAL **DE GRASSE**.

THE BRITISH SURRENDERED (THOUGH CORNWALLIS HIMSELF WAS TOO DISORIENTED TO ATTEND THE CEREMONY). UNLIKE SARATOGA, THIS WAS NOT A TURNING POINT BUT AN EXCLAMATION POINT, OR JUST A POINT, AS IN PERIOD.

AT LEAST THERE'S STILL INDIA...

AFTER YORKTOWN, BRITAIN AND THE U.S.A. HELD PEACE TALKS WHICH PRODUCED THE **TREATY** OF **PARIS** IN 1783.

ENGLAND KEPT CANADA, WHICH TURNED OUT TO BE A **GOOD THING**, ESPECIALLY IF YOU WERE LOYAL TO ENGLAND, AN ESCAPED SLAVE, OR AGAINST THE VIETNAM WAR. SEVERAL CARIBBEAN PARADISES ALSO REMAINED BRITISH, SO THAT NEW YORKERS WOULD HAVE SOMEPLACE FOREIGN TO FLY IN THE WINTER.

THE U.S.A. GOT WHAT IT WANTED, WHICH WAS EVERYTHING.

ALL THAT FOR US?

WHAT DO YOU MEAN, "US"?

FRANCE WAS CUT OUT OF THE DEAL COMPLETELY, ALTHOUGH KING LOUIS EVENTUALLY GOT MORE THAN HE BARGAINED FOR, OR LESS.

HOW WAS I TO KNOW THAT REVOLUTION IS CONTAGIOUS?

AMERICAN **TORIES** HAD A CHOICE: STAY, AND WATCH THEIR PROPERTY PILLAGED BY PATRIOTS, OR GO TO CANADA, WHERE THEY WOULDN'T HAVE TO WATCH. MOST OF THEM STAYED.

I HAD TO STAY: THEY STOLE MY SUITCASE!

ABOUT 60,000 **SLAVES** ESCAPED, TRAVELING AMAZING ODYSSEYS TO CANADA, FLORIDA, AFRICA, JAMAICA, ETC... ANOTHER 700,000 SLAVES REMAINED SLAVES, TO HELP CARRY THIS VOLUME TO ITS CONCLUSION.

AND THEY CALL IT "LIGHT READING."

AND THE **INDIANS** GOT— WELL, YOU KNOW WHAT THE INDIANS GOT.

COWBOYS...

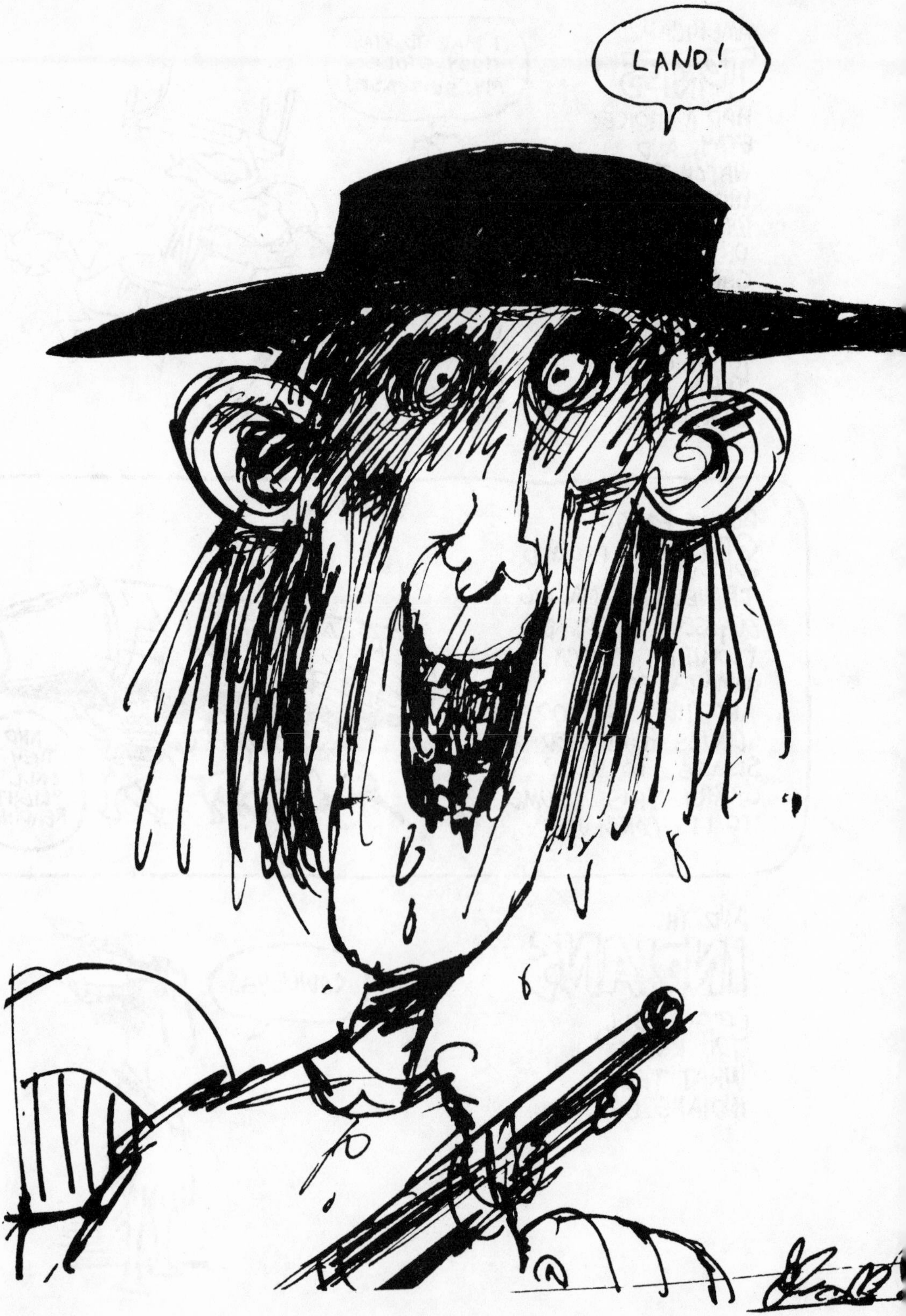
LAND!

·CHAPTER 6·

SHOES, MYTHS, THE CONSTITUTION, ETC.

And so it began... the American Dream... and the American Myth... and what could be more mythic — or more American — than the Wagon Train??

ACTUALLY, THE WAGON TRAINS OF
THE 1780's WERE PRETTY SMALL...
SMALL BUT MYTHIC... AT LEAST,
THE FRONT END WAS MYTHIC, WITH
ITS WAGONMASTERS, SCOUTS, AND
PIONEER FAMILIES HOPING TO
CARVE OUT A NEW LIFE BEFORE
IT CARVED THEM FIRST.

BUT THE SLAVE CARAVAN, OR SOUL TRAIN,
AT THE REAR, WAS LEFT OUT OF THE
FORWARD-LOOKING AMERICAN MYTH.
THE SLAVES BELONGED TO GENTLEMEN*
PIONEERS, WHOSE VISION OF TENNESSEE
AND KENTUCKY WAS IDENTICAL TO
VIRGINIA OR CAROLINA, ONLY A LITTLE
TO THE LEFT, ON THE MAP, THAT IS.

* SO-CALLED BECAUSE PEOPLE TREATED THEM GENTLY, NOT VICE VERSA

WHERE ARE WE HEADING, AS A NATION, I MEAN?

THE SPREAD OF SLAVERY WAS ALARMING, AND NOT ONLY TO THE SLAVES. A NUMBER OF WHITES HAD ALSO NOTICED SOMETHING IN THE DECLARATION OF INDEPENDENCE ABOUT "ALL MEN" HAVING A RIGHT TO LIBERTY.

I DON'T *THINK* IT SAYS "EXCEPT NEGROES..."

ANTI-SLAVERY WHITES FAILED REPEATEDLY TO HALT ITS EXPANSION. IN 1784, WHEN CONGRESS CONSIDERED A BAN ON SLAVERY IN THE WEST, THE MEASURE LOST BY A SINGLE VOTE, AND THE RELENTLESS WESTERN CLANK CONTINUED.

HEY, DID YOU HEAR THE ONE ABOUT THE NATION CONCEIVED IN LIBERTY?

IF IT WAS ANY CONSOLATION, CONTROLLING SLAVERY WASN'T THE GOVERNMENT'S ONLY PROBLEM. FOR EXAMPLE, THERE WAS ALSO THE PROBLEM OF THE SHOES — 30,000 PAIRS OF IMPORTED SHOES, TO BE EXACT, DUMPED ON THE NEW YORK MARKET AT ROCK-BOTTOM PRICES.

THIS WAS CONSIDERED (U)NFAIR (C)OMPETITION BY NEW YORK'S SHOEMAKERS, WHO BELIEVED IN AMERICAN SHOES, WITH LEATHER BOTTOMS AND PRICES TO MATCH.

ISN'T THAT WHAT THE REVOLUTION WAS ABOUT?

BUT ALAS... CONGRESS, IN ITS WISDOM, HAD FORGOTTEN TO GIVE ITSELF THE POWER TO REGULATE IMPORTS... AND SO THE COBBLERS HAD NO PIE...

TIME TO BREAK OUT THE TAR AND FEATHERS AGAIN...

THEN THERE WAS THE DEBT PROBLEM, THE PROBLEM BEING THAT EVERYONE WAS IN IT, ESPECIALLY FARMERS AND THE GOVERNMENT. (CONGRESS HAD CLEVERLY FAILED TO GIVE ITSELF THE POWER TO COLLECT TAXES.) AFTER THE REVOLUTION, DEBT-RIDDEN FARMERS FOUND THEMSELVES FACING EVICTION.

IT'S EITHER YOU OR CONGRESS, AND I CAN'T SEE HOW TO EVICT CONGRESS...

MAW, FETCH BETSY!

I'D LIKE YOU TO MEET "BETSY..."

THE FARMERS, WHO WERE VETERANS OF THE REVOLUTION, WENT FOR THEIR MUSKETS.

WHAT EVER HAPPENED TO LIBERTY **AND** PROPERTY?

THE BANKERS WERE HORRIFIED! THEY BELIEVED THAT GOVERNMENTS EXIST TO HELP COLLECT LOAN PAYMENTS, AND WHO'S TO SAY THEY WERE WRONG?

WHEN ARMED FARMERS RESISTED, AS IN SHAYS' REBELLION (1786), BIG WEALTH DECIDED THAT THE REVOLUTION HAD **GONE TOO FAR**...

THEY'RE UNCHECKED! I'M UNBALANCED!

"TOO MUCH DEMOCRACY," THEY GRUMBLED, NOTING THAT A FORMER SHOEMAKER WAS NOW LIEUTENANT GOVERNOR OF NEW YORK. WHAT WAS NEXT?

PERMANENT HOLES IN MY SOLES?

IN 1787, THE "BETTER CLASS" OF CITIZENS, WHICH INCLUDED BANKERS, BUSINESSMEN, SLAVE OWNERS, AND, FOR SOME REASON, LAWYERS, DECIDED TO DO SOMETHING.

IF THE FARMERS CAN TAKE THE LAW INTO THEIR OWN HANDS, BY GOD WE'LL TAKE THE WHOLE ☆⊙# GOVERNMENT!

ARTICLES OF CONFEDERATION

THEY CONVENED IN PHILADELPHIA TO CONSIDER CHANGES IN THE PLAN OF GOVERNMENT. AT THE TIME, THE U.S.A. WAS OPERATING, IF YOU CAN CALL IT THAT, UNDER THE ARTICLES OF CONFEDERATION, THE WONDERFUL DOCUMENT THAT PREVENTED CONGRESS FROM COLLECTING TAXES OR REGULATING COMMERCE.

THE VERY FIRST CHANGE WAS TO THROW OUT THE ARTICLES OF CONFEDERATION ENTIRELY.

ALTHOUGH VERY FEW OF THEM WERE IN THE CONSTRUCTION BUSINESS, THE CONSTITUTION-WRITERS ARE KNOWN AS THE "FRAMERS." THEY INCLUDED:

GEORGE WASHINGTON, FROM THE $1 BILL...

ALEXANDER HAMILTON, FROM THE TEN...

BEN FRANKLIN, FROM THE HUNDRED.

(JEFFERSON, WHO WAS ABSENT, LATER APPEARED ON THE $2 BILL, WHICH NOBODY USED.)

THE FRAMERS' PROBLEM: THEY BELIEVED IN REPUBLICAN GOVERNMENT (NO ONE TRUSTED ANYONE ELSE TO BE KING), BUT THEY DIDN'T BELIEVE IN "POPULAR" GOVERNMENT (TOO MUCH POWER FOR THE POOR). THEY BELIEVED IN PRIVATE WEALTH, BUT THEY KNEW HOW THE RICH COULD HOG POWER AT PUBLIC COST...

THEREFORE: A "MIXED" GOVERNMENT, WITH A POPULAR ELEMENT, BUT ENOUGH CLOUT FOR THE RICH TO SAVE THEM THE BOTHER OF OVERHAULING IT AGAIN...

WHAT A JOB!

AMERICANS, WHO BY NOW HAD THE PRACTICAL EQUIVALENT OF 3 MILLION Ph.D.'s IN POLITICAL SCIENCE, ALL KNEW WHAT THE MOST RESPONSIVE AND ACCOUNTABLE KIND OF GOVERNMENT WAS: A LEGISLATURE, ELECTED BY THE PEOPLE,* AND RE-ELECTED OFTEN, TO PRESERVE FRESHNESS.

JUST LIKE CONGRESS, UNDER THE ARTICLES OF CONFEDERATION!

THE FRAMERS KEPT ONE OF THESE IN THEIR PLAN, BUT THEY MAGICALLY SHRANK IT DOWN TO ONE HALF OF ONE OF THREE BRANCHES OF GOVERNMENT. THIS IS THE HOUSE OF REPRESENTATIVES, OR "LOWER" HOUSE.

THE CHAMBER OF HORRORS!

*BEARING IN MIND THAT POOR, BLACK, AND FEMALE PEOPLE HADN'T BEEN DISCOVERED YET.

102

ON TOP OF THE HOUSE WERE HEAPED THE SENATE, THE EXECUTIVE, AND THE JUDICIARY. THESE WERE DESIGNED TO IMPEDE AND FRUSTRATE EACH OTHER, THE IDEA BEING TO PREVENT ANY ONE BRANCH FROM BECOMING TOO POWERFUL. THIS DESIGN, WHICH SUCCEEDED, IS CALLED THE SYSTEM OF CHECKS AND BALANCES.

BECAUSE IT'S HARD TO KEEP YOUR BALANCE WHEN YOU'RE BEING CHECKED!

THE NEW GOVERNMENT WAS GIVEN POWERS TO MATCH ITS BULK: THE POWER TO TAX, TO REGULATE TRADE, TO MAKE WAR, TO RAISE A BUREAUCRACY, ETC...

HM! SOUNDS LIKE THE BRITISH GOVERNMENT...

THAT SOLVED THE PROBLEMS OF TAXES, DEBT, POWER, "EXCESS" DEMOCRACY, COMMERCE — EVERY PROBLEM BUT ONE... THE ONE THAT COULD ONLY BE DESCRIBED IN CIRCUMLOCUTIONS,* AS IT WAS TOO EMBARRASSING TO SAY IN PUBLIC, IN A REPUBLIC...

THE 5 SOUTHERN STATES, A MINORITY, WANTED GUARANTEES THAT THE NORTHERN MAJORITY WOULDN'T TAMPER WITH SLAVERY. WHENEVER A NORTHERN DELEGATE SUGGESTED THAT BLACKS HAD RIGHTS, TOO, SOUTH CAROLINA WOULD THREATEN TO GO HOME.

THE NORTH, ANXIOUS TO AVOID CIVIL WAR (AT LEAST FOR THE TIME BEING), AGREED TO MAKE SOME CONCESSIONS TO PREVENT SECESSION.

*SEE NEXT PAGE.

104

HERE WAS THE DEAL:

SOUTHERN WHITES WERE GIVEN OVER-REPRESENTATION IN THE HOUSE, BY ALLOWING 3/5 OF THE "OTHER PERSONS"* TO BE COUNTED ON TOP OF THE WHITE POPULATION, EVEN THOUGH THEY WERE REALLY UNDERNEATH IT.

IN RETURN, SOUTHERNERS IN CONGRESS AGREED TO A BAN ON SLAVERY IN THE FUTURE STATES NORTH OF THE OHIO RIVER, PROVIDED THAT THE NUMBER OF STATES THERE WAS HELD TO THREE —OHIO, INDIANA, ILLINOIS — THUS LIMITING NORTHERN INFLUENCE IN THE SENATE.

YOU REPRESENT ME?

THE NORTH PROMISED TO RETURN ANY "PERSON HELD TO SERVICE OR LABOR"* WHO ESCAPED.

AND...

ANYTHING ELSE?

THE SLAVE TRADE, OR "IMPORTATION OF SUCH PERSONS AS ANY OF THE STATES SHALL THINK PROPER TO ADMIT,"* WOULD CONTINUE UNTIL AT LEAST 1808.

...THAT WAS THE **COMPROMISE OF 1787.**

*SEE PREVIOUS FOOTNOTE.

BUT DRAFTING A CONSTITUTION WASN'T ENOUGH. IT ALSO HAD TO BE AIRED. WHEN THE PUBLIC CAUGHT WIND OF ITS CONTENTS, A STORMY DEBATE BLEW UP, WITH BOTH SIDES THUNDERING INSULTS AT EACH OTHER.

OPPONENTS BLASTED THE PLAN AS OVER-CENTRALIZED AND ANTI-DEMOCRATIC, WHILE PROPONENTS MADE BREEZY DENIALS.

THE FEDERAL GOVERNMENT WILL NEVER BECOME A BLOATED BUREAUCRACY... THE PRESIDENT CAN NEVER SEND 500,000 TROOPS TO A COUNTRY BEGINNING WITH "V" WITHOUT A CONGRESSIONAL DECLARATION OF WAR, NOT UNDER THIS CONSTITUTION, NUH-UH!

THE "ANTIS" ALSO NOTICED A FEW THINGS MISSING FROM THE DOCUMENT: LIKE ANYTHING ABOUT FREEDOM OF SPEECH, RELIGION, AND THE PRESS... THE RIGHT TO BEAR ARMS, DUE PROCESS, A SPEEDY TRIAL, ETC., ETC, ETC... THE EMBARRASSED FRAMERS PROMISED TO ADD A BILL OF RIGHTS, OR, IN MORE BIBLICAL LANGUAGE, THE TEN AMENDMENTS.

A MERE OVERSIGHT!

AFTER MANY MONTHS OF MUD-SLINGING, GUN-WAVING, POLITICAL SKULL-DIGGERY AND-DUGGERY, AND OCCASIONAL HONEST DEBATE, THE CONSTITUTION WAS ADOPTED, AND EVERYONE IMMEDIATELY FELL TO WORSHIPPING IT, WHICH IS HOW IT'S BEEN EVER SINCE, ALMOST.

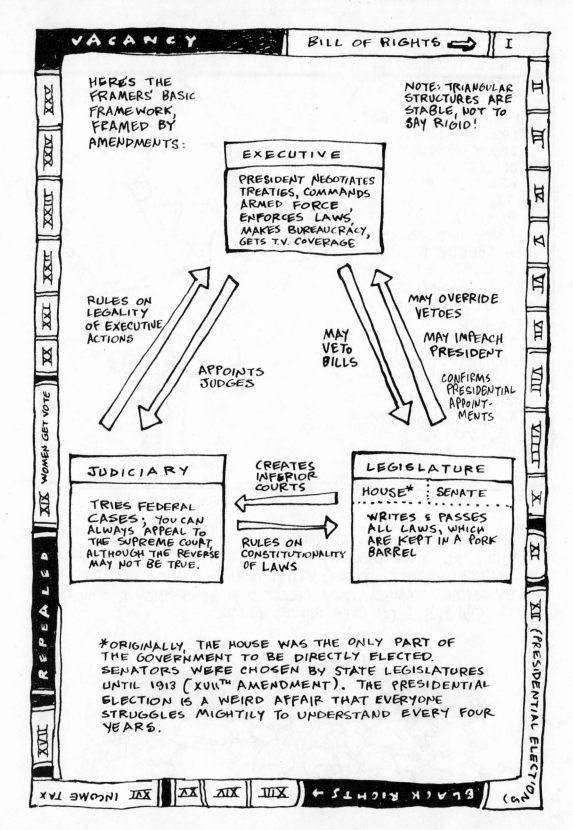

VACANCY

BILL OF RIGHTS ➡ I

HERE'S THE FRAMERS' BASIC FRAMEWORK, FRAMED BY AMENDMENTS:

NOTE: TRIANGULAR STRUCTURES ARE STABLE, NOT TO SAY RIGID!

EXECUTIVE

PRESIDENT NEGOTIATES TREATIES, COMMANDS ARMED FORCE, ENFORCES LAWS, MAKES BUREAUCRACY, GETS T.V. COVERAGE

RULES ON LEGALITY OF EXECUTIVE ACTIONS

APPOINTS JUDGES

MAY OVERRIDE VETOES

MAY IMPEACH PRESIDENT

CONFIRMS PRESIDENTIAL APPOINTMENTS

MAY VETO BILLS

JUDICIARY

TRIES FEDERAL CASES; YOU CAN ALWAYS APPEAL TO THE SUPREME COURT, ALTHOUGH THE REVERSE MAY NOT BE TRUE.

CREATES INFERIOR COURTS

RULES ON CONSTITUTIONALITY OF LAWS

LEGISLATURE

HOUSE* : SENATE

WRITES & PASSES ALL LAWS, WHICH ARE KEPT IN A PORK BARREL

*ORIGINALLY, THE HOUSE WAS THE ONLY PART OF THE GOVERNMENT TO BE DIRECTLY ELECTED. SENATORS WERE CHOSEN BY STATE LEGISLATURES UNTIL 1913 (XVIITH AMENDMENT). THE PRESIDENTIAL ELECTION IS A WEIRD AFFAIR THAT EVERYONE STRUGGLES MIGHTILY TO UNDERSTAND EVERY FOUR YEARS.

XXV · XXIV · XXIII · XXII · XXI · XX · XIX WOMEN GET VOTE · XVIII REPEALED · XVII

II · III · IV · V · VI · VII · VIII · IX · X · XI · XII (PRESIDENTIAL ELECTIONS)

XVI INCOME TAX · XV · XIV · XIII · BLACK RIGHTS ←

★ CHAPTER 7 ★

MR. JEFFERSON THROWS A PARTY

GEORGE WASHINGTON WAS UNANIMOUSLY ELECTED TO BE THE FIRST PRESIDENT UNDER THE NEW CONSTITUTION.

CONGRESS IMMEDIATELY DEBATED FOR THREE WEEKS WHETHER TO ADDRESS HIM AS "MR. PRESIDENT" OR "YOUR MAJESTY."

THIS SPLIT— BETWEEN THOSE WHO WANTED THEIR GOVERNMENT PLAIN VS. THOSE WHO WANTED IT POMPOUS— QUICKLY SPILLED OVER INTO OTHER AREAS.

YOUR MAJEST- OOF!

MR. PRESIDENT!! LOOK OUT! A FLAMING MONARCHIST!!

THE NEXT FIGHT STARTED WITH A PROVOCATIVE PROPOSAL FROM TREASURY SECRETARY ALEXANDER **HAMILTON**.

LET'S GIVE THE COUNTRY TO THE RICH!

DURING THE REVOLUTION, SAID HAMILTON, THE STATE GOVERNMENTS HAD BORROWED HEAVILY — AND NEVER REPAID THEIR DEBTS. NOW, VAST QUANTITIES OF STATE-ISSUED I.O.U.'S WERE FLOATING AROUND ... BOUGHT, SOLD, AND COLLECTED, SOMETHING LIKE BASEBALL CARDS. *

I'LL GIVE YOU TWO MARYLANDS FOR A STAN MUSIAL...

HAMILTON'S PLAN WAS FOR THE FEDERAL GOVERNMENT TO REPAY EVERY I.O.U. AT FACE VALUE — A HUGE WINDFALL FOR THE HOLDERS.

GOOD IDEA, ALEX!

* EXCEPT THAT BASEBALL CARDS SOMETIMES RISE IN VALUE.

SECRETARY OF STATE THOMAS JEFFERSON ACCUSED HAMILTON OF SCHEMING TO MORTGAGE THE NATION TO THE EASTERN MONEY ESTABLISHMENT, AT TAXPAYER EXPENSE.

"THE MORE DEBT HAMILTON COULD RAKE UP, THE MORE PLUNDER FOR HIS MERCENARIES. THIS MONEY, WHETHER WISELY OR FOOLISHLY SPENT, WAS PRETENDED TO HAVE BEEN SPENT FOR GENERAL PURPOSES, AND OUGHT, THEREFORE, TO BE PAID FROM THE GENERAL PURSE."

HAMILTON RETORTED THAT A BIG NATIONAL DEBT WAS A **GOOD THING**, BECAUSE THE RICH, HOPING TO BE REPAID, WILL SUPPORT STRONG GOVERNMENT.

MOMMY!

JEFFERSON REPLIED THAT A BIG DEBT CAUSES THE GOVERNMENT TO FAVOR THE RICH, WHO LOAN IT MONEY, AND TO CRUSH THE POOR, WHO HAVE TO PAY IT OFF.

JEFFERSON SNEERED THAT HAMILTON WAS TRYING TO BUY POLITICAL SUPPORT... HAMILTON SNARLED THAT HE SAW NOTHING WRONG WITH THAT... ENGLAND HAD BEEN RUNNING THAT WAY FOR GENERATIONS...

MONARCHIST!

FOOL! REDHEAD!

THIS FIGHT ENDED WITH A STRANGE COMPROMISE: JEFFERSON DROPPED HIS OPPOSITION TO THE TREASURY PLAN, WHILE HAMILTON BACKED JEFFERSON'S PET PROJECT, A NATIONAL CAPITAL IN THE SOUTH! AND THAT'S WHY WASHINGTON, D.C. WAS BUILT ON THE BANKS OF THE POTOMAC!

COURTESY OF THE BANKS OF N.Y.!

AH... BUT THERE WAS STILL THE MATTER OF THE

FRENCH REVOLUTION!

INSPIRED BY THE AMERICANS, THE FRENCH PEOPLE HAD RISEN UP AND GIVEN THEIR KING AN OPERATION WHICH MADE IT NECESSARY TO DECLARE A REPUBLIC.

WE DEFINITELY NEED A NEW HEAD OF GOVERNMENT...

JEFFERSON, WHO FELT LIKE ITS AMERICAN GODFATHER, WAS ALL FOR THE FRENCH REVOLUTION. HAMILTON, WHO MORE ADMIRED ENGLAND, WHERE PATRIOTISM AND PECUNIARY SELF-INTEREST WERE BLENDED TO THE POINT THAT NO ONE COULD TELL THE DIFFERENCE* WAS SUSPICIOUS OF ANYTHING BASED PURELY ON PRINCIPLES.

THE MAN HAS **NO** APPRECIATION OF THE BEAUTY OF BLOOD RUNNING IN THE STREET!

*ONLY AT THAT TIME, NO DOUBT

HAMILTON ATTACKED JEFFERSON IN THE PRESS... JEFFERSON SECRETLY STARTED HIS OWN NEWSPAPER TO SAVAGE HAMILTON AND CELEBRATE HIMSELF...

LIBERTY! EQUALITY! FRATERNITY!

THE COMMON PEOPLE, WITH JEFFERSON, HAILED REVOLUTIONARY FRANCE.

THE COMMERCIAL CLASSES, WITH HAMILTON, PREFERRED ENGLAND, THEIR MAIN SOURCE OF BUSINESS.

MONEY! PROPERTY! STABILITY!

GRADUALLY, THE COUNTRY DIVIDED INTO TWO CAMPS...

THEY CALL THEM "PARTIES"?

EVEN THO THERE'S NOT A WOMAN IN EITHER OF 'EM!

HAMILTON'S PARTY, THE

FEDERALISTS,

FAVORED A STRONG CENTRAL GOVERNMENT, THE INTERESTS OF NORTHERN BANKERS AND MANUFACTURERS, ENGLAND OVER FRANCE, AND GOVERNMENT BY THE "BETTER SORT" (READ: BANKERS AND MANUFACTURERS).

ONE FEDERALIST PROPOSED A VOTING AGE OF 50!

JEFFERSON'S PARTY, THE

REPUBLICANS,

FAVORED A MINIMAL GOVERNMENT, THE INTERESTS OF FARMERS AND BORROWERS, THE SOUTH, FRANCE OVER ENGLAND, AND WIDER POPULAR PARTICIPATION IN GOVERNMENT.

GUILLOTINISTS!

BOTH PARTIES FAVORED THEIR OWN ELECTION AND THE OTHER'S REMOVAL!

AFTER TRYING TO STAY ABOVE THE FRAY, WASHINGTON FINALLY DECLARED HIMSELF A FEDERALIST. THE REPUBLICANS BEGAN CALLING HIM "TRAITOR," "VILLAIN," AND "ENEMY OF THE REVOLUTION," INSTEAD OF "MR. PRESIDENT."

IN 1796, WASHINGTON STARTED AN AMERICAN TRADITION BY ANNOUNCING THAT EIGHT YEARS AS PRESIDENT WAS MORE THAN ENOUGH FOR ANYONE. HE DECLINED TO RUN FOR A THIRD TERM, GIVING A FAREWELL ADDRESS BUT NO FORWARDING ADDRESS.

HE RETIRED TO HIS PLANTATION AND SUCCUMBED TO AN EXCESS OF MEDICAL TREATMENT.

IN WASHINGTON'S LAST WILL & TESTAMENT, HE FREED ALL HIS SLAVES.

IN THE PRESIDENTIAL ELECTION OF 1796, THE FEDERALIST JOHN **ADAMS** WON NARROWLY OVER THE REPUBLICAN CANDIDATE, THOMAS JEFFERSON.

ASIDE FROM HIS DIAMETER, ADAMS IS BEST KNOWN FOR BUILDING UP THE NAVY WITH "OLD IRONSIDES" AND JAILING REPUBLICAN NEWSPAPER EDITORS WITH SEDITION LAWS.

SO WHY DID I LOSE IN 1800?

ADAMS' DEFEAT IN THE NEXT ELECTION SHOWS HOW IMPORTANT POLITICAL PARTIES HAD BECOME BY 1800.

A SQUABBLE BETWEEN ADAMS AND HAMILTON HAD DIVIDED THE FEDERALISTS... WHILE IN HAMILTON'S OWN NEW YORK CITY **AARON BURR** AND THE REPUBLICANS HAD BUILT A POWERFUL POLITICAL MACHINE, TAMMANY HALL, WHICH HAD BROUGHT MANY URBAN WORKERS INTO THE JEFFERSONIAN RANKS.

BURR DELIVERED THE VOTES—

MANY OF THEM PERSONALLY!

NEW YORK WENT REPUBLICAN, SWINGING THE ELECTION TO JEFFERSON.

THEN BURR, WHO WAS THE VICE-PRESIDENTIAL CANDIDATE, TRIED TO STEAL THE PRESIDENCY FROM HIS RUNNING MATE! LATER, HE RUINED HIS POLITICAL LIFE TOTALLY BY KILLING ALEXANDER HAMILTON IN A DUEL...

MY CAREER IS SHOT!

THINK HOW I FEEL...

SO THOMAS JEFFERSON BECAME PRESIDENT...

SO WHAT?

TO UNDERSTAND WHAT THIS MEANT, YOU HAVE TO REALIZE HOW THE FEDERALISTS LOATHED THE MAN.

FOR YEARS, THE FEDERALISTS HAD BEEN TRYING TO HOLD BACK THE DEMOCRATIC TIDE. JEFFERSON THEY VIEWED AS A RADICAL... AN ATHEIST... A FRIEND OF THE FRENCH REVOLUTION, WHICH HAD MADE POLITICS SYNONYMOUS WITH DECAPITATION... A DREAMER WHOSE POLICIES WERE BASED ON THE HALLUCINATION OF EQUALITY. THE "FIRE-BREATHING SALAMANDER," THEY CALLED HIM.—AND NOW HE WAS PRESIDENT!!

WE'VE ELECTED AN AMPHIBIAN!

AND WHAT DID THE FIRE-EATER DO? CUT TAXES, PAID OFF THE DEBT, AND DOUBLED THE COUNTRY'S TERRITORY — PEACEFULLY!

FOR STARTERS, HE PEACEFULLY
DOUBLED THE NATION'S TERRITORY
WITH THE

LOUISIANA PURCHASE.

THE STORY ACTUALLY BEGINS WITH ANOTHER REVOLUTION, THIS ONE IN **HAITI**, WHERE THE SLAVES THREW OFF, OR CUT OFF, THEIR FRENCH MASTERS.

THE FRENCH SET US SUCH A GOOD EXAMPLE!

(IN THE U.S.A., SOUTHERNERS CRINGED IN FEAR, AND TRIED TO KEEP THE NEWS FROM THEIR OWN SLAVES.)

MIGHTY QUIET... MUST BE AN UPRISING SOMEWHERE...

ANYWAY, FRANCE THREW HEAPS OF MEN, FRANCS, AND BEANS INTO HAITI. THE HAITIANS MADE HAMBURGER OUT OF THEM...

WHAT A BARBECUE!

HM... NOW MY WALLET'S EMPTY...

NAPOLEON, WHO WAS NOW DICTATOR OF FRANCE, DECIDED TO CASH IN HIS AMERICAN REAL ESTATE. (HE EXPECTED TO MAKE IT UP BY CONQUERING RUSSIA, WHICH HAD LOTS OF OCEANFRONT, OR AT LEAST PLENTY OF SERFS.)

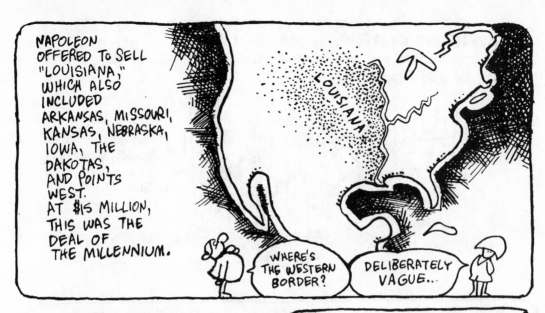

NAPOLEON OFFERED TO SELL "LOUISIANA," WHICH ALSO INCLUDED ARKANSAS, MISSOURI, KANSAS, NEBRASKA, IOWA, THE DAKOTAS, AND POINTS WEST. AT $15 MILLION, THIS WAS THE DEAL OF THE MILLENNIUM.

WHERE'S THE WESTERN BORDER?

DELIBERATELY VAGUE...

THE PRESIDENT FRANTICALLY FLIPPED THROUGH THE CONSTITUTION, LOOKING FOR A REAL ESTATE LICENSE...

C'MON! C'MON!

BONK BONK

NOT FINDING ONE, HE DID WHAT PRESIDENTS HAVE ALWAYS DONE:

WHATEVER I CAN GET AWAY WITH!

AND SO JEFFERSON CLOSED THE DEAL... AS FEDERALIST POLITICIANS MOANED HOW UNFAIR IT WAS OF HIM TO DO ANYTHING SO... SO... POPULAR...

"POPULAR!" THE VERY WORD LODGES IN MY ESOPHAGUS!

WE'LL SHOW 'EM... WE'LL DO SOMETHING POPULAR, TOO...

YEAH-- LIKE LOSE THE NEXT ELECTION...

THE PRESIDENT IMMEDIATELY SHIPPED OFF TWO VIRGINIA NEIGHBORS, **LEWIS** AND **CLARK**, TO EXPLORE LOUISIANA — ALL THE WAY TO THE PACIFIC NORTHWEST, WHERE JEFFERSON HOPED TO PUT AN AMERICAN PORT.

LOVELY PLACE, WHEN YOU CAN SEE IT...

HIS INDIAN POLICY WAS THEORETICALLY PEACEFUL, TOO... THAT IS, HE HOPED THAT THE INDIANS' CONTACTS WITH CIVILIZATION WOULD PERSUADE THEM TO ADOPT IT.

TRANSLATION: DRIVE US INTO DEBT, THEN SEIZE OUR LAND AS PAYMENT!

TRADER TIM
BLANKETS
BAUBLES
BAD BOURBON
E·Z·CREDIT

HAVE A DRINK... YOU'RE MUCH TOO RATIONAL YET TO DO BUSINESS...

AND, IN DISPUTES WITH ENGLAND, FRANCE, AND SPAIN, JEFFERSON USED ONLY <u>ECONOMIC</u> WARFARE—

BOYCOTTS AND EMBARGOES— INSTEAD OF THE SHOOTING VARIETY. THIS PINCHED AMERICANS, TOO, BUT BETTER PINCHED THAN SHOT, YES?

AND DON'T FORGET THAT JEFFERSON REDUCED TAXES, CUT THE MILITARY BUDGET, AND PAID OFF THE NATIONAL DEBT!

NATURALLY, HE WAS RE-ELECTED BY A LANDSLIDE IN 1804.*

AT THIS, THE FEDERALISTS LOST THEIR HEADS — OR RATHER, THE FEDERALIST HEADS LOST CONTROL OF THEIR BODIES.

JOHN ADAMS, THE SECOND FEDERALIST PRESIDENT, TURNED OUT TO BE THE **LAST** FEDERALIST PRESIDENT.

BUT JEFFERSON'S PARTY IS STILL AROUND... WE KNOW IT AS THE **DEMOCRATIC** PARTY. (IT CHANGED NAMES AS SOON AS IT WAS SAFE.)

HE DIDN'T GUILLOTINE US — HE JUST DECAPITATED OUR PARTY!

*DURING THE CAMPAIGN, THE PRESS SPREAD DARK RUMORS (AND LIGHT VERSE) ABOUT JEFFERSON'S ALLEGED MEDIUM-DARK MISTRESS. HER NAME WAS SALLY HEMINGS, IT WAS SAID... SHE WAS HIS SLAVE... SHE BORE HIM FOUR CHILDREN, WHO ALL LOOKED AMAZINGLY LIKE THEIR DAD... ALL REMAINED IN SLAVERY... ETC... JEFFERSON, LIKE ANY SHARP POLITICIAN CONFRONTED WITH THE TRUTH, MADE NO COMMENT, AND LOST NO VOTES, APPARENTLY!

YOU'D VOTE FOR ME, IF YOU COULD VOTE, WOULDN'T YOU, SAL?

NO COMMENT.

JEFFERSON'S LEGACY

IMPRESSIVE AS HIS ACCOMPLISHMENTS WERE, JEFFERSON'S CONTRADICTIONS WERE EQUALLY AMAZING! WHAT CAN YOU SAY ABOUT A MAN WHO—

BELIEVED THAT STATE & LOCAL GOVERNMENT WERE CLOSEST TO THE PEOPLE... ...WHEN HIS OWN STATE WAS DOMINATED BY A SLAVEOWNING ELITE?

SAW AMERICA'S FUTURE AS A NATION OF YEOMAN FARMERS... ...AT THE DAWN OF THE INDUSTRIAL AGE?

OPPOSED SLAVERY IN PUBLIC... ...ENJOYED SLAVERY IN PRIVATE?

BELIEVED THAT BLACKS WERE OPPRESSED... ...BELIEVED THAT BLACKS WERE INFERIOR?

THOUGHT URBAN WORKERS WERE IRRESPONSIBLE CITIZENS... ...WELCOMED URBAN WORKERS INTO HIS PARTY?

ADVOCATED THE SIMPLE LIFE... ...LIVED A LIFE OF LUXURY?

EXPRESSED SYMPATHY FOR THE INDIANS... ...FOUNDED THE DETESTED INDIAN BUREAU?

BELIEVED IN A FREE PRESS... ...SECRETLY SUBSIDIZED A NEWS-PAPER TO FLAY HIS ENEMIES?

DEMANDED A STRICT INTERPRETATION OF THE CONSTITUTION... ...STRETCHED THE CONSTITUTION TO BUY LOUISIANA?

WHAT, INDEED, CAN YOU SAY?

WELL, YOU CAN SAY THAT HE FOUNDED AN ENDURING POLITICAL PARTY IN HIS OWN IMAGE — FULL OF CONTRADICTIONS, THAT IS: THE PARTY OF THE WHITE RACIST AND THE BLACKS, THE ETHNIC AND THE BIGOT, THE FACTORY WORKER AND THE YUPPIE, THE SOCIALIST AND THE CONSERVATIVE, THE SOUTHERNER FOR STATES' RIGHTS AND THE NORTHERNER FOR BIG GOVERNMENT, THE EXPANSIONIST, THE CONTRACTIONIST...

AND OCCASIONALLY, THE CONTORTIONIST!

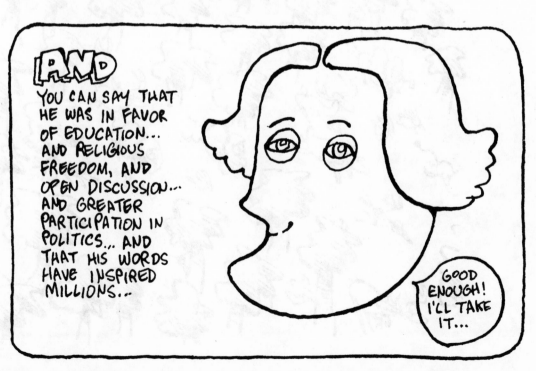

AND YOU CAN SAY THAT HE WAS IN FAVOR OF EDUCATION... AND RELIGIOUS FREEDOM, AND OPEN DISCUSSION... AND GREATER PARTICIPATION IN POLITICS... AND THAT HIS WORDS HAVE INSPIRED MILLIONS...

GOOD ENOUGH! I'LL TAKE IT...

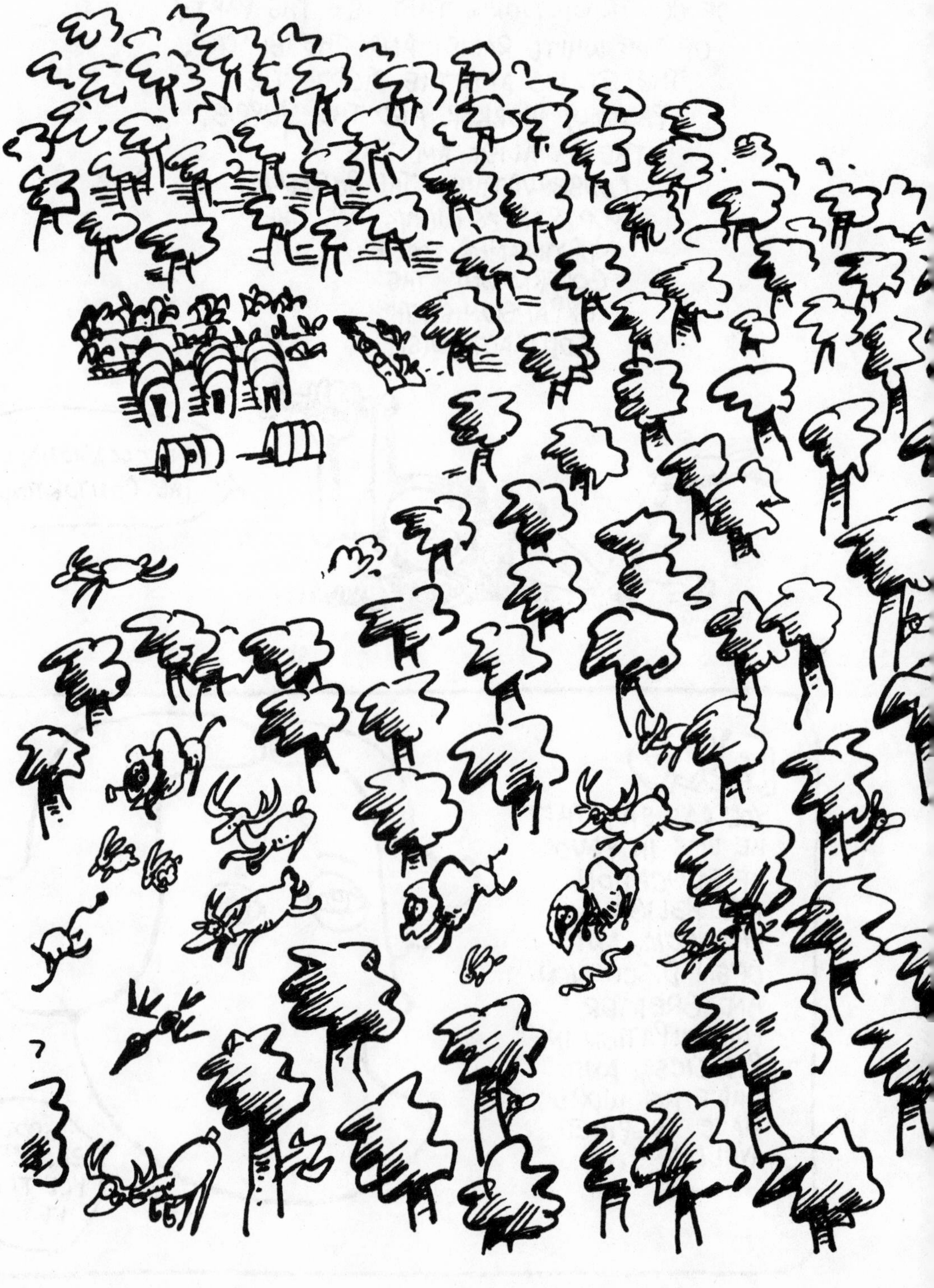

CHAPTER 8

MANIFEST DENTISTRY, OR THE GREAT UPROOTING

With Visions of Jeffersonian Rhetoric dancing in their heads, Americans flooded west in the early 1800's... The action was in Ohio, Indiana, and Illinois in the north, and Georgia, Mississippi, and Alabama, down south.

Ohio R.

Mississippi R.

By golly, Maw, let's carve us a farm from th' virgin forest inhabited only by wild beasts & nekkid savages who will quickly see the advantages of civilized life!

Unfortunately, it didn't quite work out according to the peaceable Jeffersonian plan... for some reason, the vanguard of civilization didn't exactly inspire the Indians to imitation...

Land speculators...

I'll give you a mountain of trinkets for a mountain!

Whiskey peddlers (often indistinguishable from land speculators)....

I'll throw this in for free!

And worst of all, outright Indian-killers who could never be brought to justice in any U.S. court.

Good shot, Lem! Kill her again!

INDIAN RESISTANCE WAS LED BY TWO SHAWNEE BROTHERS, **TENSKWATAWA**, "THE PROPHET," AND **TECUMSEH**, THE WARRIOR. TECUMSEH IS THE MORE FAMOUS OF THE TWO, AS HIS NAME IS EASIER TO PRONOUNCE.

"THE PROPHET"

TECUMSEH

THE PROPHET, WHO PREACHED THE REJECTION OF ALL THINGS PERTAINING TO THE U.S.A., WON MANY CONVERTS BY PREDICTING A SOLAR ECLIPSE, WHICH HE HAD HEARD ABOUT FROM SOME AMERICAN ASTRONOMERS IN 1806.

TECUMSEH, WHO RELIED MORE ON LOGIC, TRAVELED FROM CANADA TO ALABAMA, TRYING TO ORGANIZE A MILITARY ALLIANCE OF ALL THE TRIBES.

BY 1811, FEDERAL TROOPS WERE MARCHING ON THE PROPHET'S HEADQUARTERS. THE RESULT WAS THE BATTLE OF **TIPPECANOE** (INDIANA), AND THE CONCLUSION WAS INESCAPABLE: THIS WAS WAR!

THANK GOD JEFFERSON'S NOT STILL PRESIDENT!

AND SO THE U.S. DID THE ONLY LOGICAL THING: DECLARED WAR — ON **GREAT BRITAIN !!**

THIS WAS THE ⬇

WHY ME !?

IT'S TRADITIONAL!

VVAR OF 1812

(WHICH WAS PROMOTED BY WESTERN "WAR HAWKS" WHO COVETED CANADA AND HOPED TO STOP BRITISH SUPPLIES FROM REACHING TECUMSEH).

NOT TO MENTION AN EXCELLENT EXCUSE TO GRAB SOME MORE INDIAN LAND !!

AMONG OTHER REASONS...

HENRY CLAY..

WARK! WARK!

THE U.S. FOUGHT BRITAIN TO A STANDSTILL...
MOST OF THE STANDING STILL TOOK PLACE ALONG THE CANADIAN BORDER. THERE WAS ALSO SOME RUNNING, WHEN THE REDCOATS BURNED WASHINGTON, D.C., AND THE OCCASIONAL SINKING SENSATION, ESPECIALLY AFTER NAVAL BATTLES...

PASS THE DRAMAMINE...

BUT FOR THE INDIANS, THE WAR OF 1812 WAS A DISASTER... TECUMSEH FELL IN LATE 1813, NEAR THE CANADIAN BORDER.

(HE IS USUALLY CONSIDERED THE GREATEST OF MODERN INDIAN STATESMEN + WARRIORS...)

EVEN WORSE WAS THE ARRIVAL OF **ANDREW JACKSON**, WHOSE NICKNAME WAS "OLD HICKORY," BUT COULD HAVE BEEN "THE TERMINATOR." AS A BOY, JACKSON HAD LOST HIS FAMILY IN THE REVOLUTION... THIS MADE HIM A FAIRLY TESTY FELLOW... HE WAS ALWAYS CHALLENGING PEOPLE TO DUELS... AND AT TIMES IT SEEMED THAT HE TOOK GENUINE PLEASURE IN KILLING PEOPLE!!

IN 1813, JACKSON LED A CAMPAIGN AGAINST THE CREEK INDIANS IN THE SOUTH... YOU COULD FOLLOW HIS TRAIL BY THE BODIES OF SOLDIERS HANGED FOR DESERTION, INSUBORDINATION, COMPLAINING ABOUT THE FOOD, ETC...

ACKSON INVITED, OR TERRORIZED, HUNDREDS OF CREEKS AND CHEROKEES INTO HIS ARMY... AND THEN SENT THEM TO LEAD THE CHARGE AGAINST THEIR COUSINS...

THEN HE "REWARDED" HIS ALLIES WITH A TREATY THAT TOOK AS MUCH LAND FROM THEM AS FROM THEIR ENEMIES! (THIS WAS PART OF GEORGIA AND MOST OF ALABAMA...)

NEXT HE MARCHED HIS ARMY TO NEW ORLEANS AND DEFEATED THE BRITISH IN A HUGE BATTLE WHICH MADE JACKSON A Ⓝational Ⓗero... IRONICALLY, THE PEACE TREATY HAD ALREADY BEEN SIGNED, BUT WORD HADN'T ARRIVED FROM EUROPE YET...

IF THE TELEGRAPH EXISTED, I'D JUST BE ANOTHER SEMI-HOMICIDAL MANIAC FROM TENNESSEE!

AND, FOR HIS FINAL EXPLOIT OF THE 18-TEENS, JACKSON MADE A SEMI-UNAUTHORIZED INVASION OF SPANISH **FLORIDA.** THERE HE KILLED INDIANS, DESTROYED A FORTFUL OF ESCAPED SLAVES, HANGED A COUPLE ENGLISHMEN... AND CONVINCED SPAIN TO SELL FLORIDA CHEAP... WASHINGTON TOOK NOTE!

HIS METHODS ARE CRUDE, VICIOUS, ILLEGAL, AND UNCONSTITUTIONAL, BUT HIS **BODY COUNT** IS ASTONISHING!

A FUTURE IN POLITICS LOOMS...

ALL OURS!

WITHIN TEN YEARS, JACKSON WAS PRESIDENT— THE FIRST WESTERNER IN THE OFFICE...

UNTIL 1828, EVERY PRESIDENT EITHER CAME FROM VIRGINIA, OR WAS NAMED ADAMS!

JACKSON PROCEEDED TO "OPEN" THE WEST—

AS IN, "OPEN WIDE!"

(NOTE: JACKSON HIMSELF WAS A BIG SPECULATOR IN WESTERN REAL ESTATE.)

THE FEDERAL GOVERNMENT, WHICH HAD GUARANTEED CERTAIN LANDS TO THE INDIANS, NOW LOOKED THE OTHER WAY AS THEY WERE TAKEN AWAY BY WHITE SETTLERS, STATE LAWS, AND PLAIN, OLD FRAUD...

AND WHEN WE RESIST, THEY CALL IT "RAVAGING THE FRONTIER SETTLEMENTS!"

FINALLY, WHEN FIGHTING BROKE OUT AGAIN, THE PRES UNVEILED HIS REAL PLANS, WHICH TOOK THE NAME OF

REMOVAL.

AT LEAST IT'S AN HONEST NAME!

THE IDEA WAS DAZZLINGLY SIMPLE: JUST "REMOVE" ALL THE INDIANS ON THE EAST SIDE OF THE MISSISSIPPI RIVER ACROSS TO THE WEST SIDE, TO "INDIAN TERRITORY" (OKLAHOMA). SIMPLICITY ITSELF!!

CONGRESS VOTED, AND IT WAS DONE... TRIBE AFTER TRIBE WAS MARCHED OFF BY THE CAVALRY... CHICKASAWS, CHOCTAWS, CREEKS, CHEROKEES, SHAWNEES, SACS, FOXES... 70,000 IN ALL... AND ALL BADLY SUPPLIED WITH FOOD AND BLANKETS, SO THAT THOUSANDS DIED ALONG THE WAY... 4500 CHEROKEES ALONE...

MARTIN VAN BUREN, THE NEXT PRESIDENT, CALLED IT "A HAPPY AND CERTAIN CONSUMMATION" OF A "WISE, HUMANE, AND UNDEVIATING POLICY," WHILE CHEROKEES STILL CALL IT THE **TRAIL OF TEARS.**

SO—IF YOU EVER HEAR THE QUESTION ASKED, "CAN 'IT' HAPPEN HERE?"— THE ANSWER IS:

BEFORE TAKING LEAVE OF ANDREW JACKSON, WE SHOULD NOTE THAT HE WAS ONE OF ONLY TWO PRESIDENTS WHOSE NAMES BECAME ADJECTIVES, AS IN ⇒

(THE OTHER ONE WAS JEFFERSON.)

WHAT WAS DEMOCRACY, JACKSON-STYLE? ACTUALLY, IT'S EASIER TO SAY WHAT "JEFFERSONIAN" MEANT, BECAUSE JEFFERSON, A THINKER AND WRITER, HAD A THEORY OF SOCIETY. IN JEFFERSON'S VIEW, DEMOCRACY SHOULD BE BASED ON A SELF-SUFFICIENT MIDDLE CLASS OF "YEOMAN FARMERS," WHOSE IDEAS WOULD BE FORMED BY LIBERAL EDUCATION AND A FREE PRESS. GOVERNMENT SHOULD BE MINIMAL AND TAXES LOW.

THANKS, TOM!

"JACKSONIAN" DEMOCRACY, ON THE OTHER HAND, WAS NOT THE PRODUCT OF ANY ONE MIND. IT SIMPLY MEANT WHATEVER DEMOCRACY HAD BECOME BY THE TIME ANDREW JACKSON HAPPENED ALONG. (IRONICALLY, THE CONSERVATIVE JACKSON HAD ALMOST NOTHING TO DO WITH ITS DEVELOPMENT.)

I DIDN'T EVEN LIKE IT, UNTIL IT ELECTED ME PRESIDENT!

ITS ELEMENTS:

UNIVERSAL MANHOOD SUFFRAGE: BEGINNING IN THE WEST, STATES HAD BEGUN EXTENDING THE VOTE TO ALL (WHITE) MEN, REGARDLESS OF PROPERTY. THIS WAS THE DEMOCRACY OF ALL SOCIAL CLASSES.

THERE ARE GREASY STAINS ON THE WHITE HOUSE WALLS!

RAPID EXPANSION OF THE WEST: JACKSONIANS ASSAILED "EASTERN MONEY," WHOSE CONSERVATISM SLOWED WESTERN GROWTH... THEY FAVORED EASY MONEY + PLENTY OF SPECULATION, EVEN IF THESE PRODUCED A CHAOTIC, BOOM/BUST ECONOMY WITH FREQUENT BANK FAILURES.

10TH NAT'L BANK OF 11TH STREET

CLOSED

TIME TO GO WEST AGAIN!

(AND OF COURSE INDIAN REMOVAL WAS A BIG PART OF WESTERN EXPANSION.)

THE PRESIDENT AS REPRESENTATIVE OF ALL THE PEOPLE: PREVIOUSLY, CONGRESS HAD BEEN CONSIDERED THE MOST "POPULAR" BRANCH... BUT JACKSON FREELY VETOED CONGRESSIONAL BILLS AND FEUDED OPENLY WITH THE SUPREME COURT. JACKSON SET THE MODEL FOR THE BORN-ON-THE-FRONTIER, NOT-ESPECIALLY WELL-EDUCATED, MILITARY-HERO TYPE PRESIDENT.

VETO

"KING ANDREW", HIS ENEMIES CALLED HIM...

MEANWHILE

(ON ANOTHER FRONT...)

THE BROOM
OF REVOLUTION
WAS SWEEPING
SPAIN OUT OF
LATIN AMERICA...
BY 1823, ONLY
THE MOPPING
UP WAS
LEFT...

GOOD HELP IS IMPOSSIBLE TO GET THIS CENTURY...

SO THE UNITED STATES, IN THE PERSON OF PRESIDENT MONROE, ISSUED A DOCTRINE. (THIS WAS CHEAPER THAN SENDING AID TO THE REVOLUTIONARIES.) FROM NOW ON, SAID THE DOCTRINE, THE U.S. WOULD NO LONGER TOLERATE EUROPEANS WHO PILLAGED THE AMERICAS... FOR SOME REASON, THE NEWLY INDEPENDENT NATIONS TOOK THIS TO MEAN THAT ALL FUTURE PILLAGING WOULD BE DONE BY THE U.S.A. ALONE...

OH, NOTHING COULD BE FURTHER FROM THE TRUTH...

TAKE ☀ **MEXICO,** FOR EXAMPLE...

THANKS, I'D LIKE THAT!

MEXICAN INDEPENDENCE CAME IN 1821... AS YOU CAN SEE, IT WAS A BIG PLACE THEN... MUST HAVE BEEN NICE, TOO... BECAUSE AMERICANS KEPT MOVING THERE...

I WONDER WHAT'S SO BAD AT HOME THAT MAKES THEM LEAVE??

A FEW PARTS OF MEXICO
THE GRINGOS INVADED:

TEXAS

ANGLOS (AND SLAVES) BEGAN
SETTLING IN THE 1820's...
THEY RAISED BIG CATTLE WITH
LONG HORNS ON HUGE RANCHES...
EVERYTHING ABOUT THE PLACE
WAS BIG... THE QUANTITY OF **BULL**
WAS ENORMOUS... ESPECIALLY
WHEN THE TEXANS SWORE LOYALTY
TO MEXICO... WAR BROKE OUT
IN 1836 — REMEMBER THE ALAMO?
TEXAS BECAME A REPUBLIC...
THEN A STATE OF THE UNION
AND A STATE OF MIND...

HOW DO YOU FIND TEXAS?

GO EAST TILL YA SMELL IT... GO SOUTH TILL YA STEP IN IT... *

*OLD TEXAS JOKE

CALIFORNIA

CALIFORNIA WAS FAR AWAY,
BUT FAR OUT... THE
PRINCIPAL INDUSTRY
WAS GOING ON HIKES...
NEVERTHELESS, WHEN
CAPT. **JOHN FRÉMONT'S**
TROOPS SWOOPED OVER
THE SIERRA, A DOZEN
MEN BESTIRRED
THEMSELVES TO
PROCLAIM THE
BEAR FLAG
REPUBLIC IN 1846.

NOW WHAT?

UTAH

IN 1847, SALT LAKE CITY WAS FOUNDED BY THE MORMONS, WHO WERE FLEEING RELIGIOUS PERSECUTION, A GRAND AMERICAN TRADITION.* THE ONLY DIFFERENCE WAS, THIS PERSECUTION WAS IN THE UNITED STATES. UTAH SEEMED SAFE, AS WHO ELSE WOULD WANT IT?

BRIGHAM YOUNG AND FOLLOWERS

THE MORMONS GOT ALONG FINE WITH THE MEXICANS AND INDIANS... IT WAS THE AMERICANS THEY DETESTED... IN FACT, ONE OF THE WILD WEST'S MORE HEINOUS EPISODES WAS THE *MOUNTAIN MEADOWS MASSACRES*, IN WHICH MORMONS AND PAIUTES COMBINED TO SLAUGHTER OVER 100 MEN, WOMEN, & KIDS ON THEIR WAY TO CALIFORNIA...

OKAY, GUYS! GIT 'EM!

OREGON

JUST TO PROVE THAT THEY WEREN'T PICKING ON MEXICO, AMERICANS ALSO FLOODED OREGON, WHICH WAS CLAIMED BY BRITAIN, AND WAS USUALLY FLOODED ALREADY.

IT HASN'T LET UP SINCE LEWIS & CLARK...

*FLEEING, THAT IS, NOT PERSECUTION

SUDDENLY, THE AMERICAN PUBLIC AND PRESS DISCOVERED THAT THEIR COUNTRY HAD A "**MANIFEST DESTINY**" TO SPREAD FROM **SEA** TO SEA... THIS HAD NEVER BEEN PARTICULARLY MANIFEST BEFORE, ESPECIALLY TO MEXICANS...

FUNNY, IT DOESN'T **LOOK** LIKE THE UNITED STATES...

POLKING IT INTO HIM.

PRESIDENT POLK, A PROTÉGÉ OF ANDREW JACKSON, KNEW HOW TO START A FIGHT: IN 1846 HE SENT TROOPS INTO MEXICO... WHEN THE MEXICAN ARMY SHOT AT THEM, POLK SQUEALED THAT "OUR BOYS" NEEDED PROTECTION!!

CONGRESS BICKERED CONFUSEDLY... SOME SAID POLK WAS A SNEAKY, SLIMY, BALD-FACED LIAR... OTHERS SAID OF COURSE HE IS, BUT HE'S ALSO THE PRESIDENT AND COMMANDER-IN-CHIEF... WITH THAT REASSURING THOUGHT, CONGRESS VOTED MONEY FOR FIGHTING, BUT WITHHELD A DECLARATION OF WAR...

A FINE COMPROMISE!

AND SO BEGAN

THE MEXICAN WAR—

FIRST OF A LINE OF UNDECLARED WARS...
THE MARINES LANDED
IN MEXICO, AND THE
INVASION HEADED FOR
THE "HALLS OF
MONTEZUMA."

HERE'S TO
THE MONROE
DOCTRINE!

THE NAVY SAILED FOR THE COAST, WHILE THE CAVALRY VISITED SUNNY NEW MEXICO...

?

IS DIS
DA WAY
TO
HOLLYWOOD?

WHEN IT WAS OVER
IN 1848, MEXICO WAS
MINUS HALF ITS
LAND, AND THE U.S.A.
HAD SWOLLEN TO
ITS FAMILIAR
SHAPE. (OREGON
HAD BEEN ACQUIRED
PEACEFULLY.)

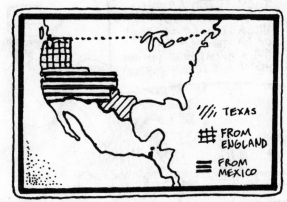

//// TEXAS

FROM
ENGLAND

= FROM
MEXICO

POSTSCRIPT TO CHAPTER 8:
THE GOLD RUSH

IN 1848, JUST AFTER CALIFORNIA WAS ACQUIRED, THE STUFF THAT DRIVES MEN MAD WAS FOUND THERE...

ACID? SPEED? OH— GOLD!

THEY CAME FROM CHILE, CHINA, CHICAGO...

DUST

NUGGETS

INGOTS

LITTLE CHUNKS...

SAN FRANCISCO EXPLODED INTO AN INSTANT CITY OF MUD, TENTS, SHACKS, HARD MEN AND EASY WOMEN, EASY MONEY AND HARD LUCK... A HARBOR OF ROTTING, ABANDONED SHIPS... PANTS CUT FROM SAILCLOTH BY LEVI STRAUSS...

EE-HAW!

WHENEVER THINGS GOT TOO FAR OUT OF HAND, THE GOOD CITIZENS WOULD STRING UP A MURDERER. THIS ENCOURAGED OTHER MURDERERS TO LEAVE TOWN...

THEY FILLED ARIZONA WITH THE "MOST VILLAINOUS COLLECTION OF WHITE MEN THAT EVER BREATHED" (IN ONE HISTORIAN'S LOVELY PHRASE).

IN JUST TWO YEARS, CALIFORNIA WAS ASKING FOR STATEHOOD, AND PLUNGING THE UNION INTO CRISIS... BUT YOU'LL HAVE TO GET THROUGH THE NEXT CHAPTER BEFORE YOU LEARN WHAT THAT WAS ABOUT...

CHAPTER 9
RAILROADS, OVER- AND UNDERGROUND

Yes, the young country was on the move, and not only westward... it was also blasting full steam ahead into the Industrial Revolution...

IT ALL
STARTED
WITH THE
COTTON GIN,
WHICH WAS
A MACHINE,
NOT A
BEVERAGE...

THE GIN
SPEEDED UP
COTTONSEED
PULLING
5000%
AND BOOSTED
PROFITS
ENORMOUSLY.

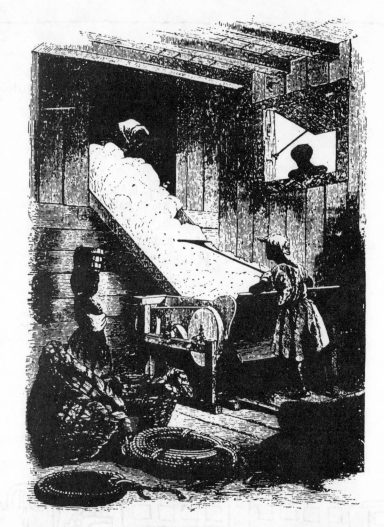

SUDDENLY, IN THE SOUTH,
COTTON FIELDS ROLLED
WESTWARD AS FAST
AS ANDY JACKSON
COULD CLEAR THE WAY...

SNAP
CRUNCH
EEYAH!
EEYAH!   ★ ☆   BANG
                  BANG BANG

THE NORTH ALSO DERIVED BENEFITS FROM THE "COTTON KINGDOM": FEDERAL TAXES ON THE SOUTH SUBSIDIZED NORTHERN EXPANSION...

THE NORTH SPROUTED HIGHWAYS, BRIDGES, CANALS, RAILROADS, AND FACTORIES THAT BELCHED SOOT WITHOUT SAYING, "EXCUSE ME!"

I'M BAD! I'M RUDE!

(THE NORTH ALSO SPROUTED NEW FORESTS, AS FARMERS ABANDONED THEIR FARMS TO SEEK WORK IN THE FACTORY TOWNS...)

INDUSTRIALIZATION CHANGED MORE THAN THE LANDSCAPE...

IT CHANGED PEOPLE'S LIVES...

LITTLE THINGS LIKE: SENDING LARGE NUMBERS OF WOMEN INTO THE FACTORIES... MAKING THEM STAND AT A MACHINE 15 HOURS A DAY... NEVER LETTING THEM SEE THE SUN... THINGS LIKE THAT...

MEANWHILE, TRANSATLANTIC STEAMSHIPS BROUGHT MILLIONS OF IMMIGRANTS TO FEED THE NEW FACTORIES.

THE IMMIGRANTS, MOSTLY IRISH AND GERMANS, FLED THE FAMINES AND FAILED REVOLUTIONS OF EUROPE.

THEY CROWDED INTO AMERICA'S CITIES, WHERE THEY FOUND OPPORTUNITY — AS WELL AS SLUMS, PERSISTENT PREJUDICE,* JOB DISCRIMINATION, AND OCCASIONAL RIOTS.

WE'LL SHOW 'EM! WE'LL TAKE OVER CITY HALL!

HELP WANTED
NO IRISH NEED APPLY

*NO IRISH CATHOLIC WAS ELECTED PRESIDENT UNTIL JOHN F. KENNEDY IN 1960!

IT WAS ALSO THE

Age of Reform

(THERE WAS SO MUCH TO REFORM!)

FREEDOM OF ASSOCIATION WAS GUARANTEED BY THE CONSTITUTION, SO AMERICANS GOT TOGETHER AND FREE-ASSOCIATED... THIS WAS SUPPOSED TO CURE SOCIETY'S ILLS...

AT LEAST IT FEELS SAFER STANDING CLOSE TOGETHER LIKE THIS...

THEY ASSOCIATED IN:

* LABOR UNIONS, TO IMPROVE WORKING CONDITIONS

* RELIGIONS, NEW AND USED

* SOCIETIES TO PROMOTE EDUCATION

* UTOPIAN COMMUNITIES, TO ACHIEVE PERFECTION

* ANTI-SLAVERY SOCIETIES

* PLAIN OLD POLITICAL PARTIES

* FACTIONS WITHIN POLITICAL PARTIES

* ASSORTED GROUPS OF PACIFISTS, PRISON REFORMERS, TEMPERANCE ADVOCATES, ETC...

AND THE WOMEN'S MOVEMENT?

NOT YET... NOT YET...

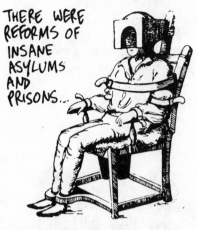

THERE WERE REFORMS OF INSANE ASYLUMS AND PRISONS...

MANY OF THESE REFORMERS HAD CAUSE FOR CELEBRATION IN THE 1820's, '30's, AND '40's. FOR EXAMPLE, THE VOTE WAS FINALLY GIVEN TO ALL WHITE MEN, REGARDLESS OF PROPERTY..

FREE PUBLIC SCHOOLS BEGAN TO OPEN HERE AND THERE...

NOW THAT I'VE GOT IT, I'M KEEPIN' IT TO MYSELF!

BALLOTS

#@!! REFORMERS!!

THE LABOR MOVEMENT MADE MODEST GAINS... AT LEAST, UNIONS WERE LEGALIZED BY THE SUPREME COURT IN 1842...

THIS IS GONNA BE A LONG STRUGGLE..

SO TELL ME — HAVE YOU NOTICED ANYTHING MISSING FROM THE LIST?

STRANGELY ENOUGH, ALL THESE CHANGES HAPPENED UP NORTH... DOWN SOUTH, THE ONLY MOVEMENT WAS THE PRICE OF SLAVES GOING UP AND DOWN...

ANTI-SLAVERY ACTIVISTS, TIRED OF SEEING EVERY OTHER REFORM GROUP MAKING PROGRESS, EXCEPT THEMSELVES, ANGRILY CHANGED THEIR TUNE — FROM FLAT TO SHARP...

NO MORE MR. NICE GUY!!

THEIR NEW LEAD VOCALIST WAS

WILLIAM LLOYD GARRISON,

AND HIS LYRICS WERE LIKE A BREATH FROM A BLAST FURNACE... SLAVEOWNERS WERE "MAN-STEALERS," "WOMAN-FLOGGERS," "RAPISTS," "MURDERERS..." THE U.S. CONSTITUTION, THANKS TO ITS PRO-SLAVERY CLAUSES, WAS A "PACT WITH HELL."

MOMMY! THAT MAN INSULTED THE CONSTITUTION!

KILL HIM!

BUT I'M ALSO FOR NON-VIOLENCE!!

GARRISON PUT ON QUITE A SHOW — EVERY PERFORMANCE WAS MOBBED... THESE WERE NOT THE SORT OF MOBS THAT TURN UGLY... THEY WERE UGLY TO BEGIN WITH... AND ALL BECAUSE GARRISON SAID THAT THE FOUNDING FATHERS WERE "HYPOCRITES" AND THAT THE NATION SHOULD BE DISMEMBERED ("NO UNION WITH SLAVEHOLDERS!").

OF COURSE THESE MOBS WERE WHITE... TO BLACKS, GARRISON MADE PERFECT SENSE. FOR YEARS, BLACK ABOLITIONISTS HAD BEEN WAITING PATIENTLY FOR A WHITE MAN THIS IMPATIENT, AND NOW HE WAS HERE. OVER HALF THE SUBSCRIBERS TO GARRISON'S NEWSPAPER, THE LIBERATOR, WERE BLACK.

HERE'S A MAN WHO SPEAKS MY LANGUAGE!

YES, PLAIN ENGLISH...

ANOTHER ABOLITIONIST NOVELTY, BESIDES THEIR RHETORIC, WAS THAT WOMEN SPOKE PUBLICLY AT THEIR MEETINGS. THIS WAS THOUGHT TO BE IMPOSSIBLE, UNTIL IT HAPPENED, AFTER WHICH IT BECAME MERELY IMPROPER, SUBVERSIVE, UNFEMININE, AND OUTSIDE "WOMAN'S PROPER SPHERE."

PIECES OF SPHERE

SARAH GRIMKÉ

ANGELINA GRIMKE

(WOMAN'S SPHERE, IN CASE YOU WONDERED, WAS COOKING, WASHING, BABIES, AND BEING SUPPORTIVE EVEN WHEN YOU'RE NOT BEING SUPPORTED.)

LET ME OUT OF HERE!

IN 1840, A WORLD ANTI-SLAVERY MEETING IN LONDON SPLIT OVER THE "WOMAN QUESTION." AFTER HEARING CIRCULAR ARGUMENTS IN FAVOR OF WOMAN'S SPHERE, THE MALE DELEGATES BANISHED THE FEMALES TO THE BALCONY.

I'VE HEARD OF PUTTING US ON A PEDESTAL, BUT A BALCONY?

152

AFTERWARDS, SEVERAL ABOLITIONIST WOMEN, TIRED OF GEOMETRY LESSONS, DECIDED THEY HAD BETTER FIGHT FOR THEIR OWN RIGHTS, TOO...

CUTE... THEY MUST BE DESIGNING A QUILT OR SOMETHING...

THE WOMEN'S MOVEMENT

WAS BORN IN 1848... THAT'S WHEN **LUCRETIA MOTT, ELIZABETH CADY STANTON, JANE HUNT, MARTHA WRIGHT,** AND **MARY ANN McCLINTOCK** CALLED THE FIRST WOMAN'S RIGHTS CONVENTION IN SENECA FALLS, N.Y. THIS MEETING WAS A SUCCESS— THE ONLY PROBLEM WAS LIMITING THE AGENDA, THERE WERE SO MANY WRONGS TO RIGHT...

MOTT

STANTON

McCLINTOCK

WRIGHT

NO PICTURE OF HUNT- SORRY!

IT TOOK MORE THAN SIXTY YEARS TO WIN THE VOTE... SO WE'LL SAVE THE STORY FOR VOLUME 2... MEANWHILE, CHECK OUT THE UNISEX FEMINIST FASHIONS OF THE 1850's:

FEMINIST   "FEMININE"

AND SPEAKING OF WOMEN, LET'S NOT FORGET THE INCREDIBLE

HARRIET TUBMAN, ALSO KNOWN AS "MOSES."

(A SMALL WOMAN WITH A LARGE PRICE ON HER HEAD)

SHE WAS THE CHIEF CONDUCTOR OF THE "UNDERGROUND RAILWAY," WHICH, UNLIKE THE REAL RAILWAY, DIDN'T RUN ON RAILS... THE PURPOSE OF THE UNDERGROUND RAILWAY WAS TO BRING SLAVES TO FREEDOM OR CANADA, WHICHEVER CAME FIRST.

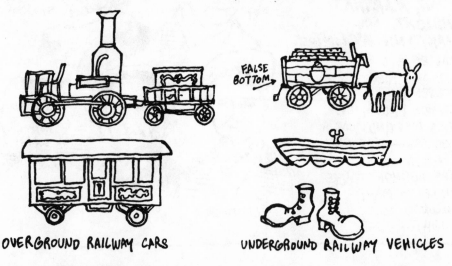

FALSE BOTTOM →

OVERGROUND RAILWAY CARS

UNDERGROUND RAILWAY VEHICLES

MS TUBMAN, AN ESCAPED SLAVE HERSELF, MADE *NINETEEN* TRIPS INTO THE SOUTH TO RESCUE HER FELLOW SLAVES...

AND BELIEVE ME, I TOOK A GUN!!

EQUALLY IMPRESSIVE WAS

FREDERICK DOUGLASS,

ANOTHER RUNAWAY... HE TURNED UP AT AN ABOLITIONIST MEETING IN 1841, AND WITHIN A YEAR OR TWO HE WAS THEIR GREATEST SPEAKER — AND A CANDIDATE FOR LARGEST HAIR OF THE 1840'S...

IN A COLOR-BLIND SOCIETY, DOUGLASS COULD HAVE BEEN PRESIDENT. AS IT WAS, HE HAD TO SETTLE FOR BECOMING THE "FIRST BLACK TO..."

⇨ RUN HIS OWN NEWSPAPER

⇨ ADVISE PRESIDENTS

⇨ BE A U.S. DIPLOMAT

⇨ MAKE A FORTUNE ON THE LECTURE CIRCUIT

AND TO THINK THAT HE LEARNED TO READ BY TRADING HIS LUNCH TO WHITE BOYS FOR LESSONS!

"THERE IS NOT A MAN BENEATH THE CANOPY OF HEAVEN, THAT DOES NOT KNOW THAT SLAVERY IS WRONG FOR HIM," HE POINTED OUT.

FORMER SLAVES TELLING THE AWFUL TRUTH... WHITE ABOLITIONISTS FLINGING INSULTS... A BLACK INTELLECTUAL SUPERIOR TO ANY WHITE IN THE SOUTH... **BLACK WOMEN WITH GUNS??** HOW WERE THE SLAVEOWNERS TO RESPOND TO *THIS?*

IT'S ALL TH' FAULT O' THET ABOLISH-NEST LIDDY-CHUR!

ONE NOT PARTICULARLY IMAGINATIVE WAY WAS WITH CENSORSHIP— LIKE THE "GAG RULE" FORBIDDING CONGRESSIONAL DEBATE ON ABOLITIONIST PETITIONS...

CONSTITUTION SEZ TH' PEOPLE HAVE A RIGHT TO PETITION, NOT THAT TH' GUMMINT GOTTA LISTEN...

...OR BANNING "INSURRECTIONARY" (I.E., ANTI-SLAVERY) MATERIAL FROM THE U.S. MAILS IN THE SOUTH...

WHUZZAT? "ALL MEN ARE CREATED EQUAL"? "ENDOWED WITH INALIENABLE RIGHTS"? GET OUTA HERE!

THEN, JUST TO PROVE THAT A CLEVER PERSON CAN DEFEND ANYTHING, THE SLAVEOWNERS TRIED TO PROVE THAT SLAVERY IS A **GOOD THING.** IN THE FIRST PLACE, THEY ARGUED, BLACKS HAD BEEN GIVEN A FREE TRIP FROM HEATHEN AFRICA TO CHRISTIAN AMERICA!

THE SURVIVORS SHOULD THANK US!

ALL THIS TALK OF MISERABLE SLAVES WAS FALSE, THEY SAID... THE SLAVES WERE HAPPY — JUST ASK THEM (IN MASTER'S PRESENCE, OF COURSE!)...

THEY RUN AWAY BECAUSE THEIR FEET ARE HAPPY!

AND BECAUSE THE WORD "SLAVERY" SOUNDED SO BAD, THEY LOOKED FOR ANOTHER NAME FOR IT... WHAT THEY CAME UP WITH WAS "THE SOUTH'S PECULIAR INSTITUTION..."

WHUPPED ANY SLAVES LATELY?

PLEASE... THAT'S "METE OUT JUST AND PROPER DISCIPLINE TO A BENEFICIARY OF OUR PECULIAR INSTITUTION..."

OF COURSE I HAVE — YOU?

HAVING MADE SLAVERY LOOK
GOOD (AT LEAST TO THEMSELVES),
THE SLAVEOWNERS WENT ON
TO MAKE FREE LABOR
SOUND BAD... FREE WORKERS
WERE TOO FOND OF STRIKES,
THEY SAID, WHEREAS SLAVES WERE
MORE ATTACHED TO
BALLS...

BY CHAINS,
THAT IS...

THEY ENVISIONED
A GLORIOUS AMERICAN
FUTURE IN WHICH
ALL WORKERS,
NORTH, SOUTH,
BLACK AND WHITE,
WOULD BE ENSLAVED!!

PLEASE...
JUST GIVE
SLAVERY A
CHANCE TO
COMPETE...

ONE THING YOU CAN
SAY FOR THE PRO-
SLAVERY PROPAGANDISTS:
THEY WEREN'T TRYING
TO BE POPULAR!!

WE MUST
HAVE A WAR
NOW AND DESTROY
THESE PEOPLE...

CHAPTER 10

IN WHICH A WAR IS FOUGHT, FOR SOME REASON...

EVERYONE HAS A THEORY OF WHY THE CIVIL WAR WAS FOUGHT...

THE SOUTH SAID IT WAS A QUESTION OF STATES' RIGHTS...

THE NORTH SAID IT WAS TO PRESERVE THE UNION...

SOME BLAMED THE SPREAD OF SLAVERY; OTHERS SAID THAT SLAVERY ITSELF WAS THE PROBLEM...

MARK TWAIN SAID IT HAPPENED BECAUSE THE SOUTH HAD READ TOO MANY NOVELS BY SIR WALTER SCOTT...

THE ANSWER IS UNDOUBTEDLY, "ALL OF THE ABOVE..." BUT WHATEVER THE UNDERLYING ISSUES, THE IMMEDIATE IRRITANT WAS THIS QUESTION: SHOULD SLAVERY BE ALLOWED IN THE VAST TERRITORIES ACQUIRED* IN THE MEXICAN WAR??

WE STOLE IT — WHY NOT ENSLAVE IT?

BETWEEN 1800 AND 1850, THE NORTH HAD BOOMED DEAFENINGLY, WHILE THE SOUTH SOMEHOW SLEPT THROUGH IT... NOW THE SOUTH WANTED TO EXPLODE, TOO... THIS REQUIRED EXPANSION... BUT FOR SOME REASON, THE SLAVEOWNER COULDN'T CONCEIVE OF DOING BUSINESS WITHOUT BEING ABLE TO BUY AND SELL HIS WORKERS.

AH'M A FAHMUH, NOT A THINKUH...

* OR, DEPENDING ON YOUR MOOD OR OPINION: CONQUERED, WRESTED, CEDED, GRABBED, JUSTLY WON, EXTORTED, ETC...

WHENEVER THE COUNTRY EXPANDED, NORTH AND SOUTH HAD MADE COMPROMISES... THE MOST RECENT HAVING BEEN THE MISSOURI COMPROMISE OF 1820. THIS ADMITTED MISSOURI AS A SLAVE STATE, WHILE LIMITING FUTURE SLAVE STATES TO THE AREA SOUTH OF MISSOURI'S SOUTHERN BORDER. NOW, IN 1850, THE COUNTRY HAD REACHED THE PACIFIC... CALIFORNIA WANTED TO BE A FREE STATE... AND SLAVEOWNERS GASPED AT WHAT WAS LEFT FOR THEM:

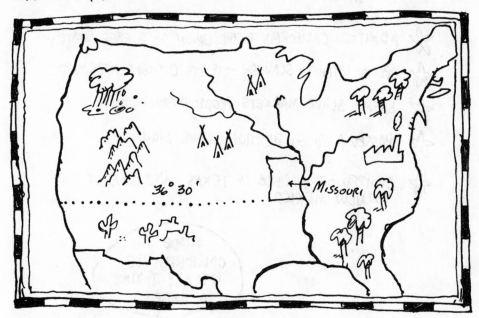

...NAMELY, ARIZONA AND NEW MEXICO!

AS USUAL, WHEN THE
SOUTH FELT WRONGED,
NORTHERNERS AND SOUTHERNERS
SCREAMED AT EACH OTHER
UNTIL THEIR VOICES GAVE OUT
AND THEN ARRANGED THE

COMPROMISE OF 1850,

WHICH —

⭐ ADMITTED CALIFORNIA TO THE UNION AS A FREE STATE...

⭐ OPENED UTAH TO SLAVERY — IF ITS CITIZENS APPROVED...

⭐ BANNED SLAVE MARKETS FROM WASHINGTON, D.C...

⭐ PASSED A TOUGH FUGITIVE SLAVE LAW...

⭐ CHOPPED OFF A PIECE OF TEXAS, AND GAVE IT
TO NEW MEXICO.

TRADE CALIFORNIA FOR UTAH?!! THANKS A HEAP!!

SINCE UTAH DIDN'T LOOK MUCH BETTER THAN ARIZONA, SOUTHERNERS TRIED TO EXPAND IN OTHER DIRECTIONS... AND WHAT BETTER DIRECTION THAN SOUTH? TENNESSEEAN **WILLIAM WALKER** RODE INTO (YES!) **NICARAGUA** AND PROCLAIMED HIMSELF PRESIDENT!

THE NICARAGUANS WERE BETTER SHOTS THAN HOSTS, SO WALKER'S HORSE HAD TO LEAVE WITHOUT HIM...

OTHER SOUTHERNERS BEGAN DROOLING OVER CUBA...

WHEN THIS FAILED TO MELT
CUBAN HEARTS, THE SOUTH
SWITCHED FROM SALIVA TO
SALINA, AS IN **KANSAS.**
IN 1854, CONGRESS OPENED
KANSAS TO "POPULAR SOVEREIGNTY,"
MEANING THAT THE QUESTION OF
SLAVERY IN KANSAS WOULD
BE DECIDED BY THE PEOPLE
OF KANSAS.

ABOLITIONISTS AND PRO-SLAVERY
MILITANTS RUSHED IN, BLASTING
EACH OTHER AS THEY WENT, ON
THE OUTMODED MEDICAL THEORY
THAT BLEEDING ANYTHING, EVEN
KANSAS, WAS THERAPEUTIC...

MEANWHILE, THERE WAS THAT "FUGITIVE SLAVE" LAW, DESIGNED TO RETURN RUNAWAYS TO THE SOUTH... AND WHAT A LAW IT WAS! IT DENIED THE ACCUSED ANY RIGHT TO A JURY TRIAL, OR EVEN TO TESTIFY IN SELF-DEFENSE... IT EVEN PAID THE JUDGE DOUBLE FOR FINDING IN FAVOR OF THE MASTER! UNDER THE CIRCUMSTANCES, MANY NORTHERN BLACKS, EVEN FREE ONES, DECIDED THAT THERE WAS ONLY ONE THING TO DO — PACK!!

WHILE HUNDREDS, IF NOT THOUSANDS, FLED INTO CANADA, OTHERS RISKED FINES, INJURY, AND JAIL BY STORMING THE PRISONS TO FREE ARRESTED FUGITIVES...

THIS TURMOIL PRODUCED, IN THE NORTH, A NEW POLITICAL PARTY, THE

REPUBLICANS.

(EVER SINCE JACKSON, THE ORIGINAL JEFFERSONIAN REPUBLICANS WERE CALLED "DEMOCRATS.") THE REPUBLICANS HAD A SINGLE PRINCIPLE:

THIS IS ONE MORE PRINCIPLE THAN MOST POLITICAL PARTIES!

IT WAS: NO SLAVERY IN THE TERRITORIES.

WITHIN A FEW YEARS, THE REPUBLICANS WERE A MAJOR PARTY. HOW DO WE ACCOUNT FOR THIS INSTANT SUCCESS, CONSIDERING THAT AMERICA IS A GRAVEYARD OF MINOR PARTIES?

FREE SOIL PARTY

AMERICAN PARTY

BULL MOOSE

PROHIBITION PARTY

WHO'S NEXT? HEE HEE

WHAT WAS ITS APPEAL? WHERE WAS THE SELF-INTEREST OF WHITE VOTERS IN AN ANTI-SLAVERY PARTY? WAS IT JUST BECAUSE IT MADE THEM FEEL VIRTUOUS?

VIRTUE

POLITICAL GRAVEYARD

SELF-INTEREST

WASHINGTON, D.C.

THE REPUBLICANS SUCCEEDED BECAUSE THEY BILLED THEMSELVES AS THE PARTY OF THE

FREE, WHITE, WORKING MAN.

HEY, THAT'S ME!

SLAVERY, THEY SAID, WAS WRONG NOT ONLY BECAUSE OF WHAT IT DID TO BLACKS, BUT BECAUSE OF WHAT IT DID TO THE WHITE WORKER.

IT'S UNFAIR COMPETITION!

THE 4 MILLION SLAVES FORMED A LOW-PAID LABOR POOL, WHICH COMPETED WITH FREE WORKERS. THE SLAVE SYSTEM LOWERED WAGES, RAISED HOURS, ERODED WORKING CONDITIONS, AND DESTROYED THE CONCEPT OF THE

☛ **DIGNITY OF LABOR.**

THE WESTERN TERRITORIES WERE SEEN AS THE LAND OF OPPORTUNITY FOR WHITE WORKERS. THEREFORE, ARGUED THE REPUBLICANS, SLAVERY MUST BE KEPT OUT OF THEM!

OR WE'LL END UP LIKE POOR WHITES DOWN SOUTH!

THIS LOGIC CARRIED MANY REPUBLICANS EVEN FURTHER — TO THE POINT OF EXCLUDING EVEN FREE BLACKS FROM THE TERRITORIES. AFTER ALL, "EVERYONE KNEW" THAT BLACKS WOULD WORK FOR LOWER WAGES THAN WHITES!

WHY IS THAT?

BECAUSE FREE WHITE EMPLOYERS PAY US LESS!

A TYPICAL, IF ESPECIALLY ELOQUENT, REPUBLICAN WAS THE ILLINOIS LAWYER **ABRAHAM LINCOLN.** BORN IN 1809, HE WAS CONVINCED BY THE EVENTS OF THE '50's THAT SLAVERY MUST SPREAD NO FARTHER... BUT HE OPPOSED ITS ABOLITION IN THE SOUTH ON CONSTITUTIONAL GROUNDS... AND HE WAS ENTIRELY UNCERTAIN WHAT TO DO ABOUT FREE BLACKS.

"LET US UNITE AS ONE PEOPLE..."

"I AM NOT... IN FAVOR OF MAKING VOTERS OF THE FREE NEGROES."

IN THE 1858 SENATE RACE, LINCOLN MADE A NAME FOR HIMSELF IN A SERIES OF DEBATES WITH THE INCUMBENT DEMOCRAT **STEPHEN DOUGLAS.** DOUGLAS

TOOK THE "POPULAR SOVEREIGNTY" POSITION THAT HAD ALREADY DRENCHED KANSAS IN BLOOD. LINCOLN TOOK THE REPUBLICAN LINE THAT SLAVERY, AS A WRONG, MUST BE STOPPED — AS FAR AS THE CONSTITUTION ALLOWED.

DESPITE DOUGLAS' EXPERIENCE AND REPUTATION, LINCOLN NEARLY WON THE ELECTION, AND THE SOUTH TOOK NOTE!

HE SURELY HAS MADE A NAME FOR HIMSELF...

CAIN'T SAY WHAT IT IS IN A FAMILY PUBLICATION...

IF THE REPUBLICANS PLANNED TO LIMIT SLAVERY TO THE SOUTH, THE SOUTHERNERS NOW DEMANDED TO PUSH IT INTO THE NORTH!

AIN'T NOTHIN' IN THE CONSTITUTION AGIN' IT!

* * * * * * * * * * * *

IN 1857, THE SOUTHERN-DOMINATED SUPREME COURT, UNDER ANDREW JACKSON'S OLD PAL, CHIEF JUSTICE **ROGER TANEY**, MADE THE DRED SCOTT DECISION, WHICH DENIED CONGRESS THE RIGHT TO RESTRICT SLAVERY ANYWHERE.

* * * * * * * * * * * *

⇒ BLACKS, WROTE TANEY, HAD "NO RIGHTS WHICH THE WHITE MAN IS BOUND TO RESPECT."

THE INFURIATED MILITANT ABOLITIONIST **JOHN BROWN** LED AN INTERRACIAL RAID ON A VIRGINIA ARSENAL, HOPING TO SPARK A SLAVE INSURRECTION. THE SPARK FIZZLED... NOBODY INSURRECTED... AND BROWN WAS HANGED ON DEC. 2, 1859.

OBSERVED BY BLACKS AS "MARTYR'S DAY"!

AND SO, WITH THE COUNTRY IN A STATE (INSTEAD OF THE OTHER WAY AROUND, WHICH IS NORMAL), THERE CAME THE ELECTION OF

1860.

AS THEIR PRESIDENTIAL CANDIDATE, THE REPUBLICANS CHOSE ABRAHAM LINCOLN... HE WASN'T THE MOST PROMINENT MAN IN THE PARTY, BUT HE HAD THE MOST PROMINENT NOSE...

AN OBSCURE MAN WITHOUT ENEMIES...

LINCOLN REALLY WAS BORN IN A LOG CABIN... A TOO-TALL, BACKWOODS LAWYER WHO TOLD CORNY JOKES AT THE WRONG TIME... A CAREER POLITICIAN WHO HAD NEVER RISEN HIGHER THAN THE HOUSE OF REPRESENTATIVES... IN SHORT, AN OBVIOUS LOSER...

DEMOCRATS, REJOICE!!

BUT THE DEMOCRATS HYSTERICALLY SPLIT INTO NORTHERN AND SOUTHERN WINGS AND NOMINATED TWO CANDIDATES —

WITH THE RESULT THAT LINCOLN WON THE ELECTION WITH 40% OF THE POPULAR VOTE!!

EVEN BEFORE HE WAS SWORN IN, LINCOLN WAS SWORN AT, MOSTLY BY THE SOUTHERN STATES... WHEN HE DIDN'T SWEAR BACK, THE SOUTH ASSUMED THERE WAS NO FIGHT IN THE MAN... AND THE WHOLE REGION PARTED WAYS WITH THE NORTH.

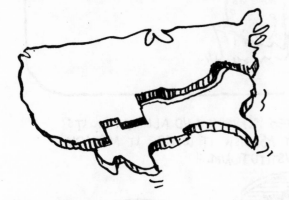

IT CALLED ITSELF THE **CONFEDERATE STATES OF AMERICA,** A NATION DEDICATED TO THE PRINCIPLE THAT ANY STATE HAD A RIGHT TO SECEDE FROM IT...

ITS PRESIDENT WAS **JEFFERSON DAVIS** OF MISSISSIPPI, A MAN AS FIRM AS LINCOLN, BUT WITHOUT ABE'S INCREDIBLE ABILITY TO MAKE PEOPLE LIKE HIM...

AND WHAT DID LINCOLN DO? HE LET HIS BEARD GROW!

> DO YOU LIKE IT?

LINCOLN, WHO WAS IN FACT A CHAMPIONSHIP WRESTLER, WAS WISELY WAITING FOR THE SOUTH TO MAKE THE FIGHTING MOVE!

> ONLY TOO GLAD TO OBLIGE!

ON APRIL 12, 1861, THE GOOD CITIZENS OF CHARLESTON, S.C., BEGAN TO BOMBARD THE U.S. FORT (SUMTER), AND THE WAR WAS ON...

AND NOW THAT THE SOUTH HAD RISEN IN REBELLION, LINCOLN COULD FREE THE SLAVES, RIGHT?

WRONG...

HUP HUP

THE REPUBLICANS SAID THEY HATED SLAVERY AND ALL THAT... ITS SPREAD SHOULD BE STOPPED... BUT ABOLISH IT WHERE IT ALREADY EXISTED? THAT WOULD BE UNCONSTITUTIONAL!!

NO... THIS WAS A WAR TO SAVE THE UNION, NOT TO ABOLISH SLAVERY!

"IF I COULD SAVE THE UNION WITHOUT FREEING ANY SLAVE, I WOULD DO IT; AND IF I COULD DO IT BY FREEING ALL THE SLAVES, I WOULD DO IT."

TO THIS, THE ABOLITIONISTS BELLOWED THAT SLAVERY WAS THE CAUSE OF THE WAR, AND AS LONG AS THERE WAS SLAVERY, THERE WOULD BE NO PEACE...

"WE HAVE ATTEMPTED TO MAINTAIN OUR UNION IN DEFIANCE OF THE MORAL CHEMISTRY OF THE UNIVERSE," WROTE FREDERICK DOUGLASS.

THE WORSE IT WENT FOR THE NORTH, THE BETTER THE ABOLITIONISTS SOUNDED— AND IT WAS GOING BADLY, AS THE SOUTH WON BATTLE AFTER BATTLE..

THE SOUTH, THOUGH OUTNUMBERED, HAD GREAT GENERALS: ROBERT E. LEE AND STONEWALL JACKSON.

THE NORTH HAD GEORGE McCLELLAN, WHOSE MEN LOVED HIM, BECAUSE HE RARELY RISKED THEIR LIVES.

AS THE GRAYS CONTINUED TO WHIP THE BLUES, THE UNION WAS FORCED TO TURN TO THE BLACKS...

173

Lincoln invited Frederick Douglass to the White House. ("I found him seated with his feet in different parts of the room," Douglass wrote.)

The abolitionist accused the president of vacillation and slowness... He urged him to abolish slavery and enlist blacks in the army...

Lincoln admitted being slow, but denied ever having wavered...

Douglass was impressed... so was Lincoln...

By the end of 1862, Lincoln had issued the ➡️

EMANCIPATION PROCLAMATION,

which freed the slaves — if only in rebel-held territories...

FREE AT LAST!

YEH... IF THE UNION ARMY EVER ARRIVES...

RED PANTS?

AT THE SAME TIME, BLACKS — FREE NORTHERNERS AND ESCAPED SLAVES — WERE FINALLY ALLOWED INTO THE ARMY... IN ALL-BLACK REGIMENTS, OF COURSE!

WITH REAL BULLETS?

TO THE SURPRISE OF SOME, THEY TURNED OUT TO BE AMONG THE NORTH'S BEST TROOPS, AND NO WONDER — THEY WERE THE MOST MOTIVATED!

AIN'T FIGHTIN' FOR NO **ABSTRACT CONCEPT**...

WHEN THEY MARCHED THROUGH THE SOUTH, SLAVES DESERTED THE PLANTATIONS IN DROVES, LEAVING THEIR DRIVERS HOLDING THE STEERING WHEEL...

HERE COME THEM YANKEES, BOYS... RUN!!

YASSUH... RUN IT IS...

JUST THEN,
ALMOST MIRACULOUSLY,
THE TIDE BEGAN TO
TURN, BUT SLOWLY...
ONE REASON WAS
THE BLACK TROOPS
PUSHING UP FROM THE
DEEP SOUTH...
ANOTHER WAS THE
DEATH OF STONEWALL
JACKSON, SHOT
ACCIDENTALLY BY HIS
OWN MEN, WHO THEN
DROPPED THE STRETCHER...

ANOTHER WAS A NAVAL BLOCKADE OF SOUTHERN PORTS... ANOTHER WAS
THE CAPTURE OF NEW ORLEANS... ANOTHER WAS THE FEROCIOUS
UNION DRIVE DOWN THE MISSISSIPPI, WHICH SPLIT THE SOUTH
AND ALLOWED THE BLUES TO PENETRATE THE CONFEDERACY FROM
THE WEST...

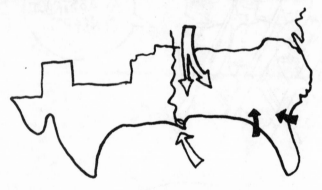

(NOTE: ALMOST
ALL THE FIGHTING
TOOK PLACE IN
THE SOUTH...)

OUT OF THE WEST
STAGGERED
GENERAL
**ULYSSES S.
GRANT.**

A HARD DRINKER... A
FAILURE AS A CIVILIAN...
AN ANTI-SEMITE... BUT
HE WON BATTLES...

IN 1864, LINCOLN PUT GRANT IN CHARGE OF ALL THE UNION ARMIES...

GO...FINISH 'EM OFF... IT'S 3 YEARS ALREADY...

GRANT WAS NO MATCH FOR LEE WHEN IT CAME TO MANUVERABILITY AND IMAGINATION, BUT HE HAD A WINNING TACTIC ALL HIS OWN—

NAMELY, A WAR OF ATTRITION, IN WHICH BODIES PILED UP UNTIL ONE SIDE RAN OUT...

(IN THE TRENCH WARFARE BEFORE RICHMOND, SOLDIERS WENT INTO BATTLE WITH THEIR NAMES AND ADDRESSES PINNED TO THEIR BACKS, FOR E-Z CLEAN-UP...)

AFTER 80,000 PERISHED IN ONE ESPECIALLY LONG BATTLE, GENERAL LEE REALIZED THAT HE WAS FACING A 20TH-CENTURY GENERAL IN THE 19TH CENTURY, WHILE DEFENDING AN 18TH-CENTURY INSTITUTION. LACKING A TIME MACHINE, LEE SURRENDERED, AND THE WAR WAS OVER.

NOW CAN WE HAVE THE COMPROMISE OF 1865?

177

YES, THE CIVIL WAR WAS THE FIRST "MODERN" WAR— THE FIRST TO USE THE TELEGRAPH... THE RAILROAD... THE ARMORED STEAMSHIP... TRENCH WARFARE — A WARM-UP FOR WORLD WAR I...

...WHERAS NUCLEAR WAR IS MORE POST-MODERN...

THE CIVIL WAR ALSO BROUGHT THE FIRST INCOME TAX... THE FIRST "GREENBACKS" (I.E., PAPER MONEY BACKED ONLY BY THE COLOR OF INK IT WAS PRINTED WITH)... AND THE FIRST TIME THE GOVERNMENT EVER BORROWED $3 BILLION— A REGULAR "DANCE OF DEBT."

BUT NOT THE LAST!

AND ABRAHAM LINCOLN — WHO HAD RISEN FROM POVERTY TO THE PRESIDENCY... WHO BEGAN AS THE CHAMPION OF THE FREE, WHITE WORKER AND BECAME THE LIBERATOR OF THE SLAVES... WHO ADMIRED JEFFERSON ABOVE ALL AND DESTROYED JEFFERSON'S OLD SOUTH... WHO ENDURED BEING ATTACKED AS A BUFFOON, A BABOON, AN INCOMPETENT, AND A TYRANT... WHOSE WONDERFUL SENSE OF HUMOR MASKED A PROFOUND SADNESS... WHO BELIEVED THAT HE HAD BEEN CONTROLLED BY EVENTS... LINCOLN, TOO, BECAME A "FIRST."

THE FIRST PRESIDENT TO BE ASSASSINATED.

TO BE CONTINUED...

THE CARTOON HISTORY
OF THE
UNITED STATES

PART II
(1865 · 1991)

INTRODUCTION
TO PART II

IN BOOKS, MOVIES, AND ON THE IMMORTAL TUBE, THE CIVIL WAR IS PORTRAYED AS A WAR BETWEEN NORTH AND SOUTH — WHICH IT WAS...

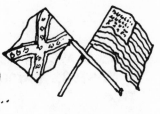

...AS A WAR BETWEEN BROTHERS, WHICH IT WAS...

...AS A WAR TO PRESERVE THE UNION, WHICH IT WAS...

BUT THE CIVIL WAR WAS ALSO SOMETHING ELSE: A WAR BETWEEN TWO SYSTEMS...

(PERHAPS THIS IDEA IS TOO COMPLEX FOR MOST BOOKS, MOVIES, AND MINISERIES.)

LUCKILY, THIS IS A COMIC BOOK, FOR WHICH NO IDEA IS TOO COMPLEX!

ONE SYSTEM — THE LOSER — WAS THE **SLAVE SYSTEM.** IT WAS AN OLD SYSTEM, AS OLD AS ANCIENT EGYPT, AT LEAST, AND DEFINITELY ON ITS LAST LEGS BY THE 1850's.

UNDER THE SLAVE SYSTEM, THE WORKER WAS THE PROPERTY OF THE MASTER, RATHER LIKE AN INTELLIGENT KIND OF LIVESTOCK.

THE MASTERS FORMED A SMALL ELITE WITH IMMENSE POWER — THOUGH RELATIVELY LITTLE MONEY. MOST OF THEIR WEALTH WAS TIED UP IN LAND AND HUMAN BEINGS.

THE WINNING SYSTEM ADVERTISED ITSELF AS THE ""SYSTEM OF FREE LABOR."" UNDER THIS SYSTEM, THE CITIZEN·WORKER WAS SUPPOSED TO BE FREE TO WORK OR NOT TO WORK, FREE TO BARGAIN FOR WAGES, FREE TO QUIT, FREE TO HEAD WESTWARD...

FREE TO BE ME !!

AS PREACHED — AND PRACTICED — BY ABRAHAM LINCOLN, THIS WAS THE AMERICAN DREAM: BEGIN AS A HIRED HAND, THEN BY DINT OF HARD WORK, THRIFT, AND OPPORTUNITY, RISE TO BECOME AN INDEPENDENT BUSINESSMAN, FARMER, OR (IN LINCOLN'S CASE) LAWYER.

IF YOU DON'T MAKE IT, IT'S YER OWN DANG FAULT!

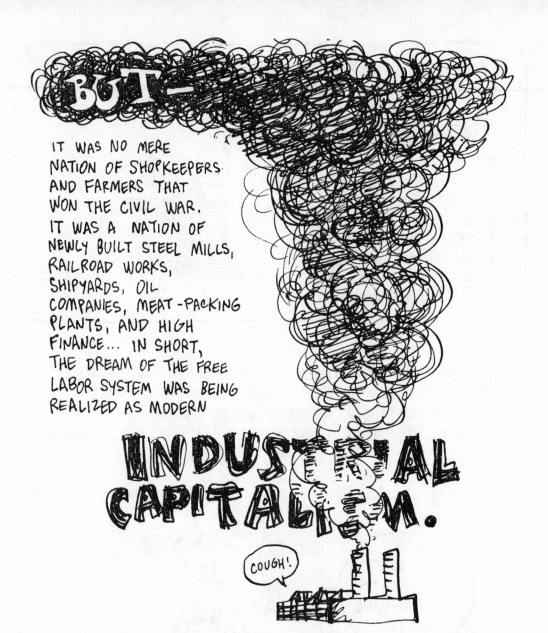

BUT—

IT WAS NO MERE NATION OF SHOPKEEPERS AND FARMERS THAT WON THE CIVIL WAR. IT WAS A NATION OF NEWLY BUILT STEEL MILLS, RAILROAD WORKS, SHIPYARDS, OIL COMPANIES, MEAT-PACKING PLANTS, AND HIGH FINANCE... IN SHORT, THE DREAM OF THE FREE LABOR SYSTEM WAS BEING REALIZED AS MODERN

INDUSTRIAL CAPITALISM.

COUGH!

THE INDUSTRIALISTS AND FINANCIERS AMASSED WEALTH BEYOND A SLAVE OWNER'S WILDEST DREAMS: ONE MAN COULD CONTROL AN ENTIRE INDUSTRY, COULD OWN MINES, FACTORIES, STOCKS, BONDS, MANSIONS, YACHTS, GOLD, SENATORS...

WHY WASTE MONEY BUYING WORKERS?

THIS RAISED MANY QUESTIONS FOR THE AMERICAN PEOPLE: IS DEMOCRACY COMPATIBLE WITH SUCH AN IMBALANCE OF WEALTH AND POWER? WHAT OPPORTUNITIES EXIST? AND FOR WHOM? HOW FREE IS THE "FREE WORKER"?

LOOK OUT! HERE COMES THE "INVISIBLE HAND" OF THE MARKET AGAIN!

THIS VOLUME TELLS THE STORY OF HOW AMERICAN DEMOCRACY CAME TO TERMS WITH THE MODERN INDUSTRIAL STATE. WE'LL LOOK AT:

THE SOUTH ADJUSTING

·

BUSINESS BOOMING AND GOING BUST

·

WORKERS', FARMERS', WOMEN'S, AND BLACK MOVEMENTS MOVING

·

AMERICA EXPANDING

·

COMMUNISM RISING

·

VALUES & MORES ROCKING AND ROLLING

·

SPUTNIKS, BEATNIKS, PEACENIKS, HIPPIES, YIPPIES, & YUPPIES DOING THEIR THING

·

AND LAST, BUT HARDLY LEAST...

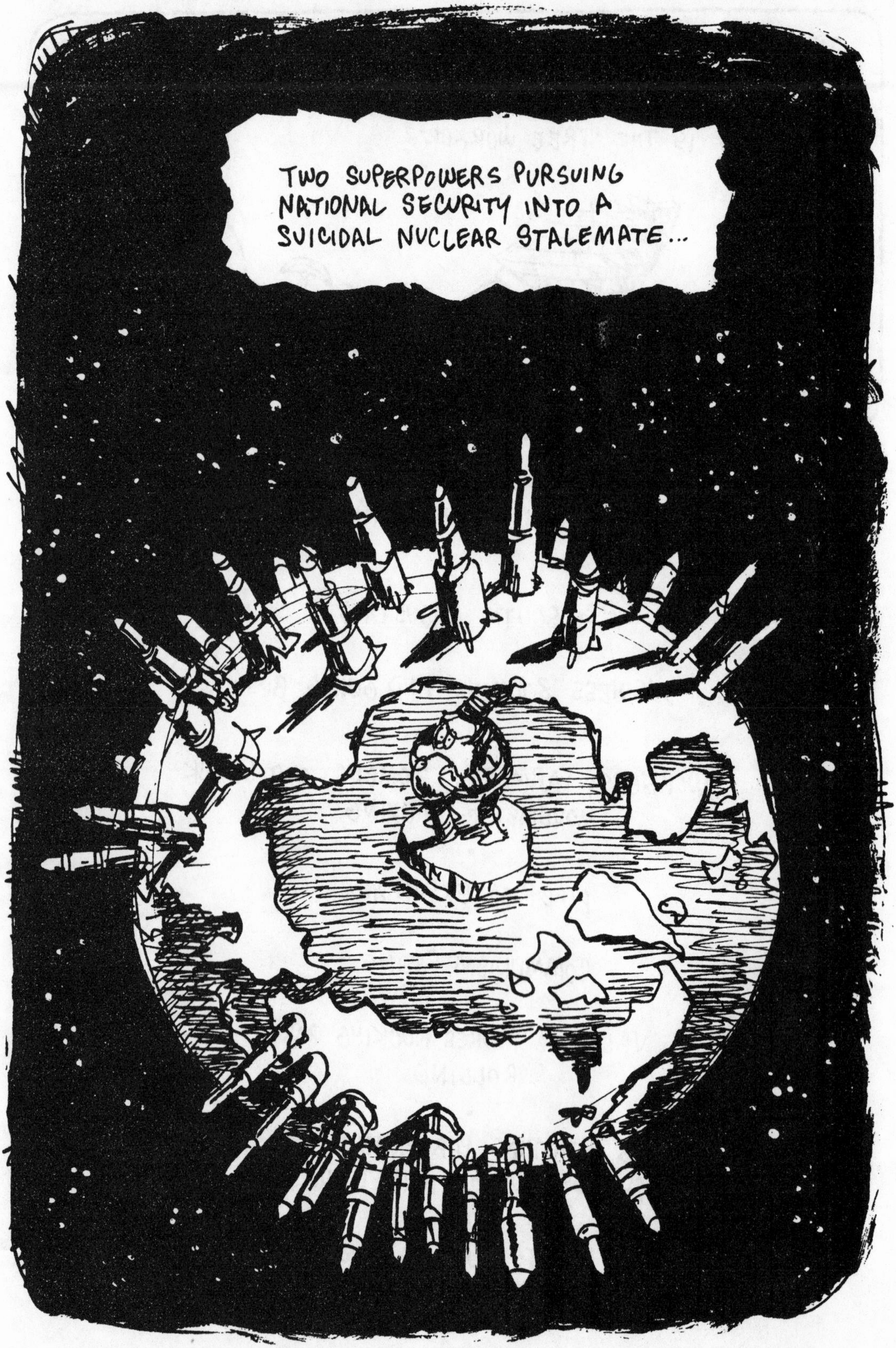
TWO SUPERPOWERS PURSUING NATIONAL SECURITY INTO A SUICIDAL NUCLEAR STALEMATE...

CHAPTER 11

DESTRUCTION AND RECONSTRUCTION

The CIVIL WAR WAS DEVASTATING: FOUR YEARS OF CARNAGE... BILLIONS OF DOLLARS DEVOTED TO DESTRUCTION... A MILLION MEN DEAD... THE COUNTRYSIDE LAID WASTE...

But MOST OF THE KILLING AND WASTING TOOK PLACE ON ONE SIDE OF THE MASON-DIXON LINE: THE SOUTHERN SIDE.

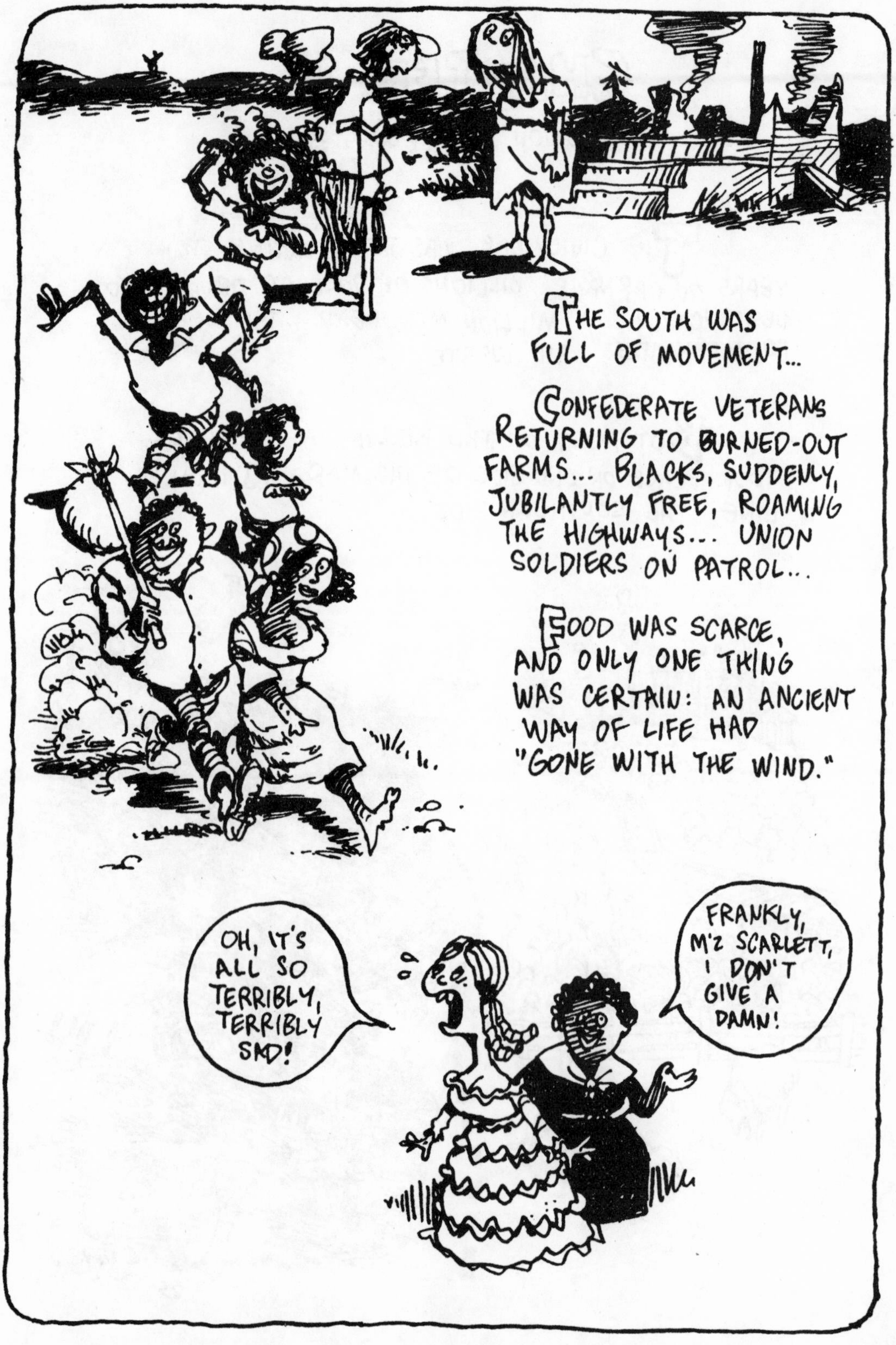
THE SOUTH WAS FULL OF MOVEMENT...
CONFEDERATE VETERANS RETURNING TO BURNED-OUT FARMS... BLACKS, SUDDENLY, JUBILANTLY FREE, ROAMING THE HIGHWAYS... UNION SOLDIERS ON PATROL...
FOOD WAS SCARCE, AND ONLY ONE THING WAS CERTAIN: AN ANCIENT WAY OF LIFE HAD "GONE WITH THE WIND."
OH, IT'S ALL SO TERRIBLY, TERRIBLY SAD!
FRANKLY, M'Z SCARLETT, I DON'T GIVE A DAMN!

MEANWHILE, THE NORTH WAS ALL HUSTLE AND BUSTLE: 900,000 IMMIGRANTS HAD MORE THAN REPLACED THE WAR DEAD.

WAR CONTRACTS HAD FATTENED INDUSTRY... WESTWARD EXPANSION PROCEEDED AS USUAL, AND A TRANSCONTINENTAL RAILROAD WAS UNDER CONSTRUCTION.

UP IN WASHINGTON, THE REPUBLICAN-DOMINATED GOVERNMENT PONDERED THE PROBLEM OF THE SOUTH: HOW TO PUT THE SOUTH TOGETHER AGAIN? AND HOW TO DO IT DIFFERENTLY FROM THE LAST TIME?

ABOVE ALL, GENTLEMEN, HOW DO WE MAKE IT VOTE **REPUBLICAN**??

WITH MALICE TOWARDS NONE...

BEFORE THE WAR'S END, PRES. LINCOLN SUGGESTED A MILD "TEN PERCENT SOLUTION."

ANY SECEDED STATE WHERE 10% OF THE ELECTORATE SWORE A LOYALTY OATH COULD FORM A STATE GOVERNMENT AND RETURN TO THE GOOD, OLD U.S.A.

WOKE UP THIS MORNIN', BLUES ALL 'ROUND MY HEAD... WITH THAT 10% SOLUTION, MIGHT AS WELL STAY IN BED...

HIS SUCCESSOR, ANDREW JOHNSON, CONTINUED THIS POLICY, WHICH IN EFFECT ALLOWED THE LOYAL WHITES TO REBUILD THE SOUTH, WITHOUT BLACK PARTICIPATION.

IN SEVERAL
SOUTHERN STATES,
10% SWIFTLY
SWORE LOYALTY!

LOYALTY? DAG
NAGTURNIPARSNIPPETY
BLANKETY SHEET!!

HE
SWEARS.

THEY FORMED NEW GOVERNMENTS, HELD ELECTIONS, AND TURNED TO
THE USUAL POLITICIANS FOR LEADERSHIP. SO THE SOUTHERN
DELEGATES TO THE 1866 CONGRESS INCLUDED NUMEROUS FORMER
CONFEDERATE OFFICIALS.

REBELS,
KILLERS,
AND
DEMOCRATS!

THE REPUBLICAN
CONGRESS
SLAMMED
THE DOOR
ON THE
"DIXIECRATS."

FRAPPE

THEY'VE
RETARDED
INDUSTRIAL
PROGRESS
TOO LONG
ALREADY!

NOW WHERE
CAN WE
FIND SOME
SOUTHERN
REPUBLICANS?

...WHICH BRINGS US TO THE EVENTFUL YEAR

WOTTA YEAR!

IT BEGAN WITH CONGRESSIONAL HEARINGS ON CONDITIONS IN THE SOUTH... AND WHAT CONGRESS HEARD WAS HAIR·RAISING (EXCEPT IN THE CASE OF REP. THADDEUS STEVENS, WHO WORE A WIG).

ALTHOUGH THE CONFEDERACY HAD SUFFERED MILITARY DEFEAT, CONGRESS WAS TOLD, THE SPIRIT OF THE OLD SOUTH LIVED ON!

BAILIFF!! ARREST THAT GHOST!!

DESPITE EMANCIPATION, THE WHITE SOUTH WAS DOING ITS UTMOST TO KEEP BLACKS "IN THEIR PLACE."

WHUT PLACE IS THAT?

ANY PLACE A WHITE MAN WON'T GO...

THE NEW SOUTHERN GOVERNMENTS ALL PASSED "BLACK CODES", SPECIAL REGULATIONS JUST FOR BLACK PEOPLE.

I DON'T LIKE THE SMELL OF THIS...

FOR EXAMPLE:

* NO BLACK COULD OWN A BUSINESS

* ALL BLACKS HAD TO SIGN A 1-YEAR LABOR CONTRACT— WAGES PAYABLE AT YEAR'S END

* NO BLACK COULD TRAVEL WITHOUT PERMISSION

* FLOGGING FOR BLACK VAGRANTS

* BLACK FELONS TO BE "SOLD" INTO SERVICE TO A "MASTER"

* NO VOTE, JURY DUTY, OR TESTIMONY IN COURT FOR ANY BLACK...

I'D SAY WE WERE SECOND-CLASS CITIZENS, BUT I'M NOT SURE WE'RE CITIZENS...

AND THAT WASN'T ALL.
IN DECEMBER, 1865, THE
KU KLUX KLAN WAS BORN.
THE KLAN AND OTHER GANGS
TERRORIZED BLACKS ACROSS
THE SOUTH, COMMITTING
MORE THAN ONE MURDER
A DAY IN LOUISIANA
ALONE. AND THE CHANCES
OF BRINGING A
KLANSMAN TO JUSTICE—?

THIS *IS*
SOUTHERN
JUSTICE!

OH,
PARDON ME,
BRUHTHUH!

ON MAY 1, IN
MEMPHIS, TENNESSEE,
A BLACK SOLDIER
TRIPPED A WHITE
POLICEMAN.

THE MEMPHIS POLICE DEPARTMENT
ATTACKED THE ARMY BASE.
AFTER A SHOOTOUT (6 DEAD),
THE POLICE TURNED AGAINST
A SOUTH MEMPHIS NEIGHBORHOOD,
AND BY THE TIME THE
INCIDENT ENDED, 46 BLACKS
LAY DEAD, AND 90 SHACKS
AND 12 SCHOOLS HAD BEEN
DESTROYED.

TO THE HORRIFIED MEMBERS OF CONGRESS, IT SOUNDED AS IF THE SOUTH WANTED TO TURN BACK THE CLOCK TO A PRE-WAR SETTING!

THEY DON'T EVEN KNOW WHAT TIME IT IS!

SO CONGRESS — WHICH WAS STILL AN ALL-NORTHERN CONGRESS, MOSTLY REPUBLICAN — BEGAN DEVISING WAYS TO PROTECT THE BLACKS AND TO KEEP THE OLD SOUTH'S MENTALITY OUT OF THE NEW SOUTH.

REP. BENJAMIN BUTLER

REP. THADDEUS STEVENS

DAMYANKS!

SEN. CHARLES SUMNER

REP. BENJAMIN WADE

FOR THIS, THE REPUBLICANS WERE HATED IN THE SOUTH FOR GENERATIONS AFTERWARD!

SOMEONE SUGGESTED GIVING BLACKS THE PLANTATIONS THEY USED TO WORK. THIS IDEA WAS REJECTED AS TOO SOCIALISTIC.

WE'RE REPUBLICANS, REMEMBER?

HEAR HEAR!

THERE WAS ALSO A LIVELY DEBATE ON ALLOWING THE BLACKS TO VOTE. SOME OBJECTED THAT IT WAS TOO SOON, THAT THE EX-SLAVES WERE TOO IGNORANT, THAT THEY HAD TOO LITTLE POLITICAL EXPERIENCE.

AND HOW AM I SUPPOSED TO GET POLITICAL EXPERIENCE IF I CAN'T VOTE?

ON THE OTHER HAND, THESE POINTS WERE MADE:

* THERE WERE PLENTY OF IGNORANT WHITE VOTERS

* BLACKS WERE NOT IGNORANT OF THEIR OWN INTERESTS

* THERE MIGHT NOT BE ANOTHER CHANCE TO EXTEND THE FRANCHISE TO BLACKS

* EVERY BLACK VOTER WOULD BE A REPUBLICAN VOTER !!

WELL, THAT CLINCHES IT!

ACTUALLY, THAT DIDN'T QUITE CLINCH IT YET... THE IDEA OF BLACK SUFFRAGE WAS STILL TOO UNPOPULAR, NORTH AND SOUTH. SOME NORTHERN STATES, LIKE ILLINOIS, EVEN BARRED BLACKS FROM MOVING THERE, MUCH LESS VOTING!

AND THIS OVER HERE IS MISTER LINCOLN'S HOUSE...

BUT CONGRESS WENT MORE THAN HALFWAY WITH A BIG CONSTITUTIONAL AMENDMENT, THE

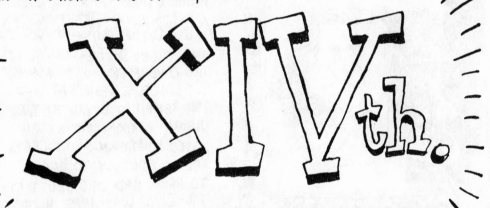

XIVth.

THE 14TH AMENDMENT, WHILE NOT ACTUALLY GRANTING BLACK SUFFRAGE, DOES REDUCE THE REPRESENTATION IN CONGRESS OF ANY STATE THAT DENIES IT. FURTHERMORE, THE GLORIOUS 14TH STATES FOR THE FIRST TIME THAT BLACKS ARE, IN FACT, CITIZENS, AND THAT—

No state shall make or enforce any law which shall abridge the privileges or immunities of citizens of the United States; nor shall any State deprive any person of life, liberty, or property, without due process of law; nor deny to any person within its jurisdiction the equal protection of the laws.

AMAZING THAT NO ONE THOUGHT OF THIS BEFORE!

CONGRESS NOW DELIVERED THE SOUTH AN ULTIMATUM: RATIFY THE 14TH AMENDMENT, OR ELSE. THIS THE SOUTH WAS UNWILLING TO DO.

A FURTHER OBSTACLE WAS NONE OTHER THAN PRESIDENT **ANDREW JOHNSON,** WHO URGED SOUTHERNERS TO RESIST THE CONGRESSIONAL "ASSASSINS." A TENNESSEE DEMOCRAT WHO HAD REMAINED LOYAL TO THE UNION, A POOR WHITE WHO HATED SOUTHERN ARISTOCRATS ABOUT EQUALLY TO BLACKS, JOHNSON HAD DECIDED THAT THE CIVIL WAR WAS HISTORY, ITS ISSUES SETTLED.

IN JULY CAME THE NEXT MASSACRE, WHEN POLICE LED AN ATTACK ON A REPUBLICAN PARTY CONVENTION IN NEW ORLEANS. ONE RIOTER'S CRY WAS:

As the congressional elections approached, the president accused the republicans of plotting a black uprising and the overthrow of the constitution!

His wild campaign speeches divided the electorate...

YUP, HE'S DRUNK!

NAW, HE'S INSANE!

When the elections were over, the republicans were stronger than ever, controlling ⅔ of both houses of congress!!

SAY, THIS IS FUN... NOW WE CAN DO WHATEVER WE WANT...

AND SO, 1866 FINALLY PASSED INTO

1867.

OVER PRESIDENT JOHNSON'S REPEATED VETOES, CONGRESS PASSED ITS OWN TOUGH RECONSTRUCTION PLAN, WHICH REQUIRED THE SOUTHERN STATES TO ———————

* CONTINUE UNDER MILITARY OCCUPATION BY THE UNION ARMY

* WRITE NEW STATE CONSTITUTIONS GUARANTEEING EQUAL RIGHTS TO BLACKS

* GIVE THE VOTE TO BLACKS

* RATIFY THE 14TH AMENDMENT

NOW CONGRESS CALLS THE TUNE!

MANY NORTHERNERS HEADED SOUTH TO SUPPORT THE CONGRESSIONAL PROGRAM. A MIXED LOT, THEY INCLUDED IDEALISTIC TEACHERS, POLITICAL ACTIVISTS, OLD ABOLITIONISTS, BUSINESSMEN, FORTUNE-HUNTERS, AND CON ARTISTS... SOUTHERN WHITES LUMPED THEM ALL TOGETHER WITH A SINGLE WORD:

CARPET-BAGGERS!

CARPETBAGGERS JOINED SYMPATHETIC LOCAL WHITES ("SCALAWAGS") AND BLACKS TO FORM NEW, "RECONSTRUCTED" STATE GOVERNMENTS. THESE FEATURED SUCH NOVELTIES AS: FREE PUBLIC SCHOOLS, INTEGRATED LEGISLATURES, BLACK U.S. SENATORS AND CONGRESSMEN, AND REPUBLICAN DOMINATION OF THE SOUTH.

REP. ROBT. DELARGE

REP. JOSIAH WELLS

REP. BENJ. TURNER

SEN. HIRAM REVELS

GAUL DAWG HICKORY HAWG!

SHH— DON'T USE MY NAME.

203

Also in 1867, Congress and President broke briefly from bickering to agree on the purchase of **ALASKA** from Russia. (Imagine if it were still Russian!)

QUIVER
TREMBLE SHIVER
CHATTER

Then, just to prove that it still hated him for obstructing Reconstruction, the House of Representatives **impeached** Pres. Johnson... but the Senate acquitted him, on the grounds that being obnoxious was neither a high crime nor a misdemeanor.

WHEW!

WHAT WOULD BE HIGH CRIME, IN CASE WE DO THIS AGAIN?

OH... BREAKING AND ENTERING, SAY...

OH, COME **ON!!** WHAT PRESIDENT WOULD EVER BE GUILTY OF **THAT?!**

THE WHOLE IMPEACHMENT
EXERCISE WAS SILLY...
JOHNSON WOULD BE OUT
OF OFFICE IN A FEW MONTHS,
ANYWAY, AS THE REPUBLICAN
CANDIDATE, WAR HERO

ULYSSES S. GRANT,

SQUEAKED INTO THE
PRESIDENCY IN 1868
(THANKS ENTIRELY TO
BLACK VOTES IN THE
SOUTH, BY THE WAY).

WITH GRANT IN THE
WHITE HOUSE, THE
REPUBLICAN CONGRESS
PASSED THE

XVth AMENDMENT,

WHICH FINALLY GAVE THE VOTE TO ALL BLACK MEN.

(UNTIL THEN,
PARADOXICALLY,
BLACKS COULD VOTE
IN THE SOUTH,
WHICH WAS CONTROLLED
BY THE FEDS,
BUT NOT IN THE
NORTH, WHERE
VOTING QUALIFICATIONS
WERE DECIDED BY THE
INDIVIDUAL STATES.)

HALLEY-
LOO-YAH!
NOW I DON'T
HAVE TO MOVE
BACK TO
MISSISSIPPI!

UNTIL 1877, THE SOUTH LIVED UNDER RECONSTRUCTION GOVERNMENTS. THESE YEARS HAVE BECOME THE SUBJECT OF A POPULAR MYTH, "THE EVILS OF RECONSTRUCTION." THIS MYTH, WHILE NOT ENTIRELY FALSE, WAS NOT ENTIRELY TRUE, EITHER.

HERE ARE SOME

RECONSTRUCTION MYTHS & REALITIES:

MYTH: SOUTHERN WHITES WERE DISENFRANCHISED AND RULED OVER BY BLACKS.

HEY! NO FAIR! REALITY USES MORE WORDS THAN MYTH!

REALITY: ALTHOUGH PARTICIPANTS IN THE REBELLION WERE DISENFRANCHISED, THE NEW STATE CONSTITUTIONS, WHICH ABOLISHED PROPERTY QUALIFICATIONS FOR VOTERS, ACTUALLY ENFRANCHISED MILLIONS OF WHITES FOR THE FIRST TIME.

AND WE VOTED!

MYTH: THE BLACK LEGISLATORS WERE IGNORANT BUFFOONS WHO LOOKED RIDICULOUS "PLAYING AT GOVERNMENT."

REALITY: WHILE SOME OF THEM WERE FRESH FROM THE FARM, MANY OTHERS WERE WELL-EDUCATED ANTI-SLAVERY ACTIVISTS.

RIDICULE IS IN THE MOUTH OF THE BEHOLDER!

MYTH: THE BLACKS WERE TOOLS OF NORTHERN "CARPETBAGGERS," DRIVEN BY GREED AND REVENGE.

MYTH: "HEEDLESS" SPENDING DROVE THE SOUTHERN GOVERNMENTS DEEP INTO DEBT.

MYTH: THE KU KLUX KLAN WAS NECESSARY TO RESTORE THE HONOR OF THE WHITE RACE.

MYTH: THE RECONSTRUCTION GOVERNMENTS WERE NOTHING BUT A "SATURNALIA OF CORRUPTION."

TO QUOTE THE ENCYCLOPÆDIA BRITANNICA!

REALITY: MANY CARPET-BAGGERS WERE IDEALISTIC REFORMERS, COOPERATING WITH BLACKS ON SUCH PROGRAMS AS: EXTENDING DEMOCRACY TO POOR WHITES AND BLACKS; REFORMING THE PENAL SYSTEM; RESTORING THE ECONOMY; AND BUILDING THE SOUTH'S FIRST PUBLIC SCHOOL SYSTEM.

REALITY: THE TAX BASE HAD BEEN DESTROYED BY WAR. URGENTLY NEEDED PROGRAMS OF EDUCATION AND ECONOMIC DEVELOPMENT HAD TO BE FINANCED BY BORROWING.

REALITY: SOME PEOPLE HAVE A FUNNY IDEA OF HONOR.

REALITY: THERE WAS, IN FACT, WIDESPREAD CORRUPTION. HOWEVER, IT IS HARDLY FAIR TO SINGLE OUT THE SOUTH HERE, BECAUSE IN THE 1870's, CORRUPTION HAD BECOME THE NATIONAL PASTIME! READ ON...

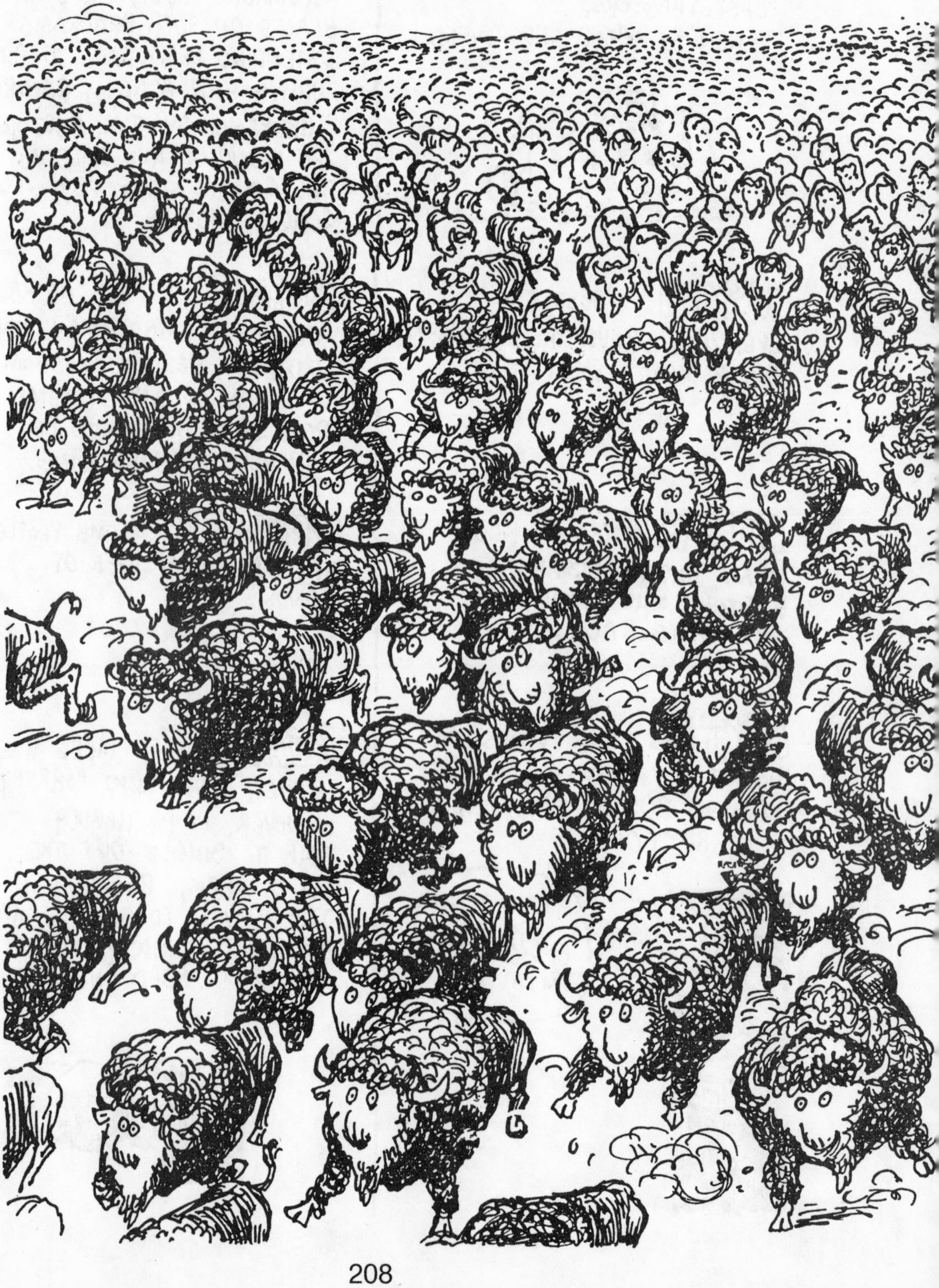

CHAPTER 12

◇ WHERE THE RAILROADS ROAM ◇

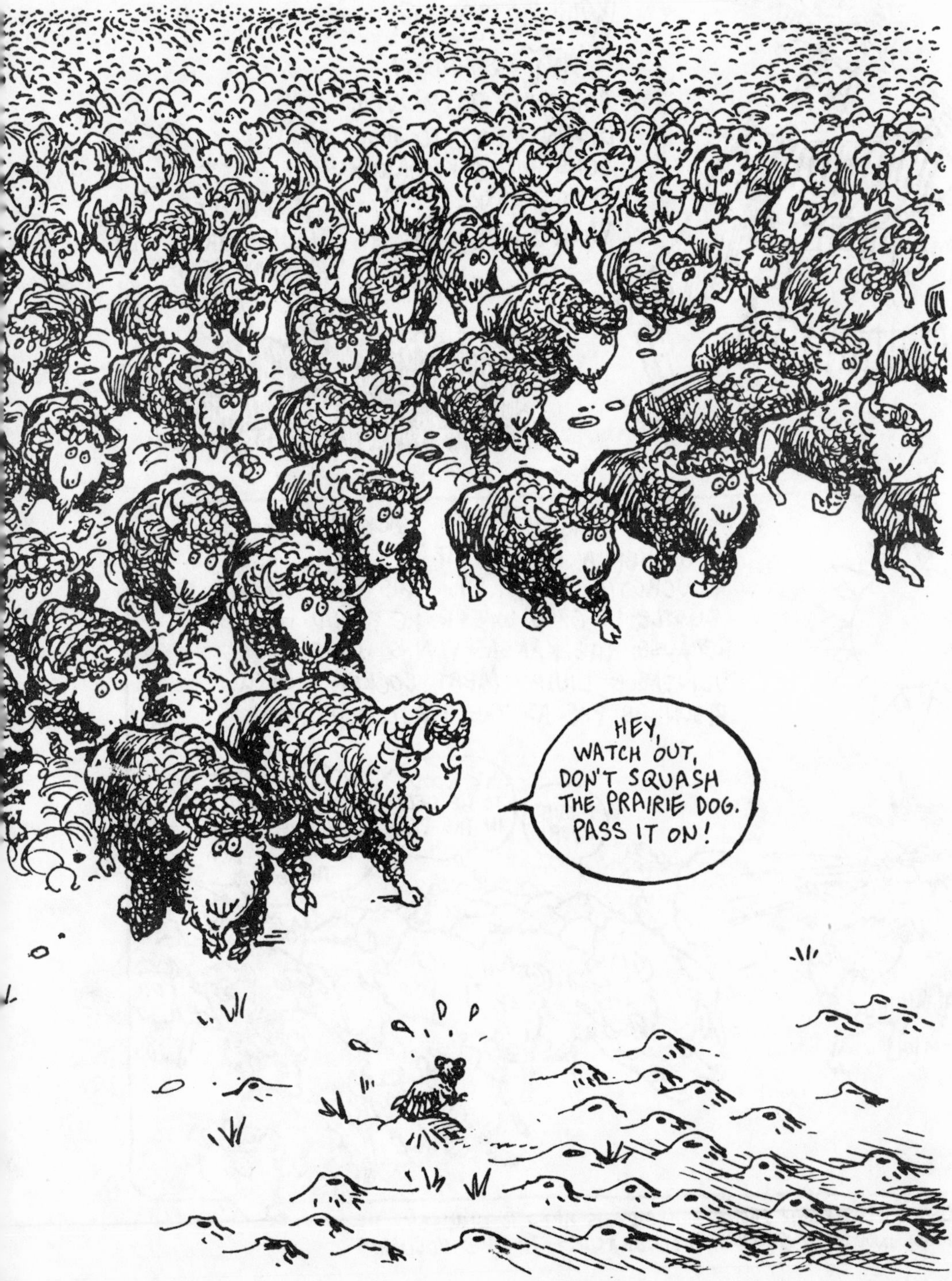
HEY, WATCH OUT, DON'T SQUASH THE PRAIRIE DOG. PASS IT ON!

IN 1866 (OR WAS IT 1867?*), THE FLAMBOYANT, YOUNG **WILLIAM F. CODY** SIGNED A CONTRACT TO PROVIDE BISON MEAT TO THE CONSTRUCTION WORKERS OF THE KANSAS PACIFIC RAILWAY.

I DON'T LIKE THE SOUND OF THIS...

CODY WAS NO MEAT PACKER... HE PACKED A GUN INSTEAD (NICKNAMED "LUCRETIA BORGIA"). HIS PLAN WAS TO RUSTLE UP GRUB WHERE HE FOUND IT... BECAUSE THE KANSAS PLAINS WERE A VERITABLE LIVING MEAT LOCKER, WITH BISON AS FAR AS THE EYE COULD SEE!

MOVE OVER!

IT'S GOOD TO BE DEEP IN THE PACK!

WHAT THE HECK ARE WE RUNNING FROM? I CAN'T SEE A THING!

* ACCURATE INFORMATION ABOUT BILL CODY IS HARD TO COME BY. HE PERSONALLY INVENTED ENOUGH INACCURACIES TO FILL VOLUMES.

210

IN EIGHT MONTHS*
CODY BAGGED OVER
4200 BISON AND
EARNED HIMSELF A
NICKNAME AS WELL:

"BUFFALO BILL."

THIS WAS JUST THE BEGINNING OF THE GREAT BUFFALO SLAUGHTER. IT WAS INCREDIBLY WASTEFUL: CODY TOOK ONLY THE HAMS AND HUMPS, LEAVING THE REST TO THE HAPPY VULTURES.

EVEN SO, HE
SUPPLIED ENOUGH
MEAT TO FEED
A SMALL ARMY
OF RAILROAD
WORKERS!

*OR EIGHTEEN. SEE PREVIOUS FOOTNOTE.

ALL THOSE WORKERS EATING ALL THOSE BUFFALO WAS A CLEAR SIGN THAT THE RAILROAD BUSINESS WAS BOOMING. IN THE 1860's, RAILROAD BARONS' FORTUNES WERE RISING EVEN FASTER THAN THE BUFFALO POPULATION WAS FALLING.

THE BOOM HAD ACTUALLY BEGUN WITH THE CIVIL WAR, WHEN CONGRESS HATCHED A TRULY GRAND SCHEME: BUILD A TRANSCONTINENTAL RAILWAY.

BUT A PROJECT SO ENORMOUS HAD SCARCELY BEEN IMAGINED BEFORE! WHO COULD POSSIBLY AFFORD IT? SUCH A HUGE INVESTMENT IN LAND, LABOR, AND EQUIPMENT WAS BEYOND THE ABILITY OF ANY PRIVATE COMPANY.

IT WAS SUGGESTED THAT THE GOVERNMENT ITSELF COULD BUILD AND RUN THE GREAT RAILROAD — BUT NO, THAT WOULD BE SOCIALISTIC!

I SAID IT BEFORE — WE'RE REPUBLICANS!

SO THE GOVERNMENT CAME UP WITH A BRILLIANT SOLUTION: SIMPLY **GIVE** THE LAND AND LEND THE MONEY TO PRIVATE RAILROAD COMPANIES! THE AMOUNT OF LAND EVENTUALLY HANDED OVER WAS INCREDIBLE: MORE THAN 200 MILLION ACRES!!

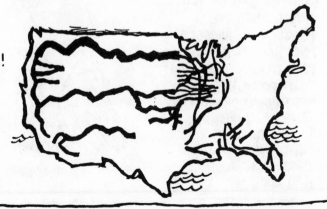

AND WHO WERE THESE RAILROAD COMPANIES? WELL, IN THOSE DAYS, WHEN THE INDUSTRY WAS YOUNG, ANYONE WHO *SAID* HE WAS A RAILROAD COULD *BE* A RAILROAD. AND WITH SUCH HIGH STAKES, THERE WERE MANY CONTENDERS!!

FOR EXAMPLE, FOUR CALIFORNIA SHOPKEEPERS, ARMED WITH SOME ENGINEERING SURVEYS, DECLARED THEMSELVES THE **CENTRAL PACIFIC** RAILROAD. ONE OF THEM HEADED TO WASHINGTON WITH A SUITCASE FULL OF CASH..

...AND "PERSUADED" CONGRESS TO GIVE THE WESTERN END OF THE TRANSCONTINENTAL PROJECT TO HIMSELF AND HIS PARTNERS. PRACTICALLY OVERNIGHT, THEIR FORTUNES MULTIPLIED FROM THE TENS OF THOUSANDS TO THE TENS OF MILLIONS. THEY WERE NOW A RAILROAD!!

HOPKINS CROCKER STANFORD HUNTINGTON

214

THE EASTERN HALF
OF THE ROUTE WAS
ASSIGNED TO THE

UNION PACIFIC

COMPANY. DESPITE THE
PATRIOTIC NAME, THE
CORPORATION'S DIRECTORS
FOUND A WAY TO MILK
CONGRESS FOR MILLIONS
OF DOLLARS...

THE SCHEME WAS SIMPLE:
THEY HIRED A FIRM NAMED
CREDIT MOBILIER TO DO THE
CONSTRUCTION WORK, THEN
OVERPAID CREDIT MOBILIER BY
AN ENORMOUS FACTOR.

THE BEAUTY OF IT WAS THAT
THE OWNERS OF CREDIT MOBILIER
AND THE OWNERS OF THE UNION
PACIFIC WERE — THE VERY
SAME PEOPLE!!

ALTHOUGH MILLIONS
IN PUBLIC FUNDS
DISAPPEARED INTO THE
RAILROADERS' BANK
ACCOUNTS, CONGRESS
WAS SILENT —
AND NO WONDER:
THE UNION PACIFIC
MEN HAD BESTOWED
MANY SHARES OF
PROFITABLE STOCK
UPON THE COMPLIANT
CONGRESSPEOPLE!

WE HAVE
TO OPERATE
THIS WAY — RUNNING
A RAILROAD IS A
RISKY BUSINESS!

ESPECIALLY
THE WAY
WE DO IT...

MOO.

RAILROADERS WEREN'T THE ONLY ONES WHO MULTIPLIED THEIR MONEY IN THE CIVIL WAR.

SEVERAL OF AMERICA'S MOST FAMOUS FORTUNES DATE FROM THE 1860's!

FOR INSTANCE (L. TO R.):
JOHN D. ROCKEFELLER (OIL),
PHILIP ARMOUR (MEAT),
ANDREW CARNEGIE (IRON & STEEL),
J.P. MORGAN (BANKING)—
ALL WERE MEN IN THEIR 20's DURING THE CIVIL WAR, AND ALL CHOSE BUSINESS OVER BATTLE!

"I HAD HOPED MY BOY WAS GOING TO MAKE A SMART, INTELLIGENT BUSINESSMAN, AND WAS NOT SUCH A GOOSE AS TO BE SEDUCED FROM DUTY [SIC] BY THE DECLAMATIONS OF BUNCOMBED SPEECHES. IT IS ONLY GREENHORNS WHO ENLIST... A MAN MAY BE A PATRIOT WITHOUT RISKING HIS OWN LIFE... THERE ARE PLENTY OF OTHER LIVES LESS VALUABLE..."
— JUDGE THOMAS MELLON TO HIS SON

"I'M RICH! I'M RICH!"
— ANDREW CARNEGIE

"WE COULD NOT BE EXPECTED TO LEAVE OUR COMFORTABLE HOMES WITHOUT SOME GREAT INDUCEMENT."
— BANKER JAY COOKE

"YOU CAN SELL ANYTHING TO THE GOVERNMENT AT ANY PRICE IF YOU'VE GOT THE NERVE TO ASK."
— JIM FISK

"TO CONTINUE MUCH LONGER WITH MOST OF MY THOUGHTS WHOLLY UPON THE WAY TO MAKE MONEY IN THE SHORTEST TIME MUST DEGRADE ME BEYOND HOPE OF PERMANENT RECOVERY."
— ANDREW CARNEGIE

"I LIKE TO TURN BRISTLES, BLOOD, BONES, AND THE INSIDES AND OUTSIDES OF PIGS AND BULLOCKS INTO REVENUE." — P. ARMOUR

AS THEIR BUSINESSES BOOMED, THESE GENIUSES OF HIGH FINANCE INVENTED NEW, FABULOUS, AND NOT ALWAYS HONEST METHODS OF MANIPULATING MONEY. FOR SOME REASON, THESE ARE OFTEN DESCRIBED IN LIQUID METAPHORS,

SUCH AS:

STOCK WATERING

SIPHONING PROCEEDS

SKIMMING ASSETS

FLOODING MARKETS

MILKING COMPANIES

FLOATING LOANS

SINKING FUNDS

POOLS

FINANCIAL RESERVOIRS

(NOTE: "LAUNDERING" MONEY WASN'T INVENTED UNTIL LATER.)

MONEY... MONEY...

AMERICANS ADMIRED THE WITS, ENERGY, AND EVEN THE RUTHLESSNESS OF THESE CORSAIRS. AFTER ALL, WASN'T COMPETITION PART OF THE NATURAL ORDER? WASN'T SUCCESS THE SURVIVAL OF THE FITTEST? IT WAS PRIMAL! IT WAS DARWINIAN!*

GEE! I WISH I'D THOUGHT OF THAT!

IN THIS ECONOMIC STRUGGLE FOR EXISTENCE, THE POST-WAR CAPITALISTS OFTEN DISPLAYED THE BUSINESS ETHICS OF A CHIMPANZEE.

*DARWIN'S *THE ORIGIN OF SPECIES* APPEARED IN 1859.

218

THEY "PURCHASED" REPRESENTATIVES, SENATORS, THE PRESIDENT'S BROTHER-IN-LAW... EVERY INDUSTRY HAD GOVERNMENT OFFICIALS IN ITS POCKET.. IN CALIFORNIA, THE RAILROAD EVEN TOSSED GOLD COINS TO THE VOTERS ON ELECTION DAY!

OOPS!

IN THE JARGON OF THE TIME, A CORRUPT NETWORK WAS A "RING." THERE WAS A WHISKEY RING, AN ERIE RAILROAD RING, THE CREDIT MOBILIER RING, A GOLD RING, A U.S. CUSTOMS RING, A CANAL RING, A MILWAUKEE RING, N.Y.'S "BOSS" TWEED RING, AND COUNTLESS OTHER STATE, COUNTY, AND MUNICIPAL RINGS.

EVERYTHING BUT A BATHTUB RING!

(AND OF COURSE, SOME OF THESE RINGS REACHED INTO THE RECONSTRUCTION SOUTH, GIVING THE RACISTS A NEW EXCUSE TO QUESTION THE BLACKS' "CAPACITY" FOR HONEST GOVERNMENT.)

MY BAG'S CAPACITY IS DEFINITELY BIGGER...

AND NOW, BACK TO BUFFALO BILL COUNTRY:

IN 1875, COL. GEORGE ARMSTRONG **CUSTER**, WITH HIS DOGS, LED AN EXPLORING PARTY INTO DAKOTA'S BLACK HILLS, LOOKING FOR GOLD. THIS WAS INDIAN COUNTRY, GUARANTEED BY SOLEMN TREATY.

CUSTER WAS FOLLOWED, AS SOON AS WORD GOT OUT, BY ANOTHER INVASION OF PROSPECTORS, SPECULATORS, HARDWARE SALESMEN, MULES, TEAMSTERS, CLAIM-JUMPERS, COOKS, LAUNDRESSES, AND CAMP-FOLLOWERS.

(IT WAS GOVERNMENT POLICY TO "DISAPPROVE" OF THIS ONSLAUGHT, WHILE DOING NOTHING TO STOP IT...)

GOLD!! IT'S NATURE'S LOTTERY!

BY THIS TIME, THE PLAINS INDIANS WERE ALREADY THREATENED BY THE DWINDLING SUPPLY OF BUFFALO.

THE GOVERNMENT URGED THE SIOUX AND CHEYENNE TO GIVE UP THEIR HOME ON THE RANGE FOR A BUNK ON THE RESERVATION... TO EXCHANGE BUFFALO ROBES FOR WOOL BLANKETS, AND BUFFALO JERKY FOR RESERVATION BEEF.

BUT NOW, WITH THE FRESH INVASION OF WHITE SETTLERS, THE INDIANS WENT ON THE WARPATH!

HOW MANY WARRIORS ARE WE TALKING ABOUT HERE?

DESPITE THE HOSTILITIES, OFFICIAL GOVERNMENT RECORDS SHOWED THAT NEARLY ALL OF THE PLAINS INDIANS WERE SAFELY ON THE RESERVATIONS.

I HAVE A FUNNY FEELING ABOUT THIS...

BUT IN AN AGE OF CORRUPTION, THE RECORDS WERE FALSIFIED BY CORRUPT GOVERNMENT AGENTS. THE AGENTS, IN CHARGE OF THE RESERVATIONS, RECEIVED FUNDS ACCORDING TO THE NUMBER OF "THEIR" INDIANS. THIS NUMBER THEY ROUTINELY INFLATED, SKIMMING OFF THE MONEY OF THOUSANDS OF IMAGINARY OR ABSENT SOULS.

NOT TO MENTION WHAT WE SAVE BY BUYING BAD BEEF!

799, 800, 801...

HALLUCINATIONS PLAY MAJOR ROLE IN WHITE MAN'S WAY OF LIFE...

RESERVATION	OFFICIAL POPULATION	ACTUAL POPULATION
SPOTTED TAIL	9,610	2,315
RED CLOUD	12,873	4,760
CHEYENNE RIVER	7,586	2,280
STANDING ROCK	7,322	2,305

ADDING UP THE NUMBERS, YOU GET A DISCREPANCY OF ROUGHLY 25,000...

... MOST OF WHOM WERE CAMPED ALONG THE BANKS OF THE LITTLE BIG HORN RIVER, MONTANA, WHEN COL. CUSTER'S CAVALRY ARRIVED ON A SEARCH-AND-DESTROY MISSION (JUNE 25, 1876).

GLEEP!

CUSTER, RECEIVING THE SURPRISE OF HIS LIFE, MADE A LAST STAND. ABOUT 265 CAVALRYMEN FELL THAT DAY — VICTIMS OF GOVERNMENT CORRUPTION!

WAS MISINFORMED...

CUSTER'S LAST STAND TURNED OUT TO BE THE NEXT-TO-THE-LAST STAND FOR THE PLAINS INDIANS... AFTER A COUPLE YEARS, THEY HAD BEEN STARVED INTO SURRENDER AND MOVED ONTO THE RESERVATION... THE BISON WERE ALL BUT WIPED OUT... AND RAILROAD TRACKS PIERCED THE WEST...

...AND SITTING BULL, HOLY MAN OF THE OGLALA NATION, WENT ON TOUR WITH BUFFALO BILL'S WILD WEST SHOW...

THINK OF THE ENDORSEMENTS! THE SPIN-OFFS! NOW LOOK FIERCE AND WAVE...

SIGH

···◇ CHAPTER 13 ◇···

LABOR PAINS

JULY 4, 1876, WAS THE UNITED STATES' HUNDREDTH BIRTHDAY.

IN THE GRAND AMERICAN TRADITION, THE NATION THREW A NOISY PARTY, WITH RINGING SPEECHES, BOOMING BELLS, BLASTING BRASS BANDS, AND EAR-INJURING FIREWORKS.

BUT THE CELEBRATION WAS A GLOOMY ONE FOR PRESIDENT GRANT AND THE REPUBLICANS.

1876 WAS ALSO AN ELECTION YEAR, AND IT LOOKED BAD FOR THE PARTY THAT GAVE US THE MOST CORRUPT ADMINISTRATION IN THE REPUBLIC'S HISTORY...

FOR PRESIDENT THE DEMOCRATS RAN A "REFORM" CANDIDATE, SAMUEL **TILDEN,** WHILE THE REPUBLICANS NOMINATED THE BUSINESS-AND-BEARDS-AS-USUAL RUTHERFORD B. **HAYES.** THE RESULT WAS SURPRISING...

AT FIRST, TILDEN SEEMED TO HAVE WON EASILY. BUT THE REPUBLICANS CHALLENGED HIS VOTES IN FOUR STATES, AND PRODUCED ALTERNATIVE RETURNS FAVORING HAYES.

THEY ACCUSED THE DEMOCRATS OF INTIMIDATING BLACK VOTERS WITH KU KLUX KLAN TACTICS, WHILE THE DEMOCRATS CHARGED THE REPUBLICANS WITH BUYING VOTES.

BOTH WERE CORRECT!

THE GOVERNMENT STOPPED DEAD ON THE ISSUE. CONGRESSIONAL DEBATE GAVE WAY TO SHOUTING, THEN SCREAMING, AND FINALLY A HIGH WHINE.

SOUNDS LIKE THE CIVIL WAR STARTING AGAIN...

A COMMISSION OF 8 REPUBLICANS AND 7 DEMOCRATS WAS APPOINTED TO RESOLVE THE IMPASSE. IT VOTED, 8-7, IN FAVOR OF HAYES.

SURPRISE!

TO SILENCE THE DEMOCRATS' COMPLAINTS, THE REPUBLICANS STRUCK AN UNHOLY DEAL: THEY PROMISED TO WITHDRAW ALL THE FEDERAL TROOPS THAT PROTECTED BLACK CIVIL RIGHTS IN THE SOUTH.

...AND THAT WAS HOW THE HAYES-TILDEN ELECTION PUT AN END TO SOUTHERN RECONSTRUCTION... WHITE DEMOCRATS TOOK BACK POLITICAL POWER, AND AN EXODUS OF BLACKS HIT THE ROAD!

All Colored People

THAT WANT TO

GO TO KANSAS,

On September 5th, 1877,

Can do so for $5.00

THE REPUBLICANS HAD SCARCELY FINISHED EXHALING THEIR SIGH OF RELIEF WHEN THE NATION WAS ROCKED BY SOMETHING CALLED ➡

THE GREAT UPHEAVAL

OF 1877...

THIS UNDER-REPORTED HISTORICAL EPISODE BEGAN IN PENNSYLVANIA WITH A STRIKE AGAINST THE B&O RAILROAD. IN PITTSBURGH, TROOPS ATTACKED THE STRIKERS, KILLING 20. THE INFURIATED WORKERS SEIZED THE TRAIN YARDS AND TORCHED THE ROUNDHOUSE.

THE STRIKE SPREAD TO SANDUSKY, BUFFALO, MILWAUKEE, CLEVELAND, ST. LOUIS. EVERYWHERE, CROWDS GATHERED TO SUPPORT THE STRIKERS, WHILE POLICE AND GUARDSMEN BACKED OFF — OR JOINED THE MOB THEMSELVES!!

I'M JUST A WORKER IN A BLUE SUIT!

228

SOON THE WORKERS WERE MANAGING THE RAILROADS THEMSELVES, MOVING STRIKE LEADERS AND INFORMATION ALMOST AT WILL.

ST. LOUIS FELL BRIEFLY UNDER THE CONTROL OF THE STRIKE COMMITTEE — A SORT OF "WORKERS' SOVIET"— WHICH SHUT DOWN THE CITY WITH A GENERAL STRIKE. RHETORIC GREW REVOLUTIONARY!

THIS MAY BE THE BEGINNING OF A GREAT CIVIL WAR IN THIS COUNTRY, BETWEEN LABOR AND CAPITAL... IT ONLY NEEDS THAT THE STRIKERS SHOULD BOLDLY ATTACK AND ROUT THE TROOPS.

THE WORKING MEN INTEND NOW TO ASSERT THEIR RIGHTS, EVEN IF THE RESULT IS SHEDDING OF BLOOD!

COMMUNISM IMPENDS!

AT LAST, THE NEW PRESIDENT ORDERED IN THE ARMY, WHICH BLOODILY CRUSHED THE STRIKE... THE WORKERS, DESPITE LOSING, WENT BACK TO WORK WITH A SPRING IN THEIR STEP!

A P.S.: AS A DIRECT RESULT OF THE 1877 UPRISING, THE GOVERNMENT NERVOUSLY BUILT THE GREAT STONE ARMORIES YOU SEE IN SO MANY AMERICAN CITIES —NOT AGAINST FOREIGN INVASION, BUT WORKERS' REBELLION!!

229

HOW HAD THIS HAPPENED?? THE GREAT UPHEAVAL HAD SEEMINGLY HEAVED UP FROM NOWHERE! WHO WOULD ATTACK THE SYSTEM IN THIS WAY? WASN'T AMERICAN INDUSTRY A WONDERFUL THING???

YOU JUST DON'T APPRECIATE THE **GOOD** IT'S DONE **ALL** OF US!

THAT'S RIGHT!

IN TRUTH, AMERICAN INDUSTRY HAD ITS WONDERFUL POINTS. IN A FEW SHORT YEARS (AND SEVERAL LONG ONES), IT HAD MECHANIZED FARM LIFE WITH LABOR-SAVING DEVICES, CREATED AN AMAZING TRANSPORTATION SYSTEM, AND MASS-PRODUCED CLOTHING, FURNITURE, AND OTHER CONSUMER ITEMS.

THE GOOD LIFE DEPENDS ON IT!

BUT ALAS... THE ECONOMY HAD THIS UNPLEASANT TENDENCY TO

WHEN THAT HAPPENED, WORKERS LOST THEIR JOBS, WAGES FELL, BANKRUPTCIES ROSE, AND PEOPLE FOUND THEMSELVES SURROUNDED BY CONSUMER GOODS THEY COULDN'T AFFORD — FOOD, FOR EXAMPLE...

AHEM...

...WHILE ROCKEFELLER AND CARNEGIE ACTUALLY GREW RICHER BY DEVOURING THEIR DISTRESSED COMPETITORS!

YOU SEE? EVERY CLOUD HAS A SILVER LINING!

THE FIRST CRASH
AFTER THE
CIVIL WAR WAS THE

PANIC OF 1873.

I AM GLAD TO SEE THAT A SYSTEM OF LABOR PREVAILS UNDER WHICH LABORERS MAY STRIKE WHEN THEY WANT TO,

ABE LINCOLN HAD SAID.

AS HARD TIMES DRAGGED ON THROUGH 1873, '74, '75, AND '76, WORKERS' FAMILIES HAD TO LIVE ON CORNBREAD AND BEANS, AND "FREE LABOR" BEGAN SOUNDING LIKE A SLOGAN AS EMPTY AS THEIR STOMACHS.

FREE TO BEEE... WHAT'S LEFT OF MEEE...

THE CIVIL WAR — WASN'T THAT THE WAR TO PROTECT FREE LABOR?

WELL, NOW I'M FREE!

LAY-OFF NOTICE

IN 1875, A WAVE OF STRIKES HIT THE COAL MINES (ACCIDENT RATE: 80 DEATHS PER YEAR). MANAGEMENT PULLED OUT ALL THE STOPS: PRIVATE ARMIES OF STRIKEBREAKERS (THE NOTORIOUS PINKERTON "DETECTIVES"), CHARGES OF TERRORISM AGAINST STRIKE LEADERS, ETC.... THIS WAS THE BACKGROUND OF 1877.

I CAN HIRE ONE HALF OF THE WORKING CLASS TO KILL THE OTHER HALF,

SAID INDUSTRIALIST JAY GOULD.

THIS PARTLY ACCOUNTS FOR
STRIKERS' MILITANT RHETORIC
DURING THE 1877 UPRISING...
ANOTHER REASON WAS THE FACT
THAT THERE WERE, IN FACT,
SOME SOCIALISTS INVOLVED!

THE SOCIALIST MOVEMENT,
IN THE OPINION OF MOST,
BEGAN IN **1848**, WHEN
A WAVE OF EUROPEAN
REVOLUTIONS SPAWNED
KARL MARX's
COMMUNIST MANIFESTO.

BY 1864, MARX HEADED
THE INTERNATIONAL
WORKING MEN'S ASSOCIATION
(WHICH WAS NICKNAMED THE
"FIRST INTERNATIONAL" SOMETIME
DURING THE ORGANIZATION OF
THE SECOND INTERNATIONAL).

BY 1877, AMERICA'S TEEMING
IMMIGRANT POPULATION INCLUDED
ENOUGH SOCIALISTS (MOSTLY
GERMAN) TO FOUND A SMALL BUT
VERY LOUD **WORKERS' PARTY**
AFFILIATED WITH THE FIRST
INTERNATIONAL.

AS THE SOCIALISTS SAW IT, WORKERS WERE LOCKED IN AN ETERNAL

CLASS STRUGGLE

WITH THE OWNERS OF CAPITAL. (CAPITAL = MONEY, STOCKS, BONDS, FACTORIES, MACHINERY, SHIPS, TRAINS, ETC. ETC. ETC.) WHAT THE WORKER NEEDS IS THE OPPOSITE OF WHAT CAPITAL NEEDS.

HIGHER WAGES!

HIGHER PROFITS!

ACCORDING TO THIS VIEW OF THE WORLD, THE WORKER ALONE CREATES VALUE BY WORKING, WHILE THE CAPITALIST TAKES IT AWAY IN THE FORM OF PROFIT. LOW WAGES, HIGH UNEMPLOYMENT, POLLUTION, UNSAFE FACTORIES ARE NECESSARY FOR PROFITABILITY.* ECONOMIC CRASHES ARE AN INEVITABLE CONSEQUENCE OF THE QUEST FOR PROFIT... AND THE GOVERNMENT, AS STRIKEBREAKER, IS A PURE TOOL OF THE BOSSES...

THE SOCIALISTS' PRESCRIPTION WAS FOR THE WORKERS TO TAKE POLITICAL POWER FROM CAPITAL AND CREATE A WORKERS' STATE. THIS WAS NOW POSSIBLE FOR THE FIRST TIME IN HISTORY, SAID MARX, BECAUSE LARGE-SCALE FACTORIES BROUGHT WORKERS TOGETHER IN INDUSTRIAL ARMIES.

FOR SUCH A SOURPUSS, I'M AN OPTIMIST!

*LOW WAGES, POLLUTION, AND INDUSTRIAL CALAMITIES IN THE PRESENT-DAY SOCIALIST WORLD ARE, OF COURSE, A COMPLETE ACCIDENT THAT DEFIES RATIONAL EXPLANATION.

ON THE OTHER HAND, MOST CAPITALISTS VIEWED THE SOCIALISTS AS LITTLE MORE THAN A GANG OF ALIEN, BOMB-THROWING BANDITTI. NO "REAL" AMERICAN WOULD FOMENT LABOR STRIFE — IT HAD TO BE THE WORK OF FOREIGNERS AND ANARCHIST-SOCIALIST-COMMUNIST AGITATORS!

SMELLS LIKE ROSES

REPUBLICAN BALLOT

DEFERENTIAL YET INTELLIGENT ATTITUDE

HAT IN HAND

"REAL" AMERICAN

SMELLS LIKE GARLIC

HAT COVERS EYES

CRINGING, SHIFTY EXPRESSION

BOMB

CONSPIRATORIAL SLOUCH

UNREAL IMMIGRANT

ALMOST WITHOUT REALIZING IT, THE BOSSES HAD INVENTED

RED-BAITING:

I.E., BREAKING UNIONS BY ATTACKING SOCIALISTS IN THE RANKS.

YOU FOLKS GO RIGHT AHEAD — WE'LL JUST JAIL YOUR PRESIDENT AND IMPUGN YOUR MOTIVES...

DESPITE MANAGEMENT'S OPPOSITION, UNION ORGANIZING STEPPED UP AFTER 1877. MOST ACTIVE WERE THE **KNIGHTS OF LABOR,** WHO CONCEALED THEMSELVES FROM THE BOSS WITH SECRET SIGNS AND HANDSHAKES.

AT THE SAME TIME, A YOUNG CIGAR ROLLER NAMED **SAMUEL GOMPERS** HELPED TO FOUND THE **A**MERICAN **F**EDERATION OF **L**ABOR. GOMPERS GUIDED THE AFL AWAY FROM PARTY POLITICS AND INTO A SIMPLE QUEST FOR "MORE" — HIGHER WAGES, SHORTER HOURS, AND BETTER WORKING CONDITIONS. THE AFL'S SKILLED CRAFT UNIONS BECAME AN "ARISTOCRACY OF LABOR."

THE RESURGENT UNION MOVEMENT MADE ITS CAMPAIGN FOR THE '80's A DEMAND FOR AN **8-HOUR DAY.**

NOW THEY WANT TO CHANGE THE COURSE OF THE SUN IN ITS ORBIT!

THE AFL AND OTHERS CALLED FOR A NATIONWIDE DEMONSTRATION: A ONE-DAY **GENERAL STRIKE** ON MAY 1, 1886... A TOTAL WORK STOPPAGE... A ZERO-HOUR DAY FOR THE EIGHT-HOUR DAY.

I'M FOR IT!

THIS EXTREME TACTIC DIVIDED THE MOVEMENT. THE RANK AND FILE GENERALLY FAVORED IT, WHILE THE NERVOUS PRESIDENT OF THE KNIGHTS OF LABOR, **TERENCE POWDERLY**, DISLIKED THE WHOLE IDEA.

ER... PREMATURE... JEOPARDIZES OUR GAINS... COMMUNISTIC... ETC. ETC. ETC.

THE GNAT OF LABOR!

THE DAY ARRIVED... AND ACROSS THE COUNTRY, UNIONISTS GATHERED IN HUGE RALLIES TO HEAR INFLAMMATORY SPEECHES.

Our war-cry is "DEATH to the foes of the human race!" *

EVER SINCE THEN, MAY DAY HAS BEEN LABOR DAY — IN EVERY COUNTRY EXCEPT THE UNITED STATES, THAT IS!!

IF THE COMMIES DO IT, WE DON'T!

* FROM A RESOLUTION OF THE ANARCHIST-LED CHICAGO CENTRAL LABOR UNION, 1885.

THE MAY DAY RALLIES WERE PEACEFUL, BUT TWO DAYS LATER, IN CHICAGO, THE POLICE ATTACKED ANOTHER DEMONSTRATION, GENEROUSLY TRYING TO PROTECT THE WORKERS' EARS FROM BECOMING INFLAMED BY THE HOT WORDS, NO DOUBT.

ON MAY 4, WHILE BREAKING UP YET ANOTHER DEMONSTRATION, SEVEN POLICEMEN WERE KILLED BY A BOMB BLAST — THE HAYMARKET EXPLOSION.

TAKE 2 ASPIRIN AND CALL ME IN THE MORNING.

WITHOUT ANY IDEA WHO TOSSED THE BOMB, THE AUTHORITIES ARRESTED — EIGHT ANARCHISTS.

IF THEY AIN'T GUILTY, THEY'RE GONNA BE!!

FIRING INTO THE FLEEING WORKERS' BACKS, THE POLICE KILLED FOUR, AND THE ANARCHIST PRESS SCREAMED BLOODY MURDER, WHICH SEEMED APPROPRIATE.

ALTHOUGH THEIR INVOLVEMENT WAS NEVER PROVED, ONE OF THE PRISONERS SHOWED AT LEAST A PASSING ACQUAINTANCE WITH EXPLOSIVES BY BLOWING HIMSELF UP IN JAIL. FOUR OTHERS WERE HANGED, AND THE REST RECEIVED LONG JAIL SENTENCES.

REVENGE! WORKINGMEN, TO ARMS!... YOU HAVE ENDURED THE MOST ABJECT HUMILIATIONS... WHY? TO SATISFY THE INSATIABLE GREED OF YOUR MASTERS? TO ARMS, WE CALL YOU, TO ARMS!

REVEN

THE HAYMARKET EVENTS COOLED THE 8-HOUR MOVEMENT, BUT NOT FOR LONG. THE '90'S BROUGHT ANOTHER CRASH AND ANOTHER WAVE OF STRIKES.

WORKERS SEIZED FACTORIES, MINES, TRAIN YARDS PINKERTONS KILLED STRIKERS' FAMILIES... BULLETS FLEW IN SEVERAL DIRECTIONS...

YOU CAN SEE WHY THEY CALL IT "CLASS WAR"

ONTO THIS WILD STAGE MARCHED THE IMPASSIONED FIGURE OF

EUGENE DEBS,

PRESIDENT OF THE AMERICAN RAILROAD UNION.

IN 1894, THE A R U BACKED A STRIKE AGAINST THE PULLMAN RAILROAD CAR COMPANY.

DEBS WAS AS AMERICAN AS THEY COME:

BORN IN INDIANA...

MARRIED IN THE EPISCOPAL CHURCH

WORKED AS A RAILROAD FIREMAN

ORGANIZED A LOCAL OF THE FIREMEN'S UNION

BECAME ITS NATIONAL SECRETARY-TREASURER

SERVED A TERM IN THE INDIANA LEGISLATURE

HE SHOULD BE PLAYED BY RONALD REAGAN!

THEN, IN 1894, HIS SUPPORT FOR THE PULLMAN STRIKE LANDED HIM IN JAIL. CONVICTED OF OBSTRUCTING THE U.S. MAIL, DEBS AND OTHER UNION OFFICIALS GOT SIX MONTHS, WHICH DEBS PASSED READING MARXIST LITERATURE.

MAYBE SENDING DEBS TO JAIL WASN'T SUCH A GOOD IDEA...

HE EMERGED FROM PRISON A CONVERT TO THE "ALIEN" PHILOSOPHY. THE AMERICAN SOCIALIST MOVEMENT WAS ABOUT TO BECOME AMERICANIZED...

MORE ON DEBS NEXT CHAPTER... NOW WE'RE LOOKING DOWN ON THE 1893 CHICAGO COLUMBIAN EXPOSITION, BUILT (A YEAR LATE) TO HONOR COLUMBUS'S 400TH ANNIVERSARY. IT'S A FITTING SYMBOL TO END THIS CHAPTER: THE ENORMOUS "PALACE OF MANUFACTURES," COVERING 30 ACRES, STUFFED WITH MODERN INDUSTRIAL WONDERS: DYNAMOS, TELEPHONES, ELECTRIC MOTORS, AUTOMOBILES, DYNAMITE, LIGHT BULBS, MACHINE GUNS...

BUT 18 WORKERS DIED BUILDING THIS EXPOSITION, AND HUNDREDS MORE WERE INJURED.

AMERICAN WORKERS HAD FOUGHT LONG AND HARD TO IMPROVE — OR EVEN TO MAINTAIN — THEIR LOT. HERE AND THERE THEY HAD WON VICTORIES ... BUT THE 40-HOUR WEEK, EXTRA PAY FOR OVERTIME WORK, UNEMPLOYMENT INSURANCE, SOCIAL SECURITY, GOVERNMENT-ENFORCED SAFETY STANDARDS WERE ALL STILL FAR IN THE FUTURE, AND WORKING MEN AND WOMEN WERE GROWING INCREASINGLY FRUSTRATED.

AND NOT ONLY WORKERS! MANY OTHER AMERICANS WERE TIRED OF THE INDUSTRIAL BLOODSHED... TIRED OF SEEING A RICH AND POWERFUL FEW DRIVE SO MANY INTO POVERTY AND DEBT...

OBVIOUSLY, SOMETHING HAD TO BE DONE !! THE ONLY QUESTION WAS...

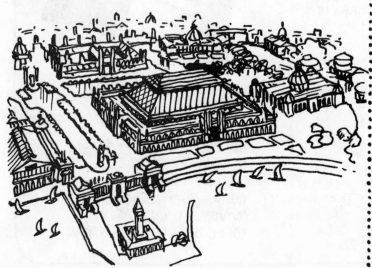

WHAT??

« CHAPTER 14 »

IN WHICH AN AWFUL LOT HAPPENS

NOW WE ENTER THE FINAL TENTH OF THE NINETEENTH...

EVERYTHING WAS IN FLUX — ELECTROMAGNETIC FLUX, THAT IS: ELECTRICITY POWERED LAMPS, STREETCARS, AND ELEVATORS IN NEW SKYSCRAPERS...

BUSINESS WAS BIGGER THAN EVER... THE LEAN, MEAN CAPITALISTS OF THE '70'S AND '80'S WERE EVOLVING INTO BLOATED ECONOMIC MONSTERS, THE **TRUSTS.**

A **TRUST** WAS SIMPLY A MONOPOLY GOING UNDER AN ANGLO-SAXON NAME...

DURING THE '60's, '70's, AND '80's, BIG COMPANIES HAD USUALLY DEALT WITH SMALLER FRY BY POUNDING THEM INTO THE DUST.

THIS TAKES TIME, ENERGY, AND MONEY!

SOMETIMES, THOUGH, IT WAS CHEAPER AND EASIER TO ABSORB COMPETITORS. THE WEAKER COMPANIES WOULD "ENTRUST" THEIR ASSETS TO THE LARGER, IN EXCHANGE FOR CASH OR STOCK, UNTIL ONLY ONE COMPANY WAS LEFT— THE **TRUST**.

EVER BEEN BODY-SNATCHED BY AN OCTOPUS?

STANDARD OIL, UNITED STATES STEEL, GENERAL ELECTRIC, THE BELL SYSTEM, THE COAL TRUST, THE SUGAR TRUST... IN INDUSTRY AFTER INDUSTRY, ONE COMPANY OR SYNDICATE EMERGED TO PLAN STRATEGY, SET PRICES, AND DEAL WITH OTHER TRUSTS.

PEACE AT LAST!

THIS WAS ALL VERY RATIONAL, AS ROCKEFELLER LIKED TO SAY... EXCEPT THAT THESE MONOPOLIES' POWER NOW RIVALED THE GOVERNMENT'S!

C'MON! WHAT GOVERNMENT HAS POWER LIKE OURS?

A RAILROAD COULD MAKE OR BREAK WHOLE CITIES AND REGIONS BY ITS CHOICE OF ROUTE. (THIS IS WHY SEATTLE, WASHINGTON, OUTGREW NEIGHBORING TACOMA — SEATTLE WAS FAVORED BY THE RAILROAD... AND MILAN, OHIO, BIRTHPLACE OF THE INVENTOR EDISON, A BOOM TOWN IN THE DAYS OF CANAL TRAFFIC, WAS BEGGARED WHEN BYPASSED BY RAIL ...) MONOPOLIES COULD CHARGE WHATEVER THE MARKET WOULD BEAR, WITHOUT WORRYING ABOUT THE COMPETITION.

COMPETITION IS OUTMODED!

ANY THREAT OF FOREIGN COMPETITION WAS PREVENTED BY HIGH TARIFFS ON IMPORTED GOODS.

AND THE LOW ETHICS OF RENTED SENATORS!

MEANWHILE, DOWN ON THE FARM, WHERE MOST AMERICANS STILL LIVED, THEY WERE FEELING MONOPOLY'S FULL EXTRACTIVE POWER.

THE HIGH COST OF MACHINERY AND SHIPPING, COMBINED WITH THE LOW PRICE OF GRAIN, DROVE THE FARMERS TO DESPERATION.

THIS WAS CLEARLY NO GOOD... HOW COULD BUSINESS SURVIVE IF NO ONE COULD AFFORD ANYTHING?

SO, IN 1887, UNDER THE PRODDING OF PRESIDENT **GROVER CLEVELAND** CONGRESS TOOK THE FIRST STEP TOWARD GOVERNMENT REGULATION OF MONOPOLY.

(FIRST DEMOCRATIC PRESIDENT SINCE THE CIVIL WAR)

244

THEY CREATED THE INTERSTATE COMMERCE COMMISSION TO CONTROL THE RAILROADS' ERRATIC RATE SCHEDULES. BIG BUSINESS RECOILED IN HORROR!

BUT A FAR SIGHTED RAILROAD LAWYER POINTED OUT, "THE COMMISSION... CAN BE MADE OF GREAT USE TO THE RAILROAD... IT SATISFIES THE POPULAR CLAMOR FOR GOVERNMENT SUPERVISION...AT THE SAME TIME THAT THAT SUPERVISION IS ALMOST·ENTIRELY NOMINAL. THE PART OF WISDOM IS NOT TO DESTROY THE COMMISSION BUT TO UTILIZE IT." THE WATCHDOG HAD NO TEETH!

COME, FIDO!

AS CONGRESS WENT ON TO PASS THE SIMILARLY TOOTHLESS **SHERMAN ANTI·TRUST ACT** IN 1890, FARMERS ROSE UP IN WHAT HAS BECOME KNOWN AS THE

POPULIST REVOLT.

RAISE LESS CORN AND MORE HELL!

—MARY LEASE

THEY FORMED THE ANTI-BANK, ANTI·BUSINESS *PEOPLE'S PARTY,* DEMANDING

☆ GOVERNMENT OWNER-SHIP OR REGULATION OF ALL MONOPOLIES

☆ EASY MONEY FOR DEBTORS

☆ AN INCOME TAX

IN THE 1892 PRESIDENTIAL ELECTION, THE POPULIST CANDIDATE CARRIED SIX STATES, AND WALL STREET FELT A NERVOUS TREMOR...

RUMBLE

THE '90'S ALSO MARKED THE END OF THE FRONTIER. THREE CENTURIES OF INDIAN WARFARE HAD FINALLY ENDED, AS DIE-HARDS LIKE THE APACHE *GERONIMO* SURRENDERED TO RESERVATION LIFE.

IN 1889, THE GOVERNMENT EVEN OPENED "INDIAN TERRITORY"—OKLAHOMA—TO WHITES. 50,000 WAITED AT THE BORDER... AT A SIGNAL, THEY MADE A MAD DASH TO SETTLE *SOONER* THAN THEIR NEIGHBORS, AND A GREAT MUSICAL WAS BORN!!

OOO OK LAHOMA!!

A BRIEF FLARE-UP OF INDIAN PRIDE, THE RELIGIOUS *GHOST DANCE* MOVEMENT, AROUSED THE WHITES' IRE. SITTING BULL HIMSELF WAS ASSASSINATED AS A SUSPECTED SYMPATHIZER, AND IN THE HYSTERIA, THE ARMY GUNNED DOWN 300 UNARMED MEN, WOMEN, AND CHILDREN AT SNOWY *WOUNDED KNEE*, S.D.

AND NOW THEY CALL THEM "GOOD" INDIANS...

246

SAY A FEW WORDS, LEROY!

INITIATIVE, REFERENDUM, AND REE-CALL OF JUDGES!

THE WEST WAS DIVIDED UP INTO TERRITORIES, WHICH WERE SETTLED BY PROUD, LEATHERY PEOPLE OF FEW WORDS AND POPULIST LEANINGS.

POSSIBLY THE WEST'S WILDEST INNOVATION WAS IN GIVING THE VOTE TO WOMEN (BEGINNING IN WYOMING IN 1870).

US PIONEER GALS AIN'T NO WEAKER SEX!

SO THIS WAS CAPITAL'S
DILEMMA IN THE 1890's:

THE ILL-PAID WORKER
CAN'T AFFORD OUR
PRODUCTS...

THE DEBT-RIDDEN
FARMER CAN'T AFFORD
OUR PRODUCTS...

THE EVER-EXPANDING
WEST HAS STOPPED
EXPANDING...

OR **HAS** IT?

FOR MANY YEARS,
AS EVERYONE KNEW,
THE EUROPEAN ANSWER
TO THESE PROBLEMS WAS

COLONIALISM.

OVERSEAS COLONIES
PROVIDED A POOL OF
LOW-PAID LABOR,
A SOURCE OF CHEAP
RAW MATERIALS, AND
A MARKET FOR
SURPLUS MANUFACTURED
GOODS!

WORKS LIKE
MAGIC!

SO—PERHAPS AMERICA
COULD KEEP EXPANDING—
INTO THE **PACIFIC!!**

WESTWARD
HO!

248

THE LIKELIEST THING IN THE PACIFIC WAS THE **PHILIPPINE ISLANDS,** A COLONY OF SPAIN.

SPAIN ALSO CONTROLLED CUBA AND PUERTO RICO, RIGHT IN THE U.S.A.'s BACK YARD...

SO...IN 1898, THE U.S. LAUNCHED THE **SPANISH-AMERICAN WAR.**

(OF COURSE, MANY AMERICANS, REMEMBERING HOW THEIR OWN NATION WAS BORN, WANTED NO COLONIES... SO THE COLONIALISTS DISGUISED THEIR AIMS UNDER A BANNER OF "LIBERATING THE FILIPINOS [CUBANS, PUERTO RICANS] FROM THE SPANISH YOKE.")

THANKS TO AMERICA'S MODERN NAVY, SPAIN WAS SUNK WITHIN FOUR MONTHS.

BUT SOME OF THE FILIPINOS MADE A FATAL MISTAKE: THEY TOOK THE RHETORIC SERIOUSLY. WHEN THE U.S. FAILED TO LEAVE THE ISLANDS, THEY ROSE UP IN AN INSURRECTION THAT ENDED ONLY AFTER THREE YEARS AND 600,000 FILIPINO DEAD.

AND SUDDENLY WE ENTER THE

20 TH

(CENTURY, THAT IS!!).

AN ANARCHIST'S BULLET FELLS PRESIDENT McKINLEY... THE VICE PRESIDENT, WAR HERO AND SPORTSMAN **THEODORE ROOSEVELT,** STEPS IN WITH A NEW AND MODERN APPROACH: *PROGRESSIVE REPUBLICANISM.*

ON THE ONE HAND, AN AGGRESSIVE FOREIGN POLICY: KEEP THE NEW COLONIES... TEAR OFF A PIECE OF COLOMBIA FOR A U.S.-CONTROLLED PANAMA CANAL... PUSH U.S. INTERESTS IN CHINA... SEND THE MARINES INTO CUBA AND THE DOMINICAN REPUBLIC...

ON THE OTHER HAND, LIBERAL REFORMS AT HOME: MORE REGULATION OF BUSINESS... ENFORCEMENT OF THE ANTI-TRUST LAWS... CONSERVATION OF NATURAL RESOURCES AND WILDERNESS AREAS.*

* MOST EARLY CONSERVATIONISTS WERE SPORTSMEN WHO WANTED TO PRESERVE WILDLIFE IN ORDER TO HAVE AN OPPORTUNITY TO SHOOT IT.

BUT MANY LIBERALS DIDN'T FEEL COMFORTABLE AMONG THE REPUBLICANS.

AND VICE VERSA!

THE MORE ARDENT AMONG THEM GRAVITATED TOWARD TWO NEW POLITICAL PARTIES, THE

SOCIALISTS

AND THE

PROGRESSIVES.

(THE POPULISTS HAD MEANWHILE DISAPPEARED INTO THE DEMOCRATS.)

(THIS WAS ALSO THE ERA OF MUCKRAKING JOURNALISM.)

EVEN AFTER ROOSEVELT LEFT OFFICE IN 1908, PROGRESSIVE PRESSURE PRODUCED SUCH REFORMS AS...

⭐ THE INCOME TAX (1913)

⭐ DIRECT POPULAR ELECTION OF SENATORS (1913)

⭐ FURTHER TRUST-BUSTING, INCLUDING THE BREAKUP OF STANDARD OIL

IN **1912**, T.R. JUMPED TO THE PROGRESSIVES, RAN FOR PRESIDENT, SPLIT THE REPUBLICAN VOTE... AND A DEMOCRAT WAS ELECTED — ONLY THE SECOND SINCE BEFORE THE CIVIL WAR —

⇒ WOODROW WILSON.

(A COLLEGE PROFESSOR!)

IN THAT SAME ELECTION, THE SOCIALIST CANDIDATE

EUGENE DEBS

POLLED ALMOST A MILLION VOTES.

DESPITE PROGRESSIVE REFORMS, WORKERS' LIVES REMAINED HARD, WITH CHILD LABOR, SWEATSHOPS, PITIFUL WAGES, MASSACRES OF STRIKERS, AND GRISLY ACCIDENTS LIKE THE TRIANGLE SHIRTWAIST FACTORY FIRE, WHICH KILLED 146 WOMEN.

WE NEED NOT REFORM BUT REVOLUTION!

ANARCHIST EMMA GOLDMAN

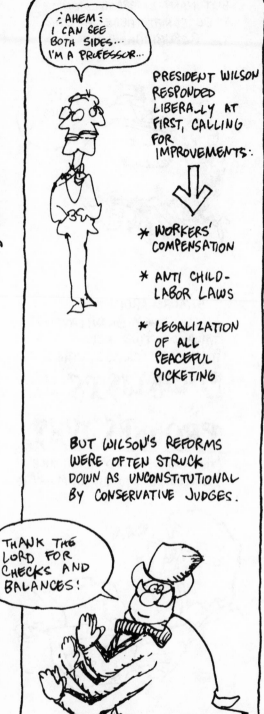

:AHEM: I CAN SEE BOTH SIDES... I'M A PROFESSOR...

PRESIDENT WILSON RESPONDED LIBERALLY AT FIRST, CALLING FOR IMPROVEMENTS:

* WORKERS' COMPENSATION

* ANTI CHILD-LABOR LAWS

* LEGALIZATION OF ALL PEACEFUL PICKETING

BUT WILSON'S REFORMS WERE OFTEN STRUCK DOWN AS UNCONSTITUTIONAL BY CONSERVATIVE JUDGES.

THANK THE LORD FOR CHECKS AND BALANCES!

BUT THESE
SOCIALISTS
WERE OPTIMISTS!

IT'S O.K.!
CAPITALISM
IS DOOMED!

SOON!

IN TIME
FOR THE
ELECTION!

ANY
DAY
NOW!

THE NATIONS OF EUROPE WERE
AT EACH OTHERS' THROATS...
THEIR CONTEST FOR COLONIES
HAD COME TO A HEAD...
TENSION MOUNTED.., ARMIES
STOOD ON ALERT...

IN THE SUMMER OF '14, A
SERB SHOT AN AUSTRIAN DUKE...
IT FOLLOWED LOGICALLY THAT—

Austria HAD TO
MENACE SERBIA ...

Russia HAD TO
GROWL AT AUSTRIA ...

Germany HAD
TO ATTACK
RUSSIA'S ALLY FRANCE...

England HAD
TO AID FRANCE ...

AND, IN THIS
RATIONAL FASHION,
A

WORLD WAR

BEGAN.

AS THE CARNAGE BEGAN, AMERICA WATCHED FROM THE SIDELINES. NOBODY WANTED TO GET INVOLVED!

YE GODS! WHO WOULD?!!

IT'S A BATTLE OF BRITISH CAPITAL AGAINST GERMAN CAPITAL, FOUGHT BY THE WORKERS!

THE SOCIALISTS WERE ESPECIALLY OUTSPOKEN AGAINST THE WAR.

THE DANGER, THEY SAW, WAS THAT AMERICAN BUSINESS WAS MUCH MORE CLOSELY TIED TO BRITAIN THAN TO GERMANY. ALREADY, U.S. MUNITIONS MAKERS WERE SHIPPING $ BILLIONS IN ARMS TO BRITAIN AND FRANCE — WITH U.S. BANKS DOING THE FINANCING...

...AND GERMAN SUBMARINES BEGAN SHOOTING TORPEDOES AT AMERICAN SHIPS.

PRESIDENT WILSON PREACHED NEUTRALITY WHILE PRACTICING PREPAREDNESS... IN THE **1916** PRESIDENTIAL CAMPAIGN, HIS SLOGAN WAS "HE KEPT US OUT OF WAR"!

BUT NO PROMISES!

BUT AMERICAN WEAPONS SHIPMENTS CONTINUED, AND SO DID THE SINKING OF AMERICAN SHIPS.

IN APRIL, 1917, ONE MONTH AFTER HIS SECOND INAUGURATION, WILSON CALLED FOR WAR AGAINST GERMANY... AND OFF MARCHED THE BOYS!

DON'T BUY THE BOSSES' WAR HYSTERIA! THINK FOR YOURSELF!

THAT WOULD BE ILLEGAL IN WARTIME.

NO TO WAR

... AND INTO THE JAILS WENT THE SOCIALISTS, FOR "OBSTRUCTING THE WAR EFFORT."

WHY SHOULD THE POOR FIGHT A WAR FOR THE RICH?

BECAUSE THERE AREN'T ENOUGH RICH TO DO IT...

BUT TURMOIL CONTINUED, AS UNIONS LIKE THE **I**NDUSTRIAL **W**ORKERS OF THE **W**ORLD KEPT UP THEIR STRIKES AND ANTI-WAR PROPAGANDA.

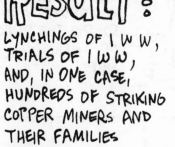

RESULT:

LYNCHINGS OF I W W, TRIALS OF I W W, AND, IN ONE CASE, HUNDREDS OF STRIKING COPPER MINERS AND THEIR FAMILIES LOCKED IN BOXCARS UNDER THE BROILING ARIZONA SUN.

WE HAVE ONE TOUGH CHAMBER OF COMMERCE!

AND THEN — A COMPLETE SURPRISE: THE COMMUNISTS CAME TO POWER IN **RUSSIA!!**

IT'S ONLY THREE MILES FROM ALASKA!

PRACTICALLY IN OUR BACK YARD!

CANADA'S NEXT!

O DEAR O DEAR

·CHAPTER 15·

WAR AND PEACE AND WARREN HARDING

NEVER! NEVER WILL WE MAKE ALLIANCES WITH THE BRITISH AND AMERICAN CAPITALISTS, UNTIL 1940!

NEVER WILL WE ENGAGE IN IMPERIALISTIC WARFARE, EXCEPT IN COUNTRIES BEGINNING WITH THE LETTERS "H", "P", "L", "E", AND "AFGH!"

LENIN

NEVER! DO YOU HEAR ME? ALMOST NEVER!

THE RUSSIAN COMMUNISTS, OR **BOLSHEVIKS** (WHOSE FONDNESS FOR THE COLOR RED MIGHT JUSTIFY THE NAME BORSCH-EVIK), IMMEDIATELY PULLED OUT OF THE WAR, MAKING A SEPARATE PEACE WITH GERMANY.

WE HAD TO! OUR ARMY HAD STOPPED FIGHTING!

THIS MADE RUSSIA'S FORMER ALLIES HATE THEM EVEN MORE THAN THEY ALREADY HATED THEM FOR BEING COMMUNISTS.

WE'LL SETTLE THEIR HASH LATER!

THE ALLIES ACTUALLY INVADED RUSSIA... A DRIVE THAT OUTLASTED THE WORLD WAR, BUT FAILED (HAVE YOU NOTICED?) TO DISLODGE THE REDS.

MAKING PEACE WITH RUSSIA FREED GERMAN ARMIES TO TURN WESTWARD AGAINST FRANCE.

WUNDERBAR! NOW WE CAN LIE IN SOME *WARM* MUD!

THERE, IN MID-1918, THE AMERICANS HELPED HOLD THE LINE, THEN PUSH THE GERMANS BACK.

TAKE US TO YOUR LARDER!

BACK THROUGH THE RUINS THEY BATTLED... A FLU EPIDEMIC ADDED 800,000 DEATHS... AUSTRIA WITHDREW... AND FINALLY, THE GERMAN KAISER AGREED TO AN ARMISTICE ON NOV. 11, 1918.

258

WHEN THE FIGHTING ENDED, EVERYONE WAS EXHAUSTED, BUT GERMANY WAS MORE EXHAUSTED THAN ANYONE ELSE.

SO WE WERE DECLARED THE LOSERS!

PRESIDENT WILSON SAILED TO EUROPE WITH A PLAN CALLED THE **14 POINTS.** THESE POINTED TOWARD A PEACE BASED ON JUSTICE, FAIRNESS, AND SELF-DETERMINATION.

AT A SUMMIT MEETING IN VERSAILLES, FRANCE, THE PRIME MINISTERS OF BRITAIN AND FRANCE ENDORSED WOODROW WILSON'S CONCEPTS OF FAIRNESS, JUSTICE, AND SELF-DETERMINATION.

THEN THEY CONCOCTED A PEACE TREATY BASED ON RECRIMINATION, RETRIBUTION, AND REVENGE.* THIS WAS THE TREATY OF VERSAILLES.

* THE FRENCH LEADER, 79-YEAR-OLD GEORGES CLEMENCEAU, LEARNED THESE 3 R's IN HIS YOUTH WHILE SERVING IN THE U.S. JUST AFTER THE CIVIL WAR.

THE TREATY OF VERSAILLES...

...DICED & SLICED GERMANY AND AUSTRIA INTO A *JULIENNE* OF NEW NATIONS.

BEFORE

AFTER

...STRIPPED GERMANY OF HER OVERSEAS COLONIES AND HANDED THEM OVER TO BRITAIN AND FRANCE...

AND DID WE GIVE UP ANY OF OUR OWN? DON'T BE SILLY!

ANYTHING LEFT?

...SQUEEZED BILLIONS IN REPARATION PAYMENTS FROM AN ALREADY IMPOVERISHED GERMANY...

...AND CREATED THE FRAMEWORK FOR A LEAGUE OF NATIONS, AN INTERNATIONAL ORGANIZATION DESIGNED TO ENFORCE THE PEACE TREATY AND PREVENT FUTURE WAR.

O.K., WILSON, GO HOME AND SELL IT!

GLEEP!

WILSON RETURNED TO A NATION IN TYPICAL POST-WAR ECONOMIC TURMOIL: 100% INFLATION... STEELWORKERS, BRASS WORKERS, MINERS, THE ENTIRE CITY OF SEATTLE, EVEN MOVIE ACTORS ON STRIKE... STRIKERS SHOT... BOMBS EXPLODING... A SHIPLOAD OF RUSSIAN WEAPONS INTERCEPTED...

A FEW LEFTISTS ORGANIZED NOT ONE BUT TWO COMMUNIST PARTIES (INEVITABLY!).

THE REVOLUTION IS AT HAND!

YES, THE LEFT HAND!

THE RIGHT HAND!

LEFT!

RIGHT...

WE LEAVE NO SHEET UNTURNED!

ATTORNEY GENERAL **MITCHELL PALMER** (WHOSE OWN HOUSE WAS BOMBED) FORMED A SPECIAL INVESTIGATIVE UNIT UNDER 24-YEAR-OLD **J. EDGAR HOOVER.** HOOVER HAD REMARKABLE VISION — HE COULD SEE COMMUNISTS UNDER EVERY BED!!

IN JANUARY, 1920, BEGAN THE PALMER RAIDS. ARMED WITH HOOVER'S INTELLIGENCE, FEDERAL AGENTS ROUNDED UP THOUSANDS OF SUSPECTED ALIEN LEFTISTS, BEAT THEM UP, ARRAIGNED THEM WITHOUT DEFENSE ATTORNEYS, AND GENERALLY VIOLATED THEIR CONSTITUTIONAL RIGHTS.

FLOUT OUR TRADITIONS, WILL THEY??

BUT HOOVER'S "FACTS" WERE FAULTY. MOST OF THE "CRIMINALS" HAD TO BE FREED. THE REST, SOME 600, WERE DEPORTED TO RUSSIA.

THEN, AFTER A ROUGH CAMPAIGN THAT LEFT WILSON CRIPPLED FROM A STROKE, THE SENATE REJECTED THE PEACE TREATY, ON THE GROUNDS THAT A LEAGUE OF NATIONS WAS UNAMERICAN.

ENTANGLING ALLIANCES HAVE BEEN UNAMERICAN SINCE GEORGE WASHINGTON!

YET EVEN IN THE TEETH OF
REACTION, THERE WERE
PROGRESSIVE BRACES.
IN 1919 AND '20's,
CONGRESS MADE TWO
FINAL ATTEMPTS TO
PROGRESSIVIZE AMERICA:

WE'LL GET IT STRAIGHT YET!!

THE 18TH AMENDMENT,
BANNING THE SALE OF ALCOHOLIC DRINK...

SNIF

AND THE 19TH,

WHICH GRANTED THE VOTE TO WOMEN.

AT LEAST WE WON'T LET 'EM INTO THE SALOONS — THERE WON'T BE ANY SALOONS!

SOB
SOB
SOB
SOB
SOB

IN A CURIOUS WAY, THESE REFORMS WERE LINKED.

HOW?

BOTH WENT BACK TO THE EARLY 1800'S, WHEN PATRIARCHAL LAWS PLACED A WIFE'S PROPERTY ENTIRELY IN HER HUSBAND'S HANDS...

AT LEAST HE HAS HANDS!

AN ALCOHOLIC MAN COULD DRINK AWAY HIS WIFE'S WAGES, BELONGINGS, INHERITANCE, BECAUSE HE OWNED THEM!

AH! WHAT A SENSE OF SECURITY!

SO SALOON-BUSTERS AND FEMINISTS FORMED A TWO-PRONGED ATTACK ON THE PROBLEM: IMPROVE WOMEN'S LEGAL STATUS, AND REDUCE ALCOHOLISM!

IF I HAVE MY PROPERTY, I CAN LEAVE THE LUSH!

LATER, PROGRESSIVES JOINED THE TEMPERANCE FORCES TO PROMOTE CIVIC EFFICIENCY, IMPROVE PUBLIC MORALS, AND PROTECT THE NATION'S STRATEGIC GRAIN SUPPLY, SO THE DOUGHBOYS WOULD HAVE BREAD IN THE WAR.

A SOBER ARMY KILLS **MUCH** MORE EFFICIENTLY!

SMESH!

THE RESULT WAS THE 18TH AMENDMENT.

MEANWHILE, WOMEN'S RIGHTS GROUPS NEVER QUIT PETITIONING, LOBBYING, MARCHING, AND DEMONSTRATING — FOR EXAMPLE, AT THE **STATUE OF LIBERTY** DEDICATION IN 1886.

CAN YOU VOTE, BABE?

THE STRUGGLE HEATED UP IN THE 19-TEENS. AT WILSON'S 1913 INAUGURAL, A SUFFRAGE MARCH TURNED INTO A RIOT!

MOST UNSEEMLY!

IN MOST WESTERN STATES, WOMEN WERE ALREADY VOTING WITHOUT DISASTER... SO IN LATE 1920, CONGRESS FINALLY GAVE IN.

AND SO CAME NOVEMBER, **1920**, AND THE FIRST ELECTION IN WHICH WOMEN VOTED NATIONWIDE.

IT'S THE END! LOOK AT THAT HEMLINE!

ANTI-FEMINISTS HAD ALWAYS SCREAMED THAT WOMEN WITH RIGHTS WOULD "TURN INTO MEN"... AND IT TURNED OUT THEY WERE RIGHT, IN ONE RESPECT, ANYWAY: WOMEN **VOTED** EXACTLY LIKE MEN!

HAD TO! THERE WERE NO WOMEN CANDIDATES!

DEBS, THE SOCIALIST, DREW 900,000 VOTES. COX, THE DEMOCRAT, MANAGED 10 TIMES THAT MANY...

IS THAT GOOD?

...WHILE THE REPUBLICAN, **WARREN HARDING**, WITH THE SLOGAN "BACK TO NORMALCY," PILED UP **16 MILLION**, AN 8-TO-5 LANDSLIDE!! AND WHAT WAS NORMALCY???

FORGETTABLE REPUBLICAN PRESIDENTS, CORRUPTION, LIGHT TAXES ON THE RICH, A BOOM, AND A CRASH!

TO SYMBOLIZE NORMALCY, THE NEW ADMINISTRATION MADE A BONFIRE OF HUNDREDS OF USED WARPLANES.

IF THIS IS NORMAL, I'M WARREN G. HARDING!

IT'S THE NORMALCY OF 1870!

THEN HARDING'S MEN CRUSHED A STEEL STRIKE, BUSTED SOME UNIONS, EASED ANTI-TRUST ENFORCEMENT, TOOK A FEW BRIBES, AND SLIPPED THE NAVY'S STRATEGIC OIL RESERVES INTO PRIVATE HANDS. THEIR PHILOSOPHY WAS EXPRESSED IN FIVE WORDS OF TREASURY SECRETARY ANDREW MELLON (A MILLIONAIRE): "LIGHT TAXES ON THE RICH."

BUT THIS WAS NORMALCY WITH A DIFFERENCE:

ALTHOUGH REPUBLICANS HAD ALWAYS WELCOMED IMMIGRANTS AS FACTORY-FODDER, NOW THEY DECIDED THAT FOREIGNERS CAUSED INDUSTRIAL INDIGESTION. THE ADMINISTRATION CUT IMMIGRATION FROM 600,000 TO 60,000 A YEAR.

* * * * * * * * * *

QUOTAS FAVORED NORTHERN EUROPEANS. THE ANNUAL LIMIT FOR JAPAN DROPPED FROM 185 TO ZERO.

WE'LL GIVE YOU A "ZERO!"

RACISM SURGED AS NEVER BEFORE... IT WAS WORLDWIDE.. WHILE HITLER SURFACED IN GERMANY, THE Ku Klux Klan HAD AMAZING SUCCESS IN THE U.S.A. THE KKK WAS NO LONGER ONLY ANTI-BLACK—

WE'RE ANTI-RED!

ANTI-JEW!

ANTI-CATHOLIC!

ANTI-IMMIGRANT!

WE DON'T THINK MUCH OF EACH OTHER!

AT ITS PEAK, THE KLAN CLAIMED SOME 5 MILLION MEMBERS!

269

THE FLIP SIDE OF RACISM IS ETHNIC NATIONALISM... AND, LIKE THE SERBS, BULGARS, ZIONISTS, AND OTHERS CRAVING NATIONHOOD, BLACK AMERICANS NOW RESPONDED *EN MASSE* TO A BACK-TO-AFRICA MOVEMENT LED BY **MARCUS** "MESSIAH" **GARVEY.**

GARVEY'S BLEND OF MUSSOLINI-STYLE UNIFORMS AND DISCIPLINE WITH BLACK PRIDE, BLACK ENTERPRISE, AND RACIAL PURITY WON MANY FOLLOWERS, ESPECIALLY AMONG THE POOR...

TO OUR KOMMON GOAL:

NO MORE KREAM IN THE KOFFEE!

WE WERE THE ORIGINAL FASCISTS,

HE SAID LATER...

...AS WELL AS THE FRIENDSHIP OF THE KU KLUX KLAN, WITH WHOM GARVEY HELD SEVERAL KOZY KOFFEE KLATCHES!!

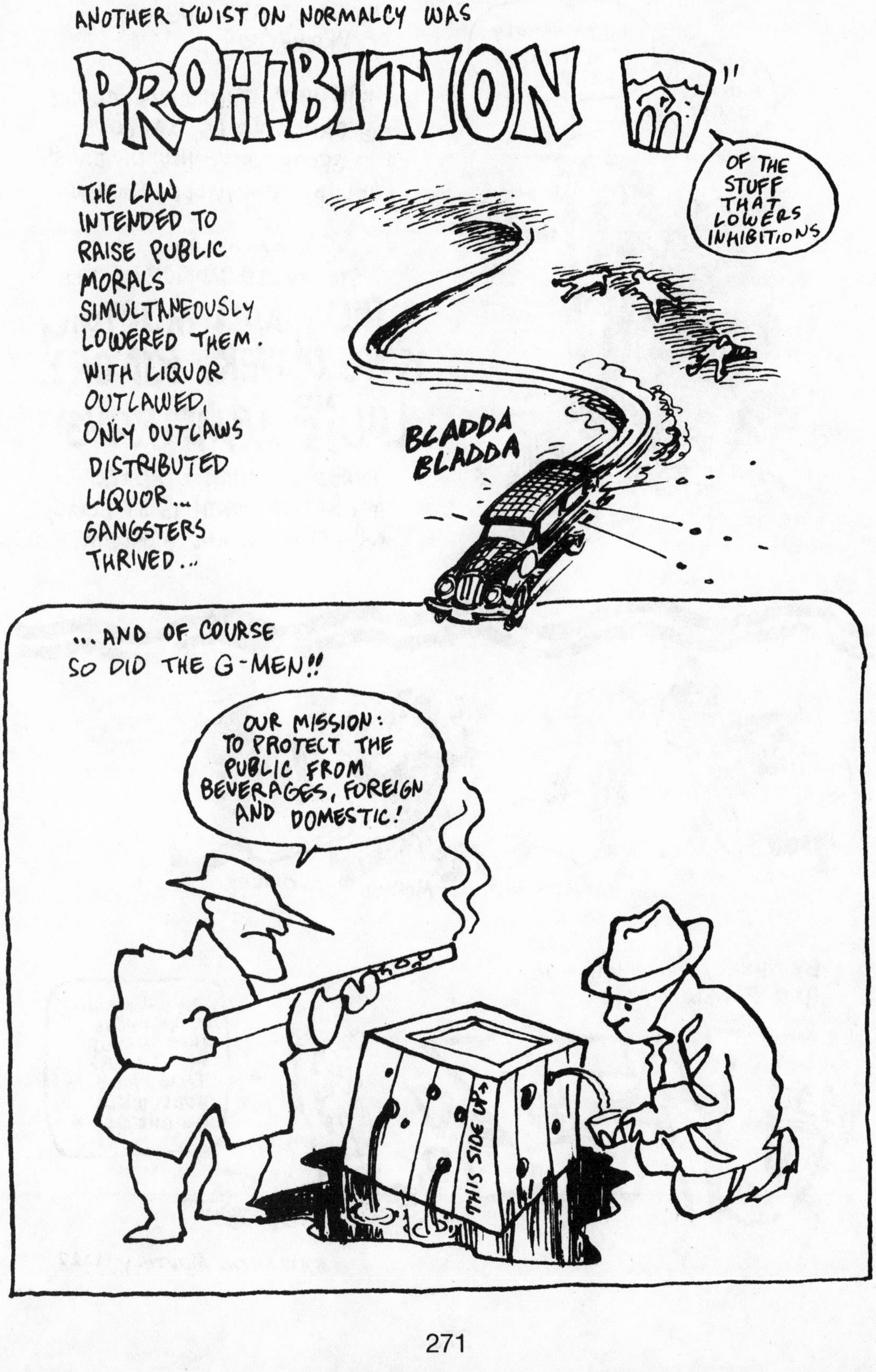
ANOTHER TWIST ON NORMALCY WAS
PROHIBITION
OF THE STUFF THAT LOWERS INHIBITIONS
THE LAW INTENDED TO RAISE PUBLIC MORALS SIMULTANEOUSLY LOWERED THEM. WITH LIQUOR OUTLAWED, ONLY OUTLAWS DISTRIBUTED LIQUOR... GANGSTERS THRIVED...
BLADDA BLADDA
...AND OF COURSE SO DID THE G-MEN!!
OUR MISSION: TO PROTECT THE PUBLIC FROM BEVERAGES, FOREIGN AND DOMESTIC!
THIS SIDE UP

A GHASTLY SIGHT!

I CAN BARELY STOP LOOKING AT IT...

COURT ORDER

ANOTHER SURPRISING EFFECT OF PROHIBITION:

IN 1917, THE "DRYS" CLOSED THE DANCE HALLS, SALOONS, AND BROTHELS OF NEW ORLEANS' FABLED STORYVILLE SECTION.

OUT-OF-WORK STORYVILLE MUSICIANS LIKE **JELLY ROLL MORTON, KING OLIVER, KID ORY,** AND **LOUIS ARMSTRONG** JOINED A GENERAL BLACK MIGRATION NORTH TO ST. LOUIS, K.C., CHICAGO, AND HARLEM.

ORY   ARMSTRONG   MORTON   OLIVER

BY THE 1920'S, THEIR MUSIC HAD A NEW NAME:

JAZZ!

"AN UNLOOSING OF INSTINCTS THAT NATURE WISELY HAS TAUGHT US TO HOLD WELL IN CHECK." *

*ATLANTIC MONTHLY, 1922

WHITE MUSICIANS JUMPED ON THE JAZZ-WAGON. WHITES FLOCKED TO BLACK CLUBS FOR ILLICIT THRILLS... SEX WAS IN... HEMLINES ROSE... HOLLYWOOD GLAMORIZED THE ACTION... THE FIRST TALKING FILM WAS "THE JAZZ SINGER" IN 1927... AND JAZZ BECAME THE FIRST AUTHENTIC ART FORM MADE IN AMERICA!

JUNK THAT JIVE! JAZZ IS **HOT!**

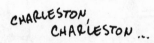

CHARLESTON, CHARLESTON...

SIGH

THEY CALLED IT THE JAZZ AGE, THE ROARING 20'S, THE WHOOPEE ERA, THE LAWLESS DECADE — BUT IN FACT, IT WAS REALLY PRETTY DRY... MORE AMERICANS THAN EVER WORKED HARD AND STAYED STONE-COLD SOBER !!

As people worked hard, business boomed...

The stock market sizzled like a Louis Armstrong solo...

...Until one horrible Wall Street week, culminating on "Black Tuesday", Oct. 29, '29.

Stock prices plunged, and so did a number of bankers and brokers!

CHAPTER 16

SHOCK THERAPY FOR A GREAT DEPRESSION

"HITLER, HAVING ENDED UNEMPLOYMENT IN GERMANY, HAD GONE ON TO END IT FOR HIS ENEMIES."
—JOHN KENNETH GALBRAITH

THE CAUSES OF THIS GREAT CRASH WERE OBSCURE, ESPECIALLY WHEN COMPARED TO ITS EFFECTS, WHICH WERE SPLATTERED ALL OVER THE SIDEWALK.

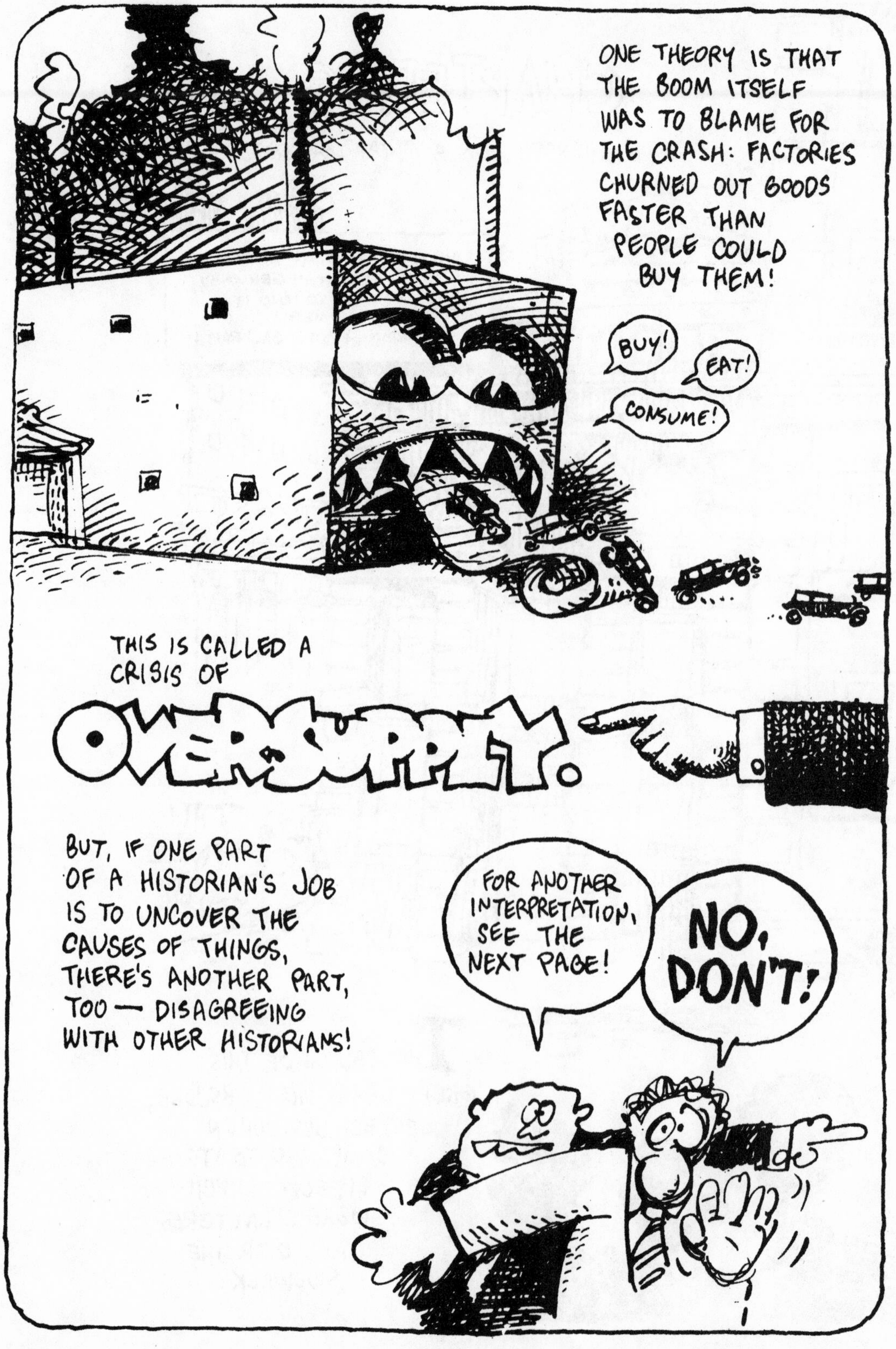
ONE THEORY IS THAT THE BOOM ITSELF WAS TO BLAME FOR THE CRASH: FACTORIES CHURNED OUT GOODS FASTER THAN PEOPLE COULD BUY THEM!
BUY!
EAT!
CONSUME!
THIS IS CALLED A CRISIS OF
OVERSUPPLY.
BUT, IF ONE PART OF A HISTORIAN'S JOB IS TO UNCOVER THE CAUSES OF THINGS, THERE'S ANOTHER PART, TOO — DISAGREEING WITH OTHER HISTORIANS!
FOR ANOTHER INTERPRETATION, SEE THE NEXT PAGE!
NO, DON'T!

CALLING IT

OVERSUPPLY, AFTER ALL, IGNORES THE HUMAN ELEMENT — JUST WHO WAS SUPPOSED TO BUY, BUY, BUY?

MILLIONS OF FARMERS

AND UNSKILLED WORKERS, UNTOUCHED BY THE BOOM, EKED OUT A LIVING ON THE EDGE OF BANKRUPTCY.

PLAYIN' BLUES, NOT JAZZ!

ANTI-UNION POLICIES

ENSURED THAT WAGES COULDN'T GROW AS FAST AS PRICES OR PROFITS...

...SO **UNDER-DEMAND** MIGHT BE A BETTER NAME FOR THE PROBLEM.

AH, FOR A CONSUMER WHO ISN'T A FARMER OR WORKER!

CONSEQUENTLY,

INVESTORS FUNNELLED PROFITS INTO SPECULATION RATHER THAN EXPANDING PRODUCTION.

PYRAMID SCHEMES, MERGERS, ETC...

STOCK PRICES

SPIRALLED UPWARD. PROFITS SWELLED — ON PAPER —

UNTIL, ONE DAY, TOO

MANY INVESTORS CASHED IN. THE MARKET DIPPED... PEOPLE BEGAN SELLING IN SELF-DEFENSE... AND THEN IN PANIC. IN SHORT, THE MARKET CRASHED.

FREE MARKET

ECONOMIES TEND TO REPEAT THIS PATTERN, MANY HISTORIANS AGREE.

OH... SWELL...

And now we pass from causes to effects...

With paper profits gone, people were forced to use real money. It turned out to be pretty scarce...

Prices plummeted...

So did wages...

Businesses folded or shrank...

Half the nation's banks failed, drained by panicky depositors...

Millions lost their jobs, houses, farms...

Breadlines swelled... (privately run, of course — the government gave no handouts!!)

A triumph of voluntarism!

THE PRESIDENT, **HERBERT HOOVER,** BELIEVED THAT PUBLIC CONFIDENCE WAS THE KEY TO RECOVERY... SO HE KEPT SAYING, "PROSPERITY IS JUST AROUND THE CORNER."

BUT IT WASN'T... IN FACT, THINGS ONLY GOT WORSE...

THIS ONE MAKES MY OTHER DEPRESSIONS LOOK LIKE LITTLE MOOD SWINGS...

PROSPERITY IS —OW!

THE ELECTORATE DID THE ONLY CONCEIVABLE THING, AND OUT WENT HOOVER IN 1932.

IN HIS PLACE THEY ELECTED THE DEMOCRAT
FRANKLIN D. ROOSEVELT,

A GOLDEN-TONGUED COUSIN OF TEDDY'S, WHO USED THE NEW-FANGLED MEDIUM OF THE RADIO NETWORK TO SPEAK DIRECTLY TO ALL.

WE HAVE NOTHING TO FEAR BUT FEAR ITSELF!
HE SAID.

THIS STATEMENT, LIKE MANY ANOTHER FAMOUS PHRASE, IS NOT ESPECIALLY EASY TO UNDERSTAND.

WOW!

WHAT?

WHAT IT MEANT WAS THAT ROOSEVELT WASN'T AFRAID TO TRY **ANYTHING!**

FOR INSTANCE...

NRA: BUSINESS SLUMPING? WAGES FALLING? LAYOFFS RISING? THE NATIONAL RECOVERY ACT SET WAGE, PRICE, AND EMPLOYMENT GUIDELINES (LATER DECLARED UNCONSTITUTIONAL).

AAA: FARM PRICES FALLING? THE AGRICULTURAL ADJUSTMENT ACT PAID FARMERS TO DESTROY PRODUCE!

NOW WAIT A MINUTE!

SSI: OLD PEOPLE DESTITUTE? SOCIAL SECURITY INSURANCE GIVES A PENSION TO EVERY RETIRED PERSON.

GERMANY HAS HAD IT SINCE THE 1870'S!

WPA: ARTISTS UNEMPLOYED? THE WORKS PROGRESS ADMINISTRATION HIRED THEM.

SUDDENLY I LOVE THE GOVERNMENT AND MUST EXPLAIN WHY IN A SERIES OF ENORMOUS MURALS...

PWA POURED MONEY INTO PUBLIC WORKS—DAMS, BRIDGES, HIGHWAYS.

FDIC SAVED BANKS BY INSURING DEPOSITS.

TVA CREATED A FEDERALLY OWNED UTILITY WHICH ELECTRIFIED THE TENNESSEE VALLEY.

AND PROHIBITION IS REPEALED!

THIS IMPROVISED STRUCTURE OF WELFARE, JOB PROGRAMS, AND ECONOMIC PLANNING WAS CALLED THE

NEW DEAL

OUR MOTTO: WHATEVER WORKS!

THE NEW DEAL TRANSFORMED AMERICA WITH A NEW SENSE OF THE GOVERNMENT'S ROLE.

IT MADE ROOSEVELT THE MOST POPULAR PRESIDENT IN OUR HISTORY — AND ONE OF THE MOST HATED. CONSERVATIVES, UNABLE TO UTTER HIS NAME WITHOUT GAGGING, DENOUNCED "THAT MAN" AS A TRAITOR TO HIS CLASS!

TWO NAMES YOU DON'T SAY OUT LOUD: GOD'S AND THAT MAN'S!!

THIS WAS ODD, BECAUSE ROOSEVELT'S PROGRAM WAS INTENDED TO STRENGTHEN CAPITALISM — TO SAVE IT FROM ITSELF, YOU MIGHT SAY. ROOSEVELT CONFISCATED NOTHING, NATIONALIZED NO INDUSTRY,* AND NOBODY SAW BUSINESSMEN GOING BROKE AS A RESULT OF THE NEW DEAL!!

THAT'S HOW SNEAKY HE IS!

* ALTHOUGH, WHEN THE MEXICAN GOVERNMENT NATIONALIZED AMERICAN OIL COMPANIES, ROOSEVELT REFUSED TO DEFEND THE COMPANIES' INFLATED CLAIMS.

SO... WHAT WAS TO HATE?? WELL... **WELFARE** AND GOVERNMENT ASSISTANCE, WHICH SUPPOSEDLY SAP PEOPLE'S INITIATIVE AND SELF-RELIANCE.

IT'S THE FREEDOM TO STARVE THAT MADE AMERICA GREAT!

DEFICIT SPENDING, I.E., FINANCING GOVERNMENT PROGRAMS THROUGH BORROWING RATHER THAN TAXES. IT STIMULATED THE ECONOMY, BUT SOUNDED UNSOUND, BUSINESSWISE!

IT'S VOODOO!

(LATER, CONSERVATIVES DID IT, TOO...)

ROOSEVELT RECOGNIZED THE **SOVIET UNION,** AND CEASED PERSECUTING COMMUNISTS AT HOME — AND PARTY MEMBERSHIP AND INFLUENCE SWELLED.

AND FINALLY, THERE WAS HIS LENIENT ATTITUDE TOWARD **ORGANIZED LABOR.**

GAH! THE WORST!!

LABOR IN THE '30's

AS THE NEW DEAL BEGAN, THE ONLY LABOR ORGANIZATION TO SPEAK OF WAS

THE **AFL.** (SEE P. 53.)

AFL UNIONS WERE **CRAFT** UNIONS— MEANING THAT EACH UNION REPRESENTED ONE SKILL:

MACHINISTS
ELECTRICIANS
WELDERS
PLUMBERS
CARPENTERS
PAINTERS

BUT

THE AFL IGNORED THE LOWEST-PAID, UNSKILLED, AND SEMI-SKILLED WORKERS.

IT RESISTED RACIAL INTEGRATION, VIEWING BLACKS AS LOW-WAGE COMPETITION.

AND KEEPING US THAT WAY!

DITTO FOR WOMEN, HISPANICS, CHINESE...

THE CHINESE MUST GO! *

* CONSTANT REFRAIN OF 1880's SAN FRANCISCO LABOR LEADER DENNIS KEARNY.

IT'S A GAIN FOR SOME ON THE BACKS OF OTHERS!

EVER SINCE DEBS, THE LEFT WING OF THE LABOR MOVEMENT HAD BLASTED THE AFL'S POLICY OF DIVIDING THE WORKING CLASS.

THE LEFTISTS FAVORED UNIONS ORGANIZED ON

INDUSTRIAL

LINES: EACH UNION REPRESENTING AN ENTIRE INDUSTRY:

MINEWORKERS
LONGSHOREMEN
STEELWORKERS
AUTO WORKERS
ETC.

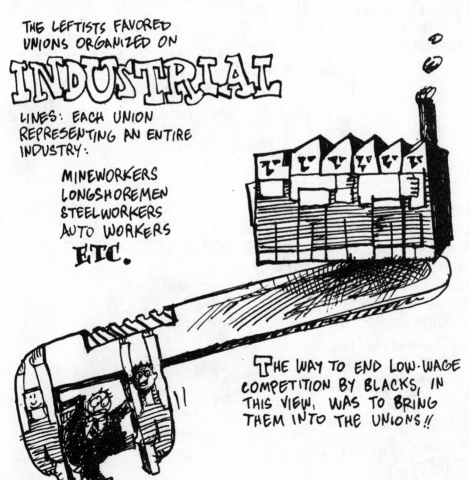

THE WAY TO END LOW-WAGE COMPETITION BY BLACKS, IN THIS VIEW, WAS TO BRING THEM INTO THE UNIONS!!

AS THE DEPRESSION DRAGGED ON, INDUSTRIAL WORKERS BEGAN DEMANDING UNION PROTECTION.. TACTICS TURNED MILITANT, WITH MASS PICKETING, 1000 AT A TIME, AND "FLYING PICKETS" ATTACKING STRIKEBREAKERS.

IN **1934** CAME THE FIRST BIG SUCCESSES: A VICTORIOUS TEAMSTER STRIKE IN MINNEAPOLIS...

A WEST COAST LONGSHORE STRIKE, WHICH BECAME A GENERAL STRIKE IN SAN FRANCISCO.

BUT THE AFL WAS PARALYZED BY JURISDICTIONAL DISPUTES. ITS CRAFT UNIONS WANTED TO DIVIDE UP THE FACTORY WORKERS— A GUARANTEED WAY TO UNIONIZE **SOME** OF THEM... BUT THE WORKERS WOULD HAVE NONE OF IT, SO IN 1935 EIGHT OF THE "PROGRESSIVE" UNIONS FORMED THE

COMMITTEE FOR **I**NDUSTRIAL **O**RGANIZATION,

HEADED BY MINEWORKERS PRESIDENT **JOHN L. LEWIS.**

PUNCHING "BIG BILL" HUTCHESON IN THE NOSE AT AFL CONVENTION

THE CIO, WHICH HAD MANY COMMUNIST ORGANIZERS, ENDORSED AN EVEN MORE MILITANT TACTIC: THE **SIT-DOWN,** OR PLANT SEIZURE.

SURPRISE!!

THE MOST FAMOUS SIT-DOWN STRIKE WAS AGAINST GENERAL MOTORS, IN DECEMBER-JANUARY, 1936.

WITH THE TEMPERATURE DOWN TO 16°, MANAGEMENT SHUT OFF THE HEAT AND STOPPED THE FOOD. WORKERS BLASTED THE POLICE WITH ICY WATER AND PELTED THEM WITH SMALL CAR PARTS — THE "BATTLE OF BULLS RUN." *

AT OTHER PLANTS, WORKERS FLOCKED TO THE UNION... THE STRIKE SPREAD... AND AT LAST GENERAL MOTORS WAS FORCED TO **SIT DOWN** WITH THE **U**NITED **A**UTO **W**ORKERS.

IT'S ALL **THAT MAN'S** FAULT!!

* "BULLS" = POLICE.

AND WHAT WAS "THAT MAN'S" ATTITUDE?

UM... ER... AH...

IN '35, ROOSEVELT HAD RELUCTANTLY SIGNED THE WAGNER ACT, CREATING THE **N**ATIONAL **L**ABOR **R**ELATIONS **B**OARD, AND LAYING THE GROUND RULES FOR UNION ORGANIZING.

GOOD ENOUGH?

THE PROBLEM WAS THAT THE BIG CORPORATIONS ROUTINELY FLOUTED THE NEW LAW.

THAT'S WHY WE HAD STRIKES!

WHAT INFURIATED THE CORPORATIONS WAS THAT ROOSEVELT WOULDN'T CALL IN THE ARMY TO CRUSH THE STRIKES. UNDER THIS STAND-OFFISH POLICY, THE C I O TRIPLED ITS MEMBERSHIP TO

3 MILLION

(INCLUDING 300,000 BLACKS!).

NOW WE ASK: HOW WELL DID THE NEW DEAL WORK??

AND WE ANSWER: GOVERNMENT SPENDING DID STIMULATE THE ECONOMY, CREATE JOBS, BUILD BRIDGES, DAMS, AND ART DECO POST OFFICES.

WELFARE PROGRAMS RELIEVED SOME ANXIETY... GOVERNMENT INSURANCE ENDED BANK PANICS... UNIONIZATION IMPROVED WAGES AND WORKING CONDITIONS FOR THE EMPLOYED.

RESULT: ROOSEVELT WON RE-ELECTION IN '36 BY A LANDSLIDE.

YEAH!

BUT — RECOVERY WAS SLOW... INDUSTRY REMAINED SLACK... AND, WHEN "PRUDENT" SPENDING TRIMS WERE MADE, THE ECONOMY TOOK A DIVE THAT SENT UNEMPLOYMENT ALMOST TO 1933 LEVELS!!

NOW WHAT?

THE ANSWER CAME FROM ABROAD, WHERE LINGERING HATREDS FROM WORLD WAR I WERE EXPLODING...
IN '31, JAPAN INVADED MANCHURIA... IN '35 ITALY INVADED ETHIOPIA... THE DEMOCRACIES STOOD BY AND DEPLORED THESE MOVES, WHICH WERE AFTER ALL, IN A TIME-HONORED TRADITION OF COLONIAL CONQUEST.

WE DEPLORE NOT DOING IT FIRST, THAT IS—

AND THEN THERE WAS GERMANY... IN '33, JUST BEFORE ROOSEVELT'S INAUGURAL, THE NAZI **ADOLF HITLER** CAME TO POWER... THIS NAZISM WAS A SORT OF GERMAN-POTENTIAL MOVEMENT...

HITLER WANTED GERMANS TO FEEL GOOD ABOUT THEMSELVES— BY THINKING ILL OF EVERYBODY ELSE, ESPECIALLY JEWS.

I'M O.K., YOU'RE DEAD!

IT ISN'T FAIR!

AT FIRST, HITLER'S ECONOMIC PROGRAM WAS AMAZINGLY LIKE ROOSEVELT'S: DEFICIT SPENDING AND PUBLIC WORKS... BUT HITLER HAD CERTAIN ADVANTAGES: A DEMONIC WORLD VIEW, ABSOLUTE POWER, NO PRUDENCE —SO HE CURED UNEMPLOYMENT MORE EFFECTIVELY THAN FDR!

BUT THAT WASN'T ENOUGH... HITLER'S DEMENTED IDEAS OF NORDIC SUPERIORITY CALLED FOR A BIGGER GERMANY, MORE GERMANS, AND FEWER "INFERIORS."

GOD! SOUNDS ALL TOO FAMILIAR!

SO, WHEN HE SWALLOWED AUSTRIA AND CZECHOSLOVAKIA, IT WAS OBVIOUS THAT WAR WAS COMING, AND THE DEMOCRACIES TREMBLED AT THE PROSPECT—

FULL EMPLOYMENT AT LAST?!!

291

1939: HITLER STUNS THE WORLD BY MAKING FRIENDS WITH HIS ARCH-ENEMY STALIN*...THEN INVADES POLAND.

BY MID-**1940** THE GERMANS HAVE OCCUPIED SCANDINAVIA, BELGIUM, HOLLAND, AND FRANCE, AND BUSILY BOMB BRITAIN...

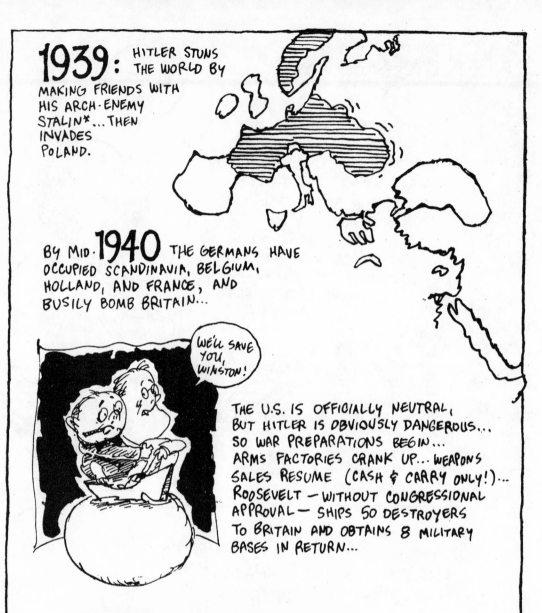

WE'LL SAVE YOU, WINSTON!

THE U.S. IS OFFICIALLY NEUTRAL, BUT HITLER IS OBVIOUSLY DANGEROUS... SO WAR PREPARATIONS BEGIN... ARMS FACTORIES CRANK UP...WEAPONS SALES RESUME (CASH & CARRY ONLY!)... ROOSEVELT — WITHOUT CONGRESSIONAL APPROVAL — SHIPS 50 DESTROYERS TO BRITAIN AND OBTAINS 8 MILITARY BASES IN RETURN...

...AND THERE'S A PRESIDENTIAL ELECTION... ROOSEVELT RUNS AGAIN AND WINS AGAIN, THE FIRST 3-TERM PRESIDENT...

* DICTATOR OF THE USSR

292

1941: JAPAN MOVES INTO FRENCH INDOCHINA (VIETNAM), THREATENING DUTCH, BRITISH, AND AMERICAN COLONIAL AND COMMERCIAL INTERESTS IN THE INDIES, BURMA, THE PHILIPPINES...

HITLER DOUBLE-CROSSES STALIN AND INVADES RUSSIA — A VAST BLUNDER, BUT IT CEMENTS AN ALLIANCE WITH JAPAN...

THE U.S. CUTS OFF OIL SHIPMENTS TO JAPAN... CONGRESS BEGINS LENDING WEAPONS TO HITLER'S FOES... JAPAN AND THE U.S. TRADE IMPOSSIBLE DEMANDS...

AND THEN...

ON DEC. 7, JAPAN BOMBED THE AMERICAN NAVY BASE AT PEARL HARBOR, HAWAII, WIPING OUT BATTLESHIPS, PLANES, AND MORE THAN 1500 LIVES.

CONGRESS NATURALLY DECLARED WAR ON JAPAN, AND WITHIN DAYS GERMANY AND ITALY HAD JOINED IN... MERRY CHRISTMAS!

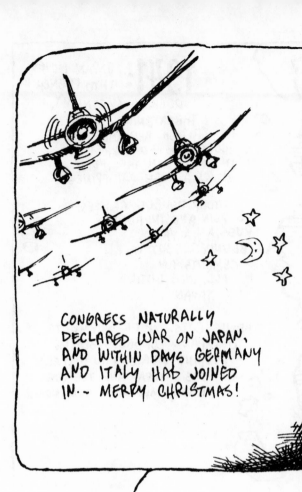

SUPERB SMELL!

WITH MOBILIZATION, THE ECONOMY BOOMED... FACTORIES RETOOLED FOR WAR... UNEMPLOYMENT VANISHED... INFLATION WAS CHECKED BY GOVERNMENT PRICE CONTROLS... UNIONS PLEDGED NOT TO STRIKE — AND NO ONE WORRIED ABOUT POLLUTION...

MASSIVE POPULATION SHIFTS TOOK PLACE... A STREAM
OF SOUTHERN BLACKS FLOWED NORTH, TOWARD
THE FACTORY JOBS OF DETROIT,
SAN FRANCISCO, CHICAGO...

TRADITIONAL DISCRIMINATION
GAVE WAY A LITTLE...
WOMEN DID HEAVY
FACTORY WORK...

MY MOM AT
THE SHIPYARDS

AND YET — OVER 100,000 JAPANESE-AMERICANS (80% OF THEM
CITIZENS) WERE ROUNDED UP AS "SECURITY RISKS" AND
INTERNED IN CAMPS FOR THE DURATION.

(AN IRONY OF THE WAR WAS
THAT AMERICAN PROPAGANDA
DEPICTED THE JAPANESE AS
INHUMAN — WHILE HITLER, WHO
REALLY WAS A MONSTER,
USUALLY APPEARED AS A
COMIC-OPERA BUFFOON.)

THAT HITLER
WAS PRETTY
SMART TO BE
BORN WHITE!

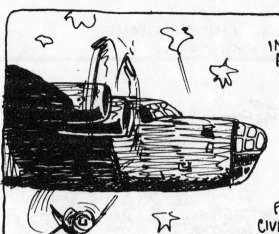

IN EUROPE, THE UNITED STATES AVOIDED A DIRECT GROUND ASSAULT AGAINST GERMANY, UNTIL THE GERMANS WERE WORN OUT BY RUSSIA... MEANWHILE, ALLIED BOMBERS BLASTED GERMAN INDUSTRY, WHICH OF COURSE WAS OFTEN LOCATED IN GERMAN CITIES. IN HAMBURG THE FIRESTORM KILLED 50,000 CIVILIANS; IN DRESDEN, 100,000 PLUS...

...WHILE ARMORED DIVISIONS INVADED NORTH AFRICA, FROM WHICH POINT THEY PUSHED INTO ITALY.

AT LAST, IN JUNE OF '44, UNDER GENERAL DWIGHT D. EISENHOWER, THE ALLIES INVADED FRANCE... AND EIGHT MONTHS LATER, MET THE RUSSIANS IN BERLIN.

ROOSEVELT, CHURCHILL, AND STALIN MET TO DIVIDE UP THE POST·WAR WORLD — RATHER TO BRITAIN'S DISADVANTAGE...

WE'LL TAKE MILITARY BASES HERE, HERE, HERE, HERE, HERE, HERE...

WE'LL TAKE THIS.

THE PACIFIC WAR COMBINED CARRIER-BASED NAVAL ENGAGEMENTS WITH JUNGLE WARFARE IN THE PHILIPPINES, OKINAWA, ETC... THE SEA BATTLES WERE THE FIRST IN HISTORY IN WHICH THE ENEMIES' FLEETS REMAINED COMPLETELY OUT OF EYESHOT!

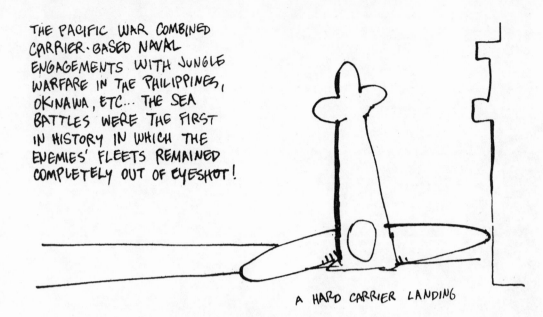

A HARD CARRIER LANDING

BY MID-1945, JAPAN WAS ENCIRCLED... FROM ISLAND BASES AMERICAN HEAVY BOMBERS LEVELLED TOKYO...

THE AMERICANS, PERHAPS TOO FULL OF THEIR SMASHING VICTORY OVER HITLER, DEMANDED NOTHING LESS THAN UNCONDITIONAL SURRENDER... THE JAPANESE SENSE OF HONOR WOULD NOT ALLOW SUCH HUMILIATION... FURTHER NEGOTIATION MIGHT HAVE PRODUCED A FACE-SAVING SOLUTION... BUT TIME WAS SHORT: THE U.S.S.R. WAS ABOUT TO DECLARE WAR ON JAPAN, AND PRESIDENT TRUMAN* DIDN'T WANT TO SHARE THE ISLANDS!!

NOT WITH THEM COM-YA-NISTS!

SO...

*ROOSEVELT HAD DIED, WITH MUCH PUBLIC MOURNING, IN APRIL, '45.

CHAPTER 17

☉ BRIGHT, WHITE LIGHT ☉

AND TECHNOLOGY BEGAT INDUSTRY...
AND INDUSTRY BEGAT CAPITALISM...
AND CAPITALISM BEGAT COMMUNISM...
AND COMMUNISM BEGAT ANTI-COMMUNISM...
AND ANTI-COMMUNISM BEGAT FASCISM...

AH, TECHNOLOGY!

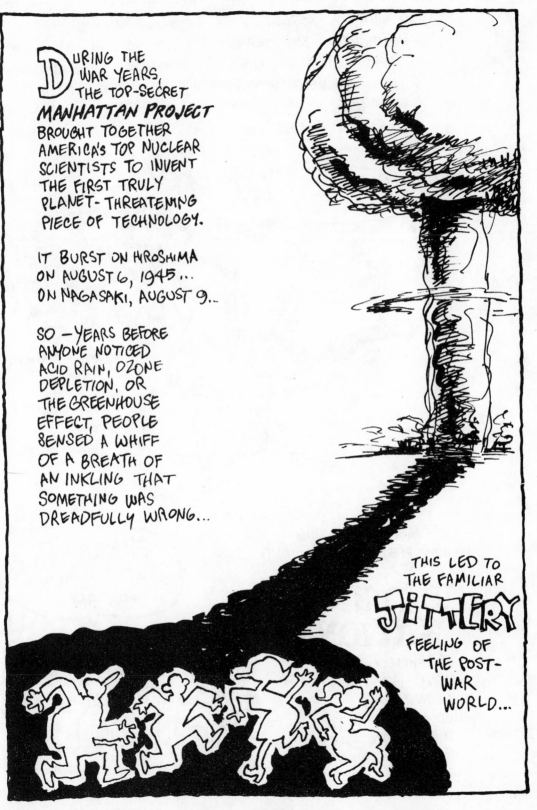

DURING THE WAR YEARS, THE TOP-SECRET **MANHATTAN PROJECT** BROUGHT TOGETHER AMERICA'S TOP NUCLEAR SCIENTISTS TO INVENT THE FIRST TRULY PLANET-THREATENING PIECE OF TECHNOLOGY.

IT BURST ON HIROSHIMA ON AUGUST 6, 1945... ON NAGASAKI, AUGUST 9...

SO — YEARS BEFORE ANYONE NOTICED ACID RAIN, OZONE DEPLETION, OR THE GREENHOUSE EFFECT, PEOPLE SENSED A WHIFF OF A BREATH OF AN INKLING THAT SOMETHING WAS DREADFULLY WRONG...

THIS LED TO THE FAMILIAR JITTERY FEELING OF THE POST-WAR WORLD...

AND WHAT A WORLD... A GLOBE SHRUNKEN BY COMMUNICATION AND TRANSPORTATION TECHNOLOGY... TWO COUNTRIES, THE U.S. & USSR, IMMENSELY SWOLLEN IN POWER... ALMOST IMMEDIATELY, THE TWO ERSTWHILE ALLIES BEGAN GROWLING LIKE A COUPLE OF MALE DOGS IN A SMALL CLOSET.

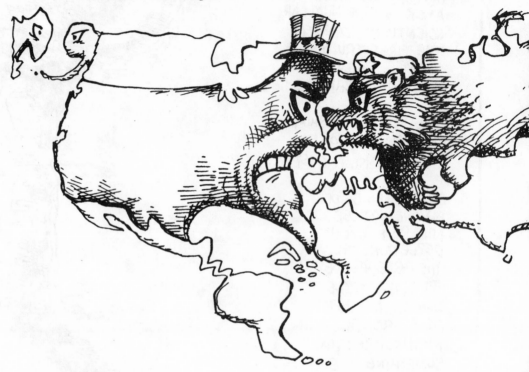

IT'S REALLY AMAZING HOW FAST THEIR ALLIANCE COLLAPSED. THE

UNITED NATIONS,

ORGANIZED IN A LOVE-FEAST MOOD IN MID-'45, DESCENDED INTO DIPLOMATIC EAR-BITING BY 1946.

THE U.S. DENOUNCED THE SOVIET OCCUPATION OF EASTERN EUROPE AND THE INSTALLATION OF COMMUNIST GOVERNMENTS THERE.

THE U S S R COMPLAINED ABOUT THE EXPANDING U.S. ROLE IN THE WORLD, TO THE EXCLUSION OF THE SOVIET UNION.

IN GREECE, A CIVIL WAR PITTED RUSSIAN-BACKED GUERRILLAS AGAINST A U.S.-BACKED FASCIST KING.

FRANCE AND ITALY BOTH HAD LARGE COMMUNIST PARTIES.

GERMANY WAS DIVIDED INTO BRITISH, FRENCH, RUSSIAN, AND AMERICAN ZONES. BERLIN, THOUGH IN THE RUSSIAN ZONE, WAS JOINTLY HELD.

WHEN NEGOTIATIONS ON GERMANY FAILED, RUSSIA BLOCKADED BERLIN. THE U.S. AIRLIFTED SUPPLIES UNTIL THE U S S R RELENTED.

WITH RELATIONS IN RUINS, PRESIDENT TRUMAN IN 1948 ANNOUNCED A NEW U.S. POLICY: THE GLOBAL

CONTAINMENT

OF COMMUNISM.

IF WE HAVE TO PEE ON EVERY TREE ON EARTH!

CONTAINMENT CALLED FOR VAST PROGRAMS, BOTH MILITARY AND ECONOMIC. THE MOST FAMOUS AND FARSIGHTED OF THESE WAS THE

MARSHALL PLAN.

I'M SUCH A SOFTY THEY SHOULD CALL IT THE MARSHMALLOW PLAN!

THIS WAS A MULTI-BILLION-DOLLAR PROGRAM OF LOANS TO REBUILD WESTERN EUROPE'S DEVASTED INDUSTRY. THE IDEA WAS THAT A PROSPEROUS EUROPE WOULD BE A PEACEFUL EUROPE, UNLIKE THE DREADFUL SITUATION AFTER WORLD WAR I.

THE MARSHALL PLAN WAS CALCULATED TO PAY CERTAIN DIVIDENDS: TO UNIFY WESTERN EUROPE AGAINST COMMUNISM; TO PENETRATE EUROPE'S ECONOMY WITH AMERICAN CAPITAL; AND TO CREATE A PROFITABLE CLIMATE FOR TRADE AND EXPANSION.

COME, LITTLE FISHIES!

THE POST-WAR PERIOD MARKED A
BASIC SHIFT IN U.S. FOREIGN POLICY:
EVER SINCE GEORGE WASHINGTON, THE
NATION HAD AVOIDED MILITARY ALLIANCES
WITH FOREIGN POWERS. NOW, THE
U.S. ORGANIZED AND LED THEM:

NATO IN WESTERN EUROPE,
ANZUS IN THE SOUTH PACIFIC,
SEATO IN SOUTHEAST ASIA.

THE U.S. WAS NOW THE WORLD'S
FOREMOST MILITARY POWER!!

WITH AN ARMY BASE NEAR YOU!

NOW, WAIT—WEREN'T YOU JUST FRIENDS WITH THE ROOSKIES?

THE WARTIME
ALLIANCE WITH
RUSSIA WAS
REINTERPRETED IN
THE NEW SCHEME
OF THINGS:
THERE MUST BE
**COMMUNIST
SYMPATHIZERS**
IN GOVERNMENT!
ROOSEVELT HAD
LOST POLAND!!
THE COMMUNIST PARTY
WAS A **FIFTH
COLUMN!!** NEVER
MIND RUSSIA—
WHAT ABOUT
COMMUNISM **WITHIN?**

305

IN 1946, A GAGGLE OF REPUBLICANS (INCLUDING RICHARD NIXON) RODE THE COMMUNISM ISSUE INTO CONGRESS.

...AND THE U.S., WITH ONE OF THE WORLD'S SMALLEST COMMUNIST PARTIES, BEGAN ONE OF THE WORLD'S BIGGEST RED HUNTS.

COMMUNISTS WERE BLAMED FOR THE STRIKE WAVE OF '46 AND '47 — THE BIGGEST IN AMERICAN HISTORY. EVEN WALT DISNEY PRODUCTIONS WENT ON STRIKE!!

NATIONAL SECURITY IS THREATENED!!

THE **H**OUSE **U**NAMERICAN **A**CTIVITIES **C**OMMITTEE DESCENDED ON HOLLYWOOD

NOW PLAYING "ARE YOU NOW OR HAVE YOU EVER BEEN?"

THE CIO DEMANDED THAT MEMBER UNIONS EJECT THEIR COMMUNISTS, EVEN FREELY ELECTED OFFICIALS. IF NOT, THE CIO EJECTED THE UNION.

AND OUT GOES DEMOCRACY!

THE RESULT WAS THE BLACKLIST, THE LOYALTY OATH, BURGLARIES & HARASSMENT BY THE FBI, AND FOR MANY, JAIL TERMS FOR "CONSPIRING TO TEACH" MARXISM!

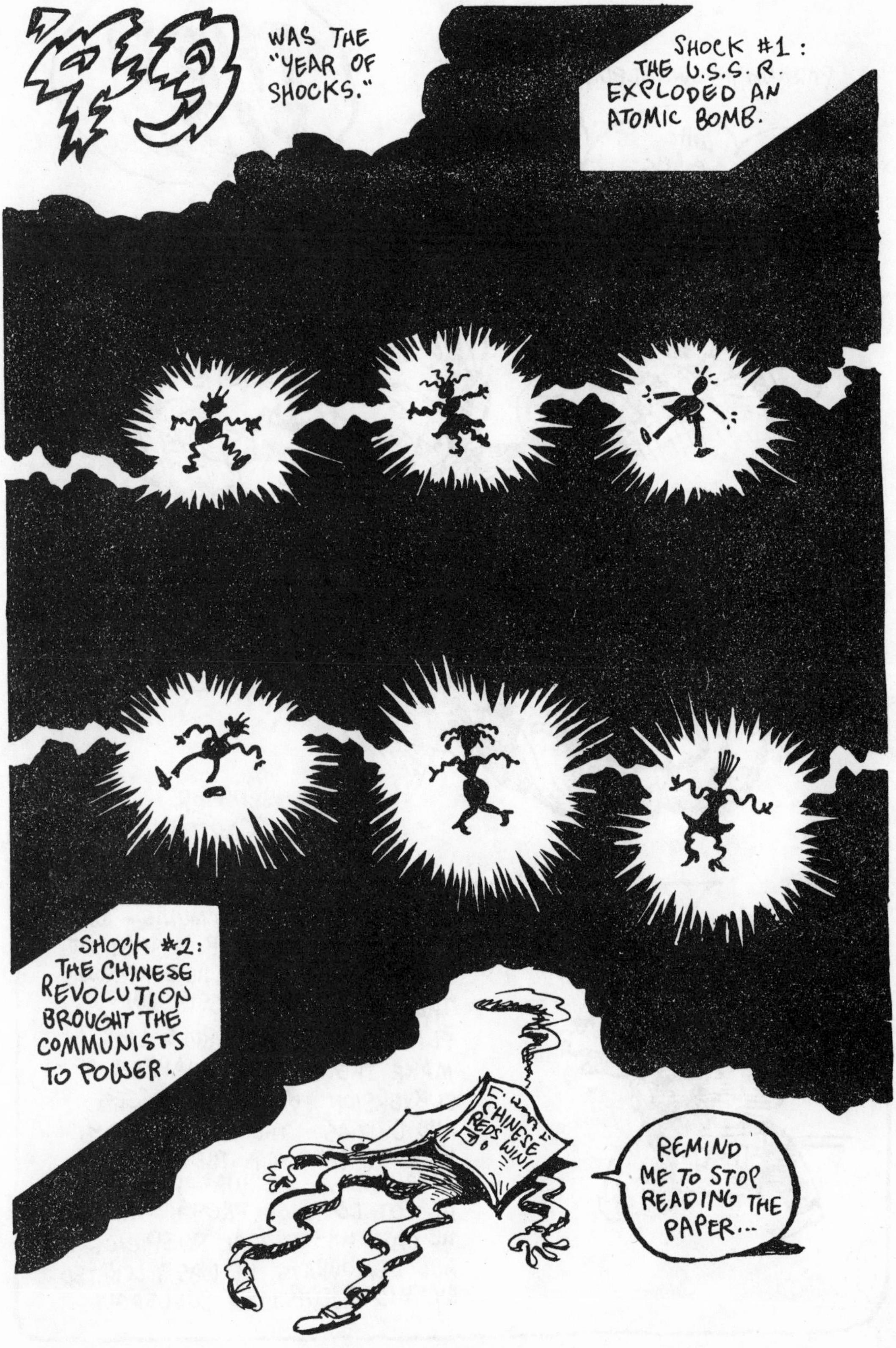
'49
WAS THE "YEAR OF SHOCKS."
SHOCK #1: THE U.S.S.R. EXPLODED AN ATOMIC BOMB.
SHOCK #2: THE CHINESE REVOLUTION BROUGHT THE COMMUNISTS TO POWER.
CHINESE REDS WIN!
REMIND ME TO STOP READING THE PAPER...

PARANOIA SWELLED...

WHO LOST CHINA?

WHO GAVE AWAY THE BOMB?

WHO ATTACKED MICKEY MOUSE?

THEY DID!!

ENTER SENATOR JOE McCARTHY...

GET 'EM, JOE!!

McCARTHY'S ANTI-COMMUNISM WAS HARDLY DIFFERENT FROM THAT OF NIXON ET AL....BUT HE SURPASSED THEM ALL IN DISHONESTY AND FLAIR... McCARTHY'S ROLE WAS TO MAKE THE WILDEST CHARGES OF SUBVERSION...BULLY WITNESSES AND CRITICS THE MOST RUDELY... WHIP UP PARANOIA THE MOST INTENSELY... HE WAS HORRIBLE... HE GOT LOTS OF PRESS... AND, AS HE CAST HYSTERICAL SUSPICION ON ALL DEMOCRATS, HE WAS TOLERATED BY HIS REPUBLICAN COLLEAGUES.

IT WAS AT THIS RELAXING MOMENT THAT THE NORTH KOREAN COMMUNISTS DECIDED TO INVADE SOUTH KOREA.

THE U.S. SENT IN TROOPS... THEY MARCHED UNDER A U.N. FLAG, TO KEEP UP APPEARANCES, BUT THEIR COMMANDER, GEN. DOUGLAS MacARTHUR, ANSWERED ONLY TO WASHINGTON.

GOT US SOME "GOOKS," LEROY!

AS THE WAR CRUNCHED UP AND DOWN THE KOREAN PENINSULA, THE AMERICAN PARADOX BECAME CLEARER... TO "DEFEND DEMOCRACY" IT WAS NECESSARY TO PROP UP A CORRUPT DICTATOR, SYNGMAN RHEE... REFUSE ELECTIONS (THE COMMIES MIGHT WIN!)... AND BOMB EVERY "TARGET" (I.E., TOWN) IN KOREA INTO RUBBLE!

WITH WORLD WAR III LOOMING, TENSION ROSE...

MCCARTHY BLAMED THE KOREAN WAR ON THE EARLIER "SOFTNESS" OF THE "COMMIECRAT" PARTY.

I AIN'T SAYIN' THEY'RE ALL SPIES, NECESSARILY.

HEY, WE CAN SHOW AS MUCH CONTEMPT FOR THE CONSTITUTION AS ANYONE!

YES, BE FAIR!

SO THE DEMOCRATS VIED WITH MCCARTHY TO ESTABLISH THEIR ANTI-COMMUNIST CREDENTIALS.

WHEN THE REPUBLICANS INTRODUCED AN "INTERNAL SECURITY ACT," LIBERAL DEMOCRATS ADDED AN AMENDMENT CREATING CONCENTRATION CAMPS FOR SUSPECTED COMMUNISTS... ULTRALIBERAL HUBERT HUMPHREY DRAFTED A LAW DECLARING THE COMMUNIST PARTY TO BE NO PARTY AT ALL, BUT A CRIMINAL CONSPIRACY!!

TOUGH ENOUGH?

NEVERTHELESS, '52 BROUGHT A REPUBLICAN INTO THE WHITE HOUSE, WAR HERO DWIGHT D. EISENHOWER.

"IKE'S" VEEP WAS NIXON, SMARTEST OF THE McCARTHYITE GROUP.

SECRETARY OF STATE WAS THE PIOUSLY ANTI-COMMUNIST JOHN FOSTER DULLES.

IN '53 THEY ENDED THE KOREAN WAR.

IN '54 McCARTHY WAS SILENCED...

...AND, OVERTLY AT LEAST, PEACE FELL...

DRINK?

WHILE, COVERTLY, DULLES'S LITTLE BROTHER ALLEN WAS LEADING THE CENTRAL INTELLIGENCE AGENCY INTO SOME NEW ARENAS: ASSASSINATION, PSY-WAR, LSD EXPERIMENTS.

OUR STRATEGIC SUPPLY OF BANANAS IS IMPERILED!

THE CIA BECAME AN ACTIVE FOREIGN POLICY ARM, SECRETLY AIDING THE OVERTHROW OF LEFTIST— THOUGH ELECTED—GOVERNMENTS IN IRAN AND GUATEMALA.

311

AND SO... UNTROUBLED BY DANGEROUS THOUGHTS, AMERICANS SET ABOUT ENJOYING THEIR NEW SUPERPOWER STATUS... GROSS NATIONAL PRODUCT CLIMBED YEAR AFTER YEAR... TRACT HOUSING SPROUTED LIKE CRABGRASS IN THE SUBURBS... THE TAILFIN WAS INVENTED IN '55... AT LAST, THE AMERICAN DREAM WAS COMING TRUE !!!...

SO WHAT IF THE TRACT HOUSE HAD A BACK-YARD BOMB SHELTER FULL OF SALTINES?

OR IF SCHOOL KIDS WERE DUCKING UNDER THEIR DESKS IN AIR-RAID DRILLS THAT NO ONE BELIEVED WOULD PROTECT THEM FROM THE BOMB?

HANDS OVER OUR NECKS, CLASS! IT'S IMPORTANT TO VAPORIZE OUR HANDS FIRST!

OR IF MOM WAS BECOMING AN ISOLATED BEING-IN-A-BOX?

M-I-C- K-E-Y...

OR IF PUBLIC HOUSING LOOKED LIKE THIS?

OR IF, WHEN 112 PEOPLE WERE ASKED TO SIGN A PETITION ENDORSING THE DECLARATION OF INDEPENDENCE, 111 REFUSED?

OR IF BLACKS STILL RODE THE BACK OF THE BUS?

OR IF THE INDUSTRIAL BOOM DEPENDED ON CHURNING OUT PRODUCTS NOBODY NEEDED — OR EVEN IMAGINED BEFORE?

FABRIC SOFTENER?

ONE LITTLE THING DISTURBED THIS PEACEFUL SCENE...
A LITTLE SATELLITE CALLED SPUTNIK...
THE FIRST SUCCESSFUL ROCKET-LAUNCHED
ARTIFICIAL MOON—AND IT
WAS **RUSSIAN!**

SPUT

UNTIL 1945, THE WORLD'S BEST ROCKET
PROGRAM WAS IN GERMANY.
AFTER THE WAR, THE U.S.
AND U.S.S.R. DIVIDED UP THE
GERMAN SCIENTISTS,
REGARDLESS OF POLITICAL
AFFILIATION OR WAR
CRIMES.   NOW, WITH
SPUTNIK, THE TRUTH
BECAME CLEAR!!

THEIR GERMANS ARE BETTER THAN OUR GERMANS!

SPAM

314

This was no mere question of national pride.

It was obvious to everyone that you could equip these missiles with H-bombs in their noses... the Russians were suddenly capable of delivering annihilation to your back yard in about half an hour.

Not long enough to get from the mall to the bomb shelter...

I'll never shop again...

Build tiny computers!

The U.S. government upped its support for the space program, scientific research, and science education... the result was a successful missile program... now both sides could deliver annihilation... everyone was relieved...

Except for a few peaceniks!

BUT IF POLITICAL PROTEST WAS MUTED, STILL, UNDER THE MINDLESS MARCH OF CONFORMITY, SOMETHING WAS BUBBLING...

...AMONG SOUTHERN BLACKS, WHO HAD BEGUN TO CHALLENGE SEGREGATION WITH LAWSUITS AND BOYCOTTS...

CIVIL RIGHTS LAWYER THURGOOD MARSHALL

...AMONG ALIENATED WHITE (AND BLACK) POETS AND DRIFTERS, WHO GATHERED IN COFFEEHOUSES WITH BONGOS AND BLACK TURTLENECKS...

LIKE... EXISTENCE IS SO~ SO...SO WHAT?

SO VERY, VERY WHAT...

316

JUST ABOUT THE ONLY SIGNS OF CULTURAL VITALITY WERE OUTSIDE THE MAINSTREAM... LIKE THE ANGRY PROSE OF JAMES BALDWIN...

THE ESOTERIC BEBOP OF PARKER, GILLESPIE, MONK...

THE POETRY OF ALLEN GINSBERG, PROSECUTED FOR OBSCENITY...

HOWL

SHOULD HAVE BEEN FOR OBSCURITY!

SATIRE LIKE KELLY'S "POGO"...

OR THE INSPIRED PARODIES OF KURTZMAN'S

MAD.

IT WAS ALSO THE "GOLDEN AGE" OF TV... THIS WAS IN THE MAINSTREAM, BUT HOW EXCITED CAN YOU GET ABOUT MILTON BERLE IN DRAG?

AND... AND... WHAT WAS WITH THOSE

TEENAGERS?

WHAT WERE THEY LISTENING TO?
IT WAS AMAZINGLY LIKE THE 1920'S ALL
OVER AGAIN: GOVERNMENT MIND CONTROL
WAS FAILING TO TAKE HOLD BELOW THE
BELT!! ONCE AGAIN, BLACK DANCE MUSIC
WAS CROSSING OVER: FATS DOMINO, CHUCK
BERRY, LITTLE RICHARD... AND THE
MESSAGE WAS... **SEXY!**

THEN CAME ELVIS, THE WHITE KID WHO COULD "SING BLACK," AND **ROCK 'N' ROLL** WENT **OUT OF CONTROL!**

AND SO, BETWEEN THE "RESPECTABLE" PARENTS AND THEIR CHILDREN, A GENERATION GAP OPENED UP...

MEANWHILE, BACK IN THE REAL WORLD, SOMETHING WAS HAPPENING THAT AFFECTED THE '60's AND EVERYTHING AFTERWARD:

DECOLONIZATION.

REMEMBER: UNTIL 1945, SEVERAL WESTERN EUROPEAN COUNTRIES WERE MORE THAN COUNTRIES — THEY WERE HEADS OF EMPIRES.

BRITAIN RULED
INDIA
BURMA
SUDAN
KENYA
UGANDA
RHODESIA
ETC ETC ETC...

PIP PIP

FRANCE RULED
ALGERIA
TUNISIA
VIETNAM
CAMBODIA
LAOS
CHAD
ETC ETC ETC...

BIEN SUR!

THE NETHERLANDS RULED INDONESIA; BELGIUM HAD THE CONGO; PORTUGAL OWNED ANGOLA, MOZAMBIQUE, GOA...

AS AMERICA VAGUELY REMEMBERED, BEING A COLONY WAS NO FUN.

OH, YEAH...

AND, LIKE AMERICA IN 1776, QUITE A FEW OF THESE 20TH-CENTURY COLONIES HAD INDEPENDENCE MOVEMENTS!

B-BUT— THEY'RE NOT WH-WHITE!

AFTER WORLD WAR II, SOME OF THESE MOVEMENTS SUCCEEDED, BEGINNING WITH THE INDEPENDENCE OF

INDIA + PAKISTAN (1947)
BURMA ('48)
VIETNAM + CAMBODIA ('55)
INDONESIA ('55)
SUDAN ('56)

CHAPTER 18

REVOLUTION NOW?

AS BRITAIN, FRANCE, HOLLAND, AND CO. WITHDREW FROM THEIR OVERSEAS POSSESSIONS, THE UNITED STATES OFTEN STEPPED IN.

THIS WAS CALLED **neo**-COLONIALISM, BECAUSE, ALTHOUGH THE COUNTRIES RETAINED NOMINAL INDEPENDENCE, THEIR POLICIES WERE SUBJECT TO U.S. PRIORITIES.

YOU CAN KEEP THE FLAG!

ECONOMIC ADVISERS

POLICE TRAINING

FOREIGN AID

CIA

AND WOE TO THE COUNTRY THAT SHOWED REAL INDEPENDENCE!

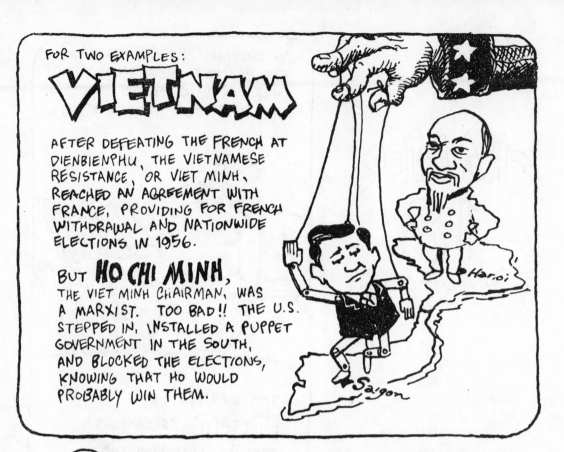

FOR TWO EXAMPLES:

VIETNAM

AFTER DEFEATING THE FRENCH AT DIENBIENPHU, THE VIETNAMESE RESISTANCE, OR VIET MINH, REACHED AN AGREEMENT WITH FRANCE, PROVIDING FOR FRENCH WITHDRAWAL AND NATIONWIDE ELECTIONS IN 1956.

BUT **HO CHI MINH,** THE VIET MINH CHAIRMAN, WAS A MARXIST. TOO BAD!! THE U.S. STEPPED IN, INSTALLED A PUPPET GOVERNMENT IN THE SOUTH, AND BLOCKED THE ELECTIONS, KNOWING THAT HO WOULD PROBABLY WIN THEM.

CUBA,

NOMINALLY INDEPENDENT, WAS IN FACT MORE OR LESS WHOLLY OWNED BY THE U.S.A. IN '59, **FIDEL CASTRO** LED A REVOLUTION WITH OTHER IDEAS... IT WASN'T EVEN KNOWN AT THE TIME IF CASTRO WAS A COMMUNIST— BUT HE THREATENED U.S. ECONOMIC INTERESTS, SO THE C I A BEGAN PLOTTING AGAINST HIM...

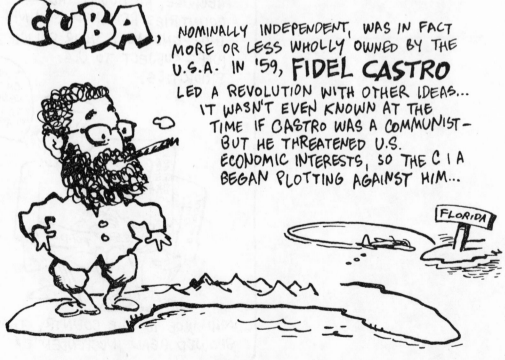

ANOTHER INGREDIENT
IN THE SOON-TO-BE-BUBBLING
BREW OF THE '60'S WAS THE

CIVIL RIGHTS MOVEMENT.

AFTER WORLD WAR II, THE GOVERNMENT
REALIZED THAT RACISM WAS
A BLOT ON AMERICA'S IMAGE
AS WORLD LEADER... SO
BARRIERS AGAINST BLACKS
BEGAN COMING DOWN.

"AHEM"
WE'RE DOING THE
BEST WE CAN!
AND WE'VE BEEN
DOING IT FOR
MANY, MANY
MONTHS!

WHITES ONLY

WHITES ONLY

THE FIRST COLOR BARRIER TO FALL,
IN 1947, WAS IN MAJOR-LEAGUE
BASEBALL. NEXT, IN '48,
TRUMAN ORDERED
THE MILITARY
DESEGREGATED...

...AND THE SUPREME COURT
ISSUED A SERIES OF ANTI-
DISCRIMINATION RULINGS,
MOST NOTABLY **BROWN** VS.
BOARD OF EDUCATION,
BANNING SEGREGATED
PUBLIC SCHOOLS.

THE COURT RULED THAT SEGREGATION MUST FALL "WITH ALL DELIBERATE SPEED." THIS WAS OPEN TO INTERPRETATION, ESPECIALLY DOWN SOUTH,* WHERE BLACKS EMPHASIZED THE SPEED, WHILE WHITES STRESSED DELIBERATION.

WE DEE-LIBERATIN' AS DEE-LIBERATELY AS WE CAN...

MONTGOMERY, ALA., WAS TYPICAL: BY LAW, BLACKS SAT IN THE BACK OF THE BUS — UNTIL A WHITE PERSON DEMANDED A SEAT, WHEN THEY STOOD...

...UNTIL DEC. 1, 1955, WHEN CIVIL RIGHTS ACTIVIST *ROSA PARKS* SAID NO...

PARKS WAS PUT OFF THE BUS, ARRESTED, AND JAILED.

THIS SPARKED THE *MONTGOMERY BUS BOYCOTT*, THE FIRST DIRECT ACTION OF THE CIVIL RIGHTS MOVEMENT. FOR A YEAR, BLACKS WALKED AND CARPOOLED, ENDURING HEAT, HARASSMENT, THREATS, JAIL, AND EVEN BOMBS — AND WON VICTORY WITH A SUPREME COURT RULING AGAINST MONTGOMERY'S SEGREGATED BUSES.

* BUT NOT ONLY IN THE SOUTH. FOR EXAMPLE, THE ARMY TOOK YEARS TO INTEGRATE FULLY, WHILE THE AIR FORCE DID IT IN ONE DAY.

THE BOYCOTT'S LEADER WAS A 27-YEAR-OLD MINISTER, **MARTIN LUTHER KING, JR.,** AN EXCEPTIONAL COMBINATION OF BRAVERY, VISION, ELOQUENCE, MORAL FORCE, AND TACTICAL KNOW-HOW. WHEN HIS HOUSE WAS BOMBED, KING DISPERSED AN ANGRY CROWD OF BLACKS WITH THESE WORDS:

WE MUST MEET VIOLENCE WITH NON-VIOLENCE.

WHO'S NON-VIOLENT?

KING THEN ORGANIZED THE SOUTHERN CHRISTIAN LEADERSHIP CONFERENCE TO CONTINUE NON-VIOLENT DIRECT ACTION.

TENSION ROSE IN THE SOUTH, AND FBI CHIEF J. EDGAR HOOVER DECIDED THAT KING WAS SOME KIND OF SUBVERSIVE.

AND I HAVE TAPE RECORDINGS OF HIS SEX LIFE TO PROVE IT!

1960: IKE BOWS OUT WITH AN ASTONISHING WARNING AGAINST AMERICA'S GROWING "MILITARY-INDUSTRIAL COMPLEX"... AND IN COMES A YOUNG, VIGOROUS, AND CHARMING BOSTONIAN,

JOHN F. KENNEDY.

(HIS OPPONENT, NIXON, FORGETS TO POWDER HIS 5 O'CLOCK SHADOW ON TV, AND LOSES THE ELECTION BY A WHISKER.)

GRRR

"ASK NOT WHAT YOUR COUNTRY CAN DO FOR YOU, BUT WHAT YOU CAN DO FOR YOUR COUNTRY."

KENNEDY APPEALS TO YOUNG AMERICANS' IDEALISM. HE CALLS HIS PROGRAM THE **NEW FRONTIER.**

?

AND THEY RESPOND, SOME BY JOINING THE PEACE CORPS AND SEEING THE WORLD... OTHERS BY JOINING THE CIVIL RIGHTS MOVEMENT AND SEEING THE SOUTH.

IN 1963, CIVIL RIGHTS DEMONSTRATIONS TOOK PLACE IN 186 CITIES ACROSS THE COUNTRY... A BLACK STUDENT ENROLLED AT THE UNIVERSITY OF ALABAMA... SEGREGATION RECEDED... IN JUNE, KENNEDY PROPOSED A CIVIL RIGHTS ACT TO CONGRESS... IN AUGUST, 250,000 PEOPLE MARCHED PEACEFULLY TO WASHINGTON, WHERE MARTIN LUTHER KING GAVE HIS FAMOUS SPEECH...

"I HAVE A DREAM THAT ONE DAY ON THE RED HILLS OF GEORGIA THE SONS OF FORMER SLAVES AND THE SONS OF FORMER SLAVE OWNERS WILL BE ABLE TO SIT DOWN TOGETHER AT THE TABLE OF BROTHERHOOD..."

MEANWHILE, IN CUBA, KENNEDY
CARRIED OUT EISENHOWER'S PLAN:
IN 1961, CIA-TRAINED CUBANS
INVADED THE ISLAND'S BAY OF
PIGS AND WAITED FOR THE MASSES
TO RISE UP AND EMBRACE THEM.
DREAM ON!!

MASSES!
YOO.
HOO!
OH,
MASSES!

SHH...
I THINK
THE MASSES
ARE SHOOTING
AT US...

WE'LL SET
FIRE TO HIS
BEARD...

SOAK
HIS CIGAR
IN LSD!

THE CIA TURNED TO
MORE EXOTIC IDEAS,
WHILE CASTRO TURNED
TO THE USSR FOR
MILITARY AID.

RUSSIA SENT BALLISTIC MISSILES...
KENNEDY SENT THE NAVY TO
CONFRONT THE RUSSIAN
CONVOY... FOR
SEVERAL DAYS THE
WORLD TEETERED
ON THE BRINK...

FINALLY, THE CRISIS ENDED WHEN THE USSR AGREED TO
WITHDRAW THE MISSILES AND THE U.S. PROMISED TO
LEAVE CASTRO IN PEACE.

AND IN SOUTH VIETNAM, A MESS: SAIGON, THE CAPITAL, A VAST SLUM... LAND REFORM IN THE HANDS OF A LANDLORD... GROWING OPPOSITION TO DIEM'S CORRUPT GOVERNMENT...

KENNEDY, CONCLUDING THAT DIEM WAS NO LONGER USEFUL, GAVE THE NOD, AND THE VIETNAMESE PRESIDENT WAS ASSASSINATED ON NOV. 1, 1963.

THREE WEEKS LATER, THE AMERICAN PRESIDENT WAS ASSASSINATED...

A FEW DAYS LATER, KENNEDY'S ASSASSIN WAS ASSASSINATED, ON LIVE TV — AND NOW THE '60'S HAD REALLY BEGUN...

THE SAME DAY KENNEDY WAS SHOT, TWO OF MY HIGH-SCHOOL FRIENDS — 16 AND 17 YEARS OLD (!!) — TOOK PEYOTE* FOR THE FIRST TIME. THEY HAD VISIONS OF EVIL UNLEASHED.

HOME-MADE THELONIOUS MONK SWEATSHIRTS

LET'S LOOSEN OUR NECKTIES...

PSYCHEDELIC DRUGS HAD HIT THE MEDIA THE PREVIOUS YEAR, WHEN HARVARD'S TIMOTHY LEARY WAS FIRED FOR TURNING ON TO LSD WITH HIS STUDENTS.

BY '65, A DRUG CULTURE AROSE, COMPLETE WITH A FABRIC (PAISLEY), A MUSIC (ACID ROCK'), AND AN OFFICIAL OUTBURST:

OH, WOW!

* THEN LEGALLY AVAILABLE FROM A TEXAS CACTUS FARM.

UNAWARE OF THIS DISTURBANCE IN THE PSYCHIC ATMOSPHERE, VICE PRESIDENT

LYNDON JOHNSON

TOOK THE OATH OF OFFICE.

THE TALL TEXAN FULFILLED KENNEDY'S PROMISE WITH FIVE YEARS OF STRONG CIVIL RIGHTS AND SOCIAL LEGISLATION.

THE CIVIL RIGHTS ACT

THE VOTING RIGHTS ACT

FOOD STAMPS

MEDICARE

OFFICE OF ECONOMIC OPPORTUNITY

OCCUPATIONAL SAFETY AND HEALTH ADMINISTRATION

THE WAR ON POVERTY

UNFORTUNATELY, THE WAR ON POVERTY WASN'T JOHNSON'S ONLY WAR...

PAUSING BRIEFLY TO CELEBRATE A LANDSLIDE ELECTION VICTORY ON A PEACE PLATFORM, JOHNSON NOW BEGAN SENDING GROUND TROOPS TO VIETNAM.

JOHNSON'S STRATEGISTS WERE "THE BEST AND THE BRIGHTEST," INTELLECTUALS WHO UNDERSTOOD THE SUBTLETIES OF DEFENDING DEMOCRACY IN A COUNTRY WHERE YOU HAD REFUSED TO HOLD ELECTIONS.

THEIR POLYSYLLABIC PREFERENCES PERHAPS PROMOTED THE PENTAGON'S PENCHANT FOR PRETENTIOUS PROSE. FOR EXAMPLE:

TRI-CIRCUMVOLUTORY TRANSLOCATION DEVICE

"STRATEGIC HAMLET PROGRAM" (UPROOTING VILLAGERS AND MOVING THEM TO CAMPS)

"PROTECTIVE REACTION" ("REACTING" TO SOMETHING THAT HADN'T HAPPENED YET)

"SURGICAL BOMBING" (BOMBING)

"ANTI-PERSONNEL DEVICE" (NAPALM, WHITE PHOSPHORUS, FRAGMENTATION GRENADES)

"PACIFICATION" (KILLING AND TORTURE)

UP THE ESCALATOR

IN 1964, THE U.S. HAD 20,000 "MILITARY ADVISERS"* IN SOUTH VIETNAM, PROPPING UP DIEM'S SUCCESSOR. THE OPPOSITION NATIONAL LIBERATION FRONT, SUPPORTED BY THE NORTH, WAGED A GUERRILLA WAR, AND THEY SEEMED TO BE ON THE VERGE OF WINNING.

ON AUG. 5, JOHNSON ACCUSED NORTH VIETNAM OF ATTACKING U.S. SHIPS IN THE GULF OF TONKIN. ON AUG. 7, CONGRESS PASSED THE "TONKIN GULF RESOLUTION," A BLANK CHECK FOR JOHNSON TO DO "WHATEVER IS NECESSARY..."

PAY TO THE ORDER OF *Lyndon Johnson*
THE AMOUNT OF: _____

AND JOHNSON BEGAN TO BOMB NORTH VIETNAM — 2 DAYS BEFORE THE RESOLUTION WAS PASSED !!

* MOSTLY HELICOPTER PILOTS.

BERKELEY, 1964, THE FIRST BIG STUDENT DEMONSTRATION: THE **FREE SPEECH MOVEMENT** PROTESTS A UNIVERSITY BAN ON "POLITICAL TABLES" ON THE CAMPUS PLAZA.

CIVIL RIGHTS VETERANS FOUNDED THE **S**TUDENTS FOR A **D**EMOCRATIC **S**OCIETY (SDS) TO SPONSOR ANTI-WAR "TEACH-INS" AND DEMONSTRATIONS. DRAFT CARDS BURNED TO THE SMOLDERING CHANT OF "GIRLS SAY YES TO BOYS WHO SAY NO."

334

MEANWHILE, BLACKS WERE LOSING PATIENCE WITH WHITE RACISM... THE VIETNAM WAR DEVOURED THEM...

ELIJAH MOHAMMED,

PREACHING THAT WHITES ARE DEVILS, ATTRACTED MANY BLACKS TO HIS MUSLIM SECT. THE MESSAGE WAS "BLACK IS BEAUTIFUL"... THE AFRO EXPANDED...

BUT THE MUSLIMS' MOST ELOQUENT SPEAKER,

MALCOLM X,

HAD A VISION OF RACIAL HARMONY ON A TRIP TO MECCA. HE BROKE WITH ELIJAH MOHAMMED... AND IN 1965, MALCOLM X WAS ASSASSINATED.

...BY THE MUSLIMS? BY THE CIA? BY MUSLIMS WHO WERE CIA? NO ONE KNOWS...

IN '66 THE SWELLING RAGE BROKE IN THE TIDAL WAVE OF LOS ANGELES'S WATTS RIOTS. FINAL TOLL: 40 DEAD, HUNDREDS OF ACRES CHARRED.

WHY YOU WANNA BURN DOWN THE NEIGHBORHOOD?

AIN'T YOU NEVER HEARD OF URBAN RENEWAL?

3 POWERS OF 1967:

FIRE POWER: 400,000 G.I.'S (DISPROPORTIONATELY BLACK) IN "THE NAM", TRYING TO WIN VIETNAMESE HEARTS & MINDS WHILE WASTING THEIR COUNTRY... FOR THE G.I., A YEAR OF HELL,... FOR THE VIETNAMESE, MORE THAN A YEAR.

M·60 MACHINE GUN – "THE P...

BLACK POWER: ERUPTIONS IN THE GHETTOS OF DETROIT, NEWARK, ETC. ETC. ETC... THE CHANT OF "BURN, BABY, BURN..." POLICE SHOOTING TO KILL... THEIR FIRE RETURNED... MORE LIKE A REVOLT THAN A RIOT!

FLOWER POWER: IN SAN FRANCISCO, THE "SUMMER OF LOVE" (??!!)... HIPPIES, BIKERS, BLACK PANTHERS, THE FARM, THE FAMILY, THE FAMILY DOG... PAINTED FACES, ACID ROCK... THE LOVE·IN, THE BE·IN, SPEED, ACID, GRASS...

EXCUSE ME, I'M FROM THE MEDIA...

(WITH APOLOGIES TO R. CRUMB AND GILBERT SHELTON)

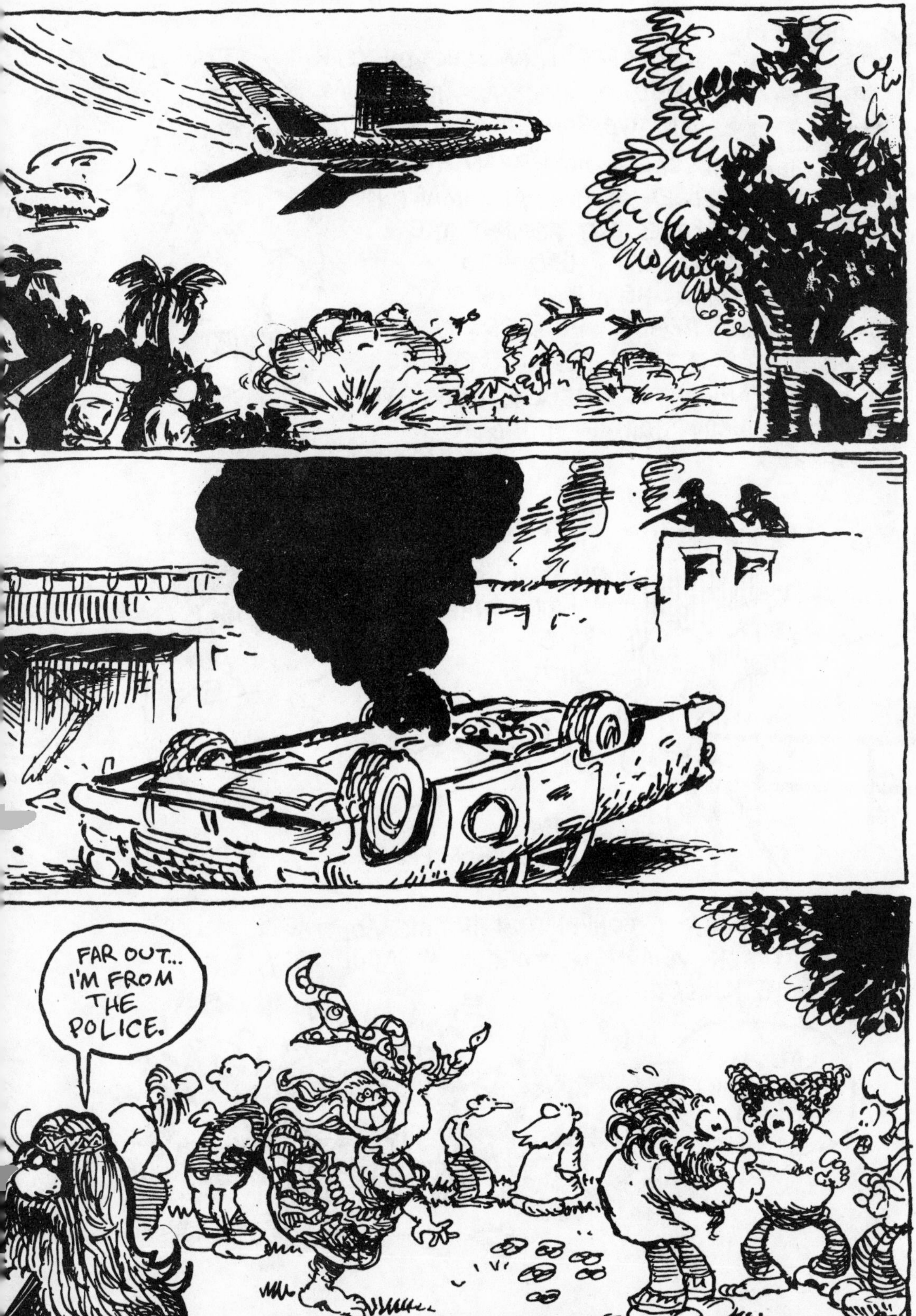
FAR OUT... I'M FROM THE POLICE.

 **68** (SHUDDER!), AN ELECTION YEAR... 550,000 AMERICANS IN VIETNAM... MASSIVE BOMBING OF THE NORTH...

"THINGS AIN'T GOIN' ACCORDIN' TO PLAN."

U.S. SOLDIERS MASSACRE MORE THAN 400 WOMEN AND CHILDREN AT MY LAI... MARTIN LUTHER KING SPEAKS OUT AGAINST THE WAR... THE DEMOCRATS BEGIN TO DESERT JOHNSON... HE ANNOUNCES THAT HE WON'T RUN AGAIN... HE EASES THE BOMBING... PEACE TALKS BEGIN... SEVERAL ANTI-WAR CANDIDATES EMERGE, INCLUDING ROBERT KENNEDY, JOHN'S YOUNGER BROTHER.

ON APRIL 4, MARTIN LUTHER KING IS SHOT...

IN JUNE, ROBERT KENNEDY FALLS...

AT THE DEMOCRATIC CONVENTION IN CHICAGO, THE POLICE ATTACK DEMONSTRATORS... MIRACULOUSLY, NO ONE IS KILLED.

"CALL US PIGS, WILL YOU?"

BUT IN NOVEMBER, THE CANDIDATES' WERE: PRO-WAR DEMOCRAT HUBERT HUMPHREY, ALABAMA GOV. GEORGE WALLACE (WHOSE CAMPAIGN HAD FASCIST OVERTONES), AND THE WINNER, WITH 43% OF THE POPULAR VOTE.........??!!

HI!! I'M BACK!

NIXON CLAIMED TO HAVE A "SECRET PLAN" TO END THE WAR...

THE PLAN, "OPERATION DUCK HOOK," WAS TO MAKE A SERIES OF ESCALATING THREATS AGAINST NORTH VIETNAM, CULMINATING, IF NECESSARY, IN THE USE OF NUKES. IN NOV., '69, NIXON SECRETLY* PUT U.S. FORCES ON FULL NUCLEAR ALERT.

MORE THAN A PLAN TO END THE WAR, IT'S A PLAN TO END THE WORLD!

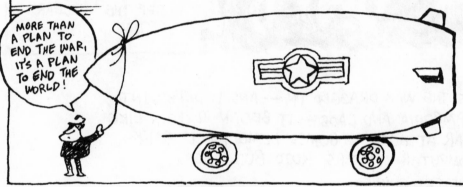

BEFORE SEEING HOW THIS TURNED OUT, LET'S NOTE A COUPLE OF OTHER EVENTS FROM 1969.

AN AMERICAN, NEIL ARMSTRONG, LANDED ON THE MOON...

ANOTHER AMERICAN, CHARLES MANSON, PROGRAMMED TEEN-AGE GIRLS WITH LSD TO COMMIT POINT-LESS, GRUESOME MURDERS.

* THAT IS, IT WAS A SECRET FROM THE AMERICAN PEOPLE, MOST OF WHOM PROBABLY THOUGHT THAT NIXON WAS SIMPLY LYING ABOUT HAVING A PLAN. THE SOVIET GOVERNMENT, HOWEVER, WAS KEPT FULLY INFORMED!

NIXON'S ESCALATION BEGAN:
HE MINED HAIPHONG HARBOR;
BOMBED NORTH VIETNAM'S
IRRIGATION DIKES; AND
EVENTUALLY WASTED THE
LITTLE COUNTRY WITH MORE
EXPLOSIVE POWER THAN ALL
THE BOMBS OF WORLD WAR II.

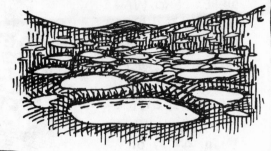

☆◉#!

250,000 PROTESTERS
DESCENDED ON
WASHINGTON...
THE OUTCRY WAS
SO LOUD THAT
NIXON BACKED
OFF THE NUCLEAR
OPTION.

AS THE WAR DRAGGED ON — AND WIDENED INTO
CAMBODIA AND LAOS — IT BEGAN TO LOOK LIKE
WAR AT HOME... BOMBS DEMOLISHED BANKS,
COMPUTER CENTERS, ROTC BUILDINGS...

THE FBI GUNNED
DOWN BLACK RADICALS
IN BED...GUARDSMEN
KILLED STUDENTS
AT KENT STATE
(OHIO) AND
JACKSON STATE
(MISSISSIPPI).

IT'S THE
REVOLUTION!

ISN'T
IT?

IN 1971, A DISGRUNTLED
PENTAGON ANALYST,
DANIEL ELLSBERG,
LEAKED THE
"PENTAGON PAPERS"
TO THE PRESS,
DOCUMENTING
GOVERNMENT LIES
AND SELF-DECEPTION
ON VIETNAM.
THE PUBLIC WAS
ALMOST AS AGHAST
AS THE PRESIDENT!

(EXPLETIVE DELETED)

NY TIMES

NIXON CREATED THE "PLUMBERS," A SECRET TEAM TO
PLUG LEAKS. THEY BURGLED ELLSBERG'S PSYCHIATRIST'S
OFFICE, VAINLY SEEKING SOMETHING TO SMEAR HIM WITH.

THEN — AS THE '72 ELECTIONS DREW NEAR, THE
PLUMBERS WERE CAUGHT TAPPING PHONES IN THE
DEMOCRATS' HEADQUARTERS AT THE WATERGATE
APARTMENT COMPLEX IN WASHINGTON, D.C.

GAH!
HIPPIES WITH GUNS!!

(PLAIN CLOTHES OFFICERS)

BUT NIXON ESCAPED RESPONSIBILITY UNTIL AFTER THE ELECTION, WHICH HE WON BY A LANDSLIDE — AND THEN THE AMAZING STORY CAME OUT:

* THE EXISTENCE OF THE PLUMBERS

* THE ELLSBERG BURGLARY

* "ENEMIES" HARASSED BY THE IRS AND BEATEN BY THUGS

* THE ATTORNEY GENERAL'S PRIOR KNOWLEDGE

* SUITCASEFULS OF $100 BILLS FOR "HUSH MONEY"

* AN INTERNATIONAL MONEY-LAUNDERING OPERATION

* MASSIVE INFLUENCE-PEDDLING

I AM NOT A CROOK!

* A COVER-UP INVOLVING THE FBI, CIA, + WHITE HOUSE...

SAID NIXON.

...AND THE MOST INCREDIBLE THING: A SECRET WHITE HOUSE TAPING SYSTEM, RECORDING IT ALL FOR POSTERITY!!

THIS IS ☆◎#⁑ ⅋#◎ HISTORY, BOB!

☆·⅋# RIGHT, BOSS!

(EIGHTEEN CRUCIAL MINUTES HAD BEEN ERASED, THOUGH... TOO BAD!)

NOT A CROOK... NOT A CROOK... NOT A CROOK...

FACING IMPEACHMENT, NIXON RESIGNED IN 1974. HIS TOP AIDES, AN ATTORNEY GENERAL OR TWO, AND A SLEW OF JUNIOR ASSISTANTS WENT TO JAIL— AN AMERICAN FIRST!

HE'S A CROOK!

HE'S A CROOK!

...BUT BEFORE RETIRING, NIXON "VIETNAMIZED" THE WAR — I.E., TURNED THE FIGHTING OVER TO THE SOUTH VIETNAMESE ARMY.

JUST REMIND ME WHAT WE'RE FIGHTING FOR...?

WHERE'S THE DAMN TICKER TAPE?

...AND THE AMERICAN BOYS FINALLY CAME HOME (ALTHOUGH CAPTURED PILOTS RETURNED LATER).

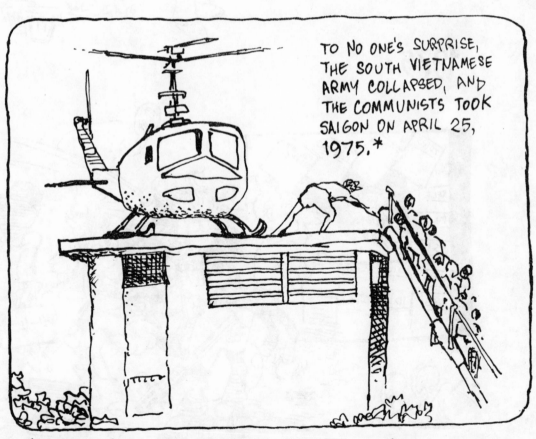

TO NO ONE'S SURPRISE, THE SOUTH VIETNAMESE ARMY COLLAPSED, AND THE COMMUNISTS TOOK SAIGON ON APRIL 25, 1975.*

*EXACTLY ONE WEEK AFTER THE KICK-OFF OF THE U.S. BICENTENNIAL.

1960:

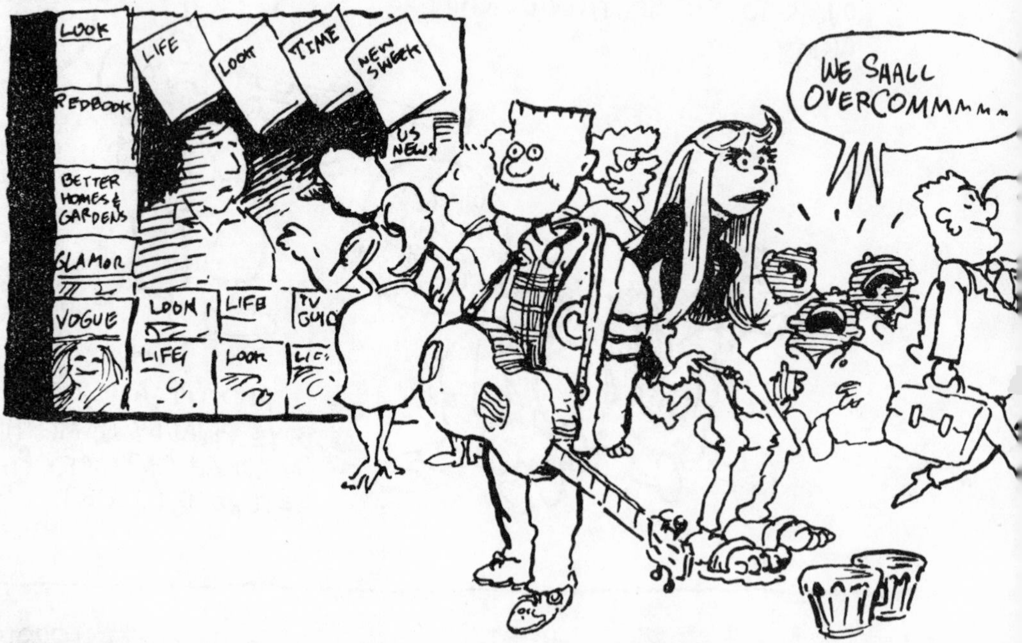
LOOK
LIFE
LOOK
TIME
NEWSWEEK
REDBOOK
US NEWS
BETTER HOMES & GARDENS
GLAMOR
VOGUE
LOOK!
LIFE
LIFE!
LOOK
WE SHALL OVERCOMMMMM

1975:

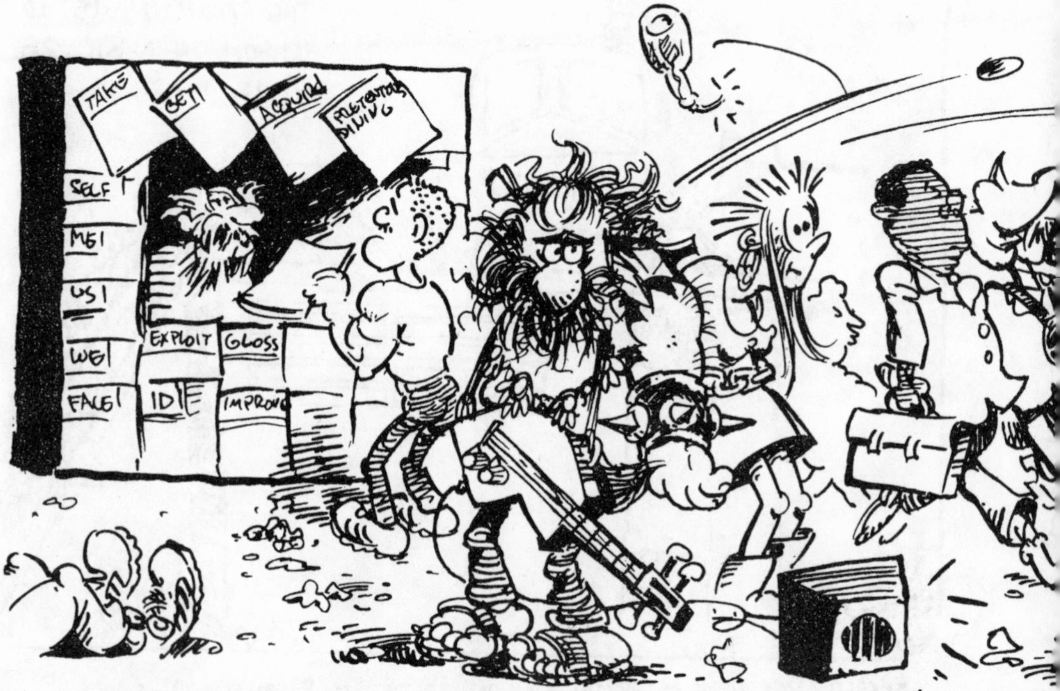
TAKE
GET
ACQUIRE
OSTENTATIOUS DINING
SELF
ME!
US!
WE!
FACE!
EXPLOIT
GLOSS
ID

CHAPTER 19
AND THEY LIVED HAPPILY EVER AFTER

READING THAT LAST CHAPTER, YOU MIGHT WELL WONDER **WHAT WAS SO GREAT ABOUT THE SIXTIES?**

ALL THAT BLOOD AND GUTS — WHAT'S TO BE NOSTALGIC ABOUT?

NOSTALGIC? WHY, ARE THEY OVER?

WELL, I LIVED THROUGH IT — LET'S SEE IF I CAN DUST OFF MY BRAIN CELLS AND REMEMBER...

"PICTURE YOURSELF ON A BOAT ON A RIVER..." THE MUSIC, OF COURSE!! NOT JUST THE BEATLES & STONES, BUT THE SOUL SOURCE: THE TEMPTATIONS, THE IMPRESSIONS, THE MIRACLES, JAMES BROWN, ARETHA FRANKLIN, WILSON PICKETT, RAY CHARLES...

BIRTH CONTROL PILLS... THEY MADE THE SEXUAL REVOLUTION POSSIBLE.

MYSTIC ECSTACY AT THE DROP OF A "TAB"... A SENSE THAT ANYTHING WAS POSSIBLE... COMMUNAL LIVING... FREE FOOD... A LOOSENING... AN INFORMALITY... HITCHHIKING WAS COMMON... TELEPHONE OPERATORS (IN L.A.) WOULD CHAT AIMLESSLY AS LONG AS YOU LIKED!!

FAR OUT!

SOME UNPLEASANT '60'S SIDE EFFECTS ARE STILL WITH US — DRUGS, FOR EXAMPLE. THE POST-'60'S GENERATION WENT FOR COCAINE, TO BUILD CONFIDENCE, AND PCP, FOR THAT DELIGHTFUL SENSATION OF BEING A RAMPAGING BULL ELEPHANT.

DON'T FORGET THE ASSASSINATON FAD — BOTH GOVERNMENT-SPONSORED AND FREE-LANCE.

THE SEXUAL REVOLUTION, WHEN COMBINED WITH A TRADITIONAL PURITAN RESISTANCE TO SEX EDUCATION, CREATED THE WORLD'S HIGHEST TEEN PREGNANCY RATE AND SPREAD VARIOUS VENEREAL DISEASES, MOST RECENTLY THE DREAD

A FLOWERING OF CULTS, FROM THE BENIGN TO THE RIDICULOUS.

FREE-FLOATING ANGER... A SERIES OF MASS MURDERERS, SOME OF WHOM WERE ALSO CULT LEADERS.

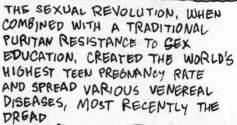

CHARLIE MANSON, YOU'RE A PIKER!

AND, MAYBE FROM DRUGS, OR FROM TV, OR FROM NUKE-THINK (SEE P.184) OR FROM AN INABILITY TO LOOK VIETNAM IN THE FACE — THE "PERCEPTION GAP." THIS IS THE NOTION THAT PERCEPTION IS AS IMPORTANT AS REALITY, IF THERE IS A REALITY.

I CAN PACKAGE THAT!

AND—

ON THE MORE POSITIVE SIDE, BLACKS WON VISIBLE, MAINSTREAM JOBS: BROADCASTERS, MANAGERS, TEACHERS (IN INTEGRATED SCHOOLS), DOCTORS, COPS, LAWYERS, SHERIFFS, JUDGES, MAYORS, CONGRESSIONAL REPS...

GOOD EVENING... I'M YOUR HIGHLY VISIBLE *BLACK* ANCHORPERSON... WELCOME TO EYEWITNESS NEWS...

GOOD. THE MOVEMENT SUCCEEDED. LET'S GO TO BED.

(...WHILE, AT THE SAME TIME, BLACK POVERTY AND UNEMPLOYMENT ACTUALLY INCREASED!)

YOU SURE YOU BLACK?

AND THEN THERE WAS WOMEN'S LIBERATION

REMEMBER THAT CHANT, "GIRLS SAY YES TO BOYS WHO SAY NO".? THIS CHANT OFFENDED SOME GIRLS!

DO WE HAVE ANY ROLE BEYOND SAYING "YES" TO BOYS?

NO! NO! NO!

THEY LOOKED AT THE ANTI-WAR MOVEMENT'S PERSONAL POLITICS — THE MEN DIDN'T TAKE THE WOMEN SERIOUSLY.

ER— I THINK...

DOES ANYONE HEAR A VOICE? I DON'T HEAR A VOICE!

ALSO — THE SEXUAL REVOLUTION CREATED THE MINISKIRT (DESIGNED BY A WOMAN, NO LESS!). THIS WAS LIBERATION?

FIDGET

TUG

SQUIRM

SOME MOVEMENT WOMEN DENOUNCED THE MINI-SKIRT AS SLAVE CLOTHES!

ONLY PANTS ARE POLITICALLY CORRECT!

UNLESS EVERYONE WEARS LEOTARDS + TIGHTS!

LIKE THEIR ABOLITIONIST SISTERS OF 1848, MODERN FEMINISTS REACTED FIRST TO MALE CHAUVINISM IN THE BROADER MOVEMENT. SMALL CONSCIOUSNESS-RAISING (C.R.) GROUPS SPONTANEOUSLY FORMED ALL OVER THE COUNTRY.

CONSPIRE

VENT

EXPLORE

MEDITATE

350

WOMEN'S LIBERATIONISTS REJECTED SEXUAL OBJECTIFICATION, SEXUAL COMPETITION, BEAUTY PAGEANTS, STRUCTURAL UNDERGARMENTS, FEMALE PASSIVITY, INFANTILE BEHAVIOR, AND MINDLESS SUPPORTIVENESS. THE SLOGAN WAS:

"SISTERHOOD IS POWERFUL!"

INDEED — SO IMPRESSED WERE THEY TO DISCOVER EACH OTHER'S WHOLE PERSONALITIES, THAT SOME FEMINISTS FELL IN LOVE — WITH EACH OTHER!!

THEIR SLOGAN: "A WOMAN WITHOUT A MAN IS LIKE A FISH WITHOUT A BICYCLE!"

THE C.R. GROUPS COALESCED INTO AN IMPRESSIVE ARRAY OF NATIONAL ORGANIZATIONS AND PUBLICATIONS.

MS. MAGAZINE FOUNDER GLORIA STEINEM

SOME OF THEIR GOALS:
- ANTI-DISCRIMINATION LAWS
- EQUAL RIGHTS AMENDMENT
- ABORTION ON DEMAND
- EQUAL PAY FOR EQUAL WORK
- PROSECUTION OF WIFE-BEATERS
- MORE SENSITIVE MEN

A RETURN TO GODDESS-WORSHIP!

SENSITIVE? B-BUT WE'RE **MEN!!**

NOT TO BE OUTDONE IN SENSITIVITY, HOMOSEXUAL MEN CAME OUT PROUDLY, AND **GAY LIBERATION** WAS BORN.

IT'S GOOD TO BE DIFFERENT

IT'S GOOD TO BE DIFFE

IT'S GOO

SEE? CASTRO STREET! PROOF OF A COMMIE PLOT!

IT'S ALL THIS PRESSURE TO BE SENSITIVE THAT ACCOUNTS FOR THE AWKWARD HUGGING THAT GOES ON NOW...

...CAN I LET GO YET?

THE ECOLOGY MOVEMENT

'60'S SPACECRAFT BEAMED HOME THE FIRST PHOTOS OF THE WHOLE EARTH. UNTIL THEN, NO ONE HAD REALIZED HOW BEAUTIFUL, BLUE, SMALL, AND FRAGILE IT LOOKED...

SCIENTISTS SUDDENLY WOKE UP TO GLOBAL PROBLEMS: ACID RAIN; SMOG; PAVING OVER FOREST, MARSH, AND FARM; WATER AND SOIL POLLUTION; DESERTIFI-CATION; RADIOACTIVE WASTE; CONSUMPTION OF NON-RENEWABLE RESOURCES LIKE METALS AND FUELS; DESTRUCTION OF OZONE BY AEROSOL CANS; THE GREENHOUSE EFFECT... ADD YOUR OWN!

IT WAS DISCOVERED
THAT DOLPHINS
WERE AS INTELLIGENT
AS HUMAN BEINGS —
THAT WHALES
SANG SONGS!!

BUT WE PUT OUR MINDS TO SOMETHING IMPORTANT — HAVING FUN!

THE CONCEPT OF HUMANITY'S
DOMINION OVER NATURE
GAVE WAY TO ONE OF
INTERDEPENDENCE AND
HARMONY — THE IDEA OF AN

ECOSYSTEM.

THE DETAILS INCLUDED:
RECYCLING
ORGANIC FARMING
POLLUTION CONTROL
ALTERNATIVE ENERGY SOURCES
CONSERVATION
"SMALL IS BEAUTIFUL"
WILDLIFE PROTECTION

HUMANS, BLESS 'EM — THEY TRY SO HARD!!

➡ ON A GLOBAL SCALE!!

WHAT REALLY BROUGHT THIS HOME TO AMERICANS WAS THE OIL CRISIS.

OIL-PRODUCING NATIONS, MINDFUL THAT THEIR RESERVES WOULD RUN OUT SOMEDAY, FORMED A CARTEL TO RAISE PRICES. THIS WAS THE

ORGANIZATION OF **P**ETROLEUM **E**XPORTING **C**OUNTRIES.

THE RESULT IN THE U.S.A.:

DOLLAR REGULAR.

£@

≸#¢

☆●¢

IT'S THE BEGINNING OF THE END...

GAS AND FUEL BILLS SUDDENLY DOUBLED AND TRIPLED. THE PRICE OF EVERYTHING THAT DEPENDED ON OIL FOR PRODUCTION OR TRANSPORTATION — I.E., EVERYTHING — WENT UP AND UP AND UP!

RECESSION AND INFLATION TOGETHER! A FIRST!

THE ECONOMY STAGNATED...

BURP

AMERICANS TURNED TO FUEL-EFFICIENT JAPANESE CARS, LEAVING DETROIT TO CHOKE ON THEIR EXHAUST.

SOME POLITICIANS ANNOUNCED THAT WE HAD ENTERED AN ERA OF LIMITS: LIMITS ON RESOURCES, GROWTH, AND WEALTH.

CALIF. GOV. JERRY "MOONBEAM" BROWN

LIMITS ALSO EXISTED
ON U.S. POWER ABROAD:
VIETNAM PROVED THAT!
AFTER VIETNAM,
REVOLUTIONS
FOLLOWED IN
LAOS, CAMBODIA,
ETHIOPIA, ANGOLA,
GUINEA-BISSAU,
MOZAMBIQUE,
SOUTH YEMEN,
IRAN,
NICARAGUA...

ANOTHER GLOBAL EVENT!

ANTI-AMERICANISM RAN HIGH, BECAUSE WHEREVER YOU LOOKED,
THE U.S. OPPOSED POPULAR GOVERNMENTS AND BACKED DICTATORS:

GIT THEM COMMIES!

THE PHILIPPINES?
          THE DICTATOR MARCOS
S. KOREA?
          THE DICTATOR CHUN
NICARAGUA?
          THE   "   SOMOZA
GREECE?
          THE COLONELS
IRAN?
          A SHAH, FOR HEAVEN'S
              SAKE!
ARABIA?
          A KING...

BETWEEN DEMOCRATIC INDIA AND AUTOCRATIC PAKISTAN? WE
LIKE PAKISTAN... DEMOCRATIC CHILE? NIXON'S CIA TOPPLED
PRESIDENT ALLENDE AND INSTALLED THE MONSTROUS PINOCHET

BUT WE LIKE
THE DEMOCRACIES
OF ISRAEL AND
SOUTH AFRICA!

AFTER THE VIETNAM HORROR, THE U.S. BACKED OFF THE HEAVY-HANDED IMPERIAL ACTION. NIXON'S SUCCESSOR, GERALD FORD, WAS THE ONLY PRESIDENT SINCE WORLD WAR II NOT TO CONSIDER ALERTING THE NUCLEAR FORCES.

I COULDN'T FIND THE BUTTON.

THE NEXT PRESIDENT, JIMMY CARTER, SENT AID TO THE NEW NICARAGUAN GOVERNMENT, WHOSE ANTHEM CALLS YANKEES THE "ENEMIES OF MANKIND."*

IT'S O.K. AH'M NOT A YANKEE... AH'M FROM GEORGIA...

HAVE SOME PEANUTS.

BUT EVEN CARTER COULDN'T DEAL WITH THE FUNDAMENTALIST ISLAMIC REVOLUTIONARIES IN IRAN. THEY COMPARED THE U.S. WITH SATAN (UNFAVORABLY).

JUST TRY AND BE FRIENDS WITH US!

THE IRANIANS SEIZED THE U.S. EMBASSY IN TEHRAN, HOLDING 50 PEOPLE HOSTAGE...

*BUT ONLY IN THE SECOND VERSE, SO PROBABLY NOBODY KNOWS IT...

DESPITE INTENSIVE NEGOTIATIONS, CARTER FAILED TO FREE THE HOSTAGES IN TIME FOR THE 1980 ELECTION. A NEWSPAPER EDITORIAL DESCRIBED HIS SPEECHES AS "MUSH FROM THE WIMP."

WRING WRING WRING

AND SO THE ELECTORATE BROUGHT IN A NEW MAN WHO WAS ALSO OLD—

RONALD REAGAN

A 69-YEAR-OLD FORMER ACTOR— PERFECT FOR THE ERA OF THE PERCEPTION GAP!!

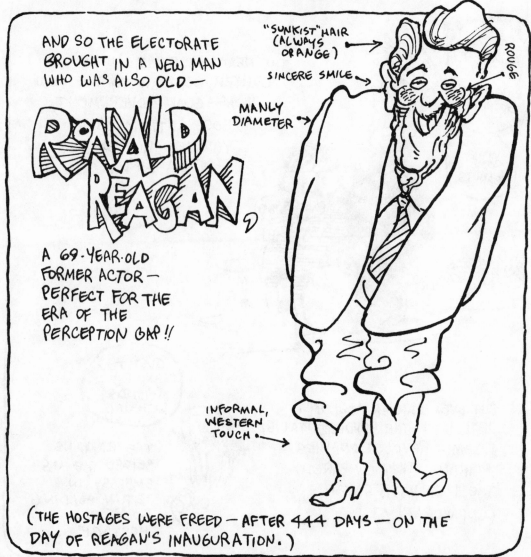

"SUNKIST" HAIR (ALWAYS ORANGE)

ROUGE

SINCERE SMILE

MANLY DIAMETER

INFORMAL, WESTERN TOUCH.

(THE HOSTAGES WERE FREED — AFTER 444 DAYS — ON THE DAY OF REAGAN'S INAUGURATION.)

REAGAN'S SUPPORTERS CALLED HIM FIRM AND CONSISTENT. HIS DETRACTORS SAID HIS IDEAS HAD BEEN FIXED IN STONE LONG AGO.

REAGAN BELIEVED IN LIMITS, TOO, THE OLD-FASHIONED KIND: ON TAXES, FEDERAL SPENDING, AND GOVERNMENT REGULATIONS. THE REAGAN ADMINISTRATION BEGAN TO CUT — POLLUTION CONTROLS, FOOD STAMP BENEFITS, MEDICARE AND EDUCATION OUTLAYS, AND TAXES.

MEANWHILE, HE CALLED FOR MORE SHIPS, MORE TANKS, MORE PLANES, MORE NUKES!

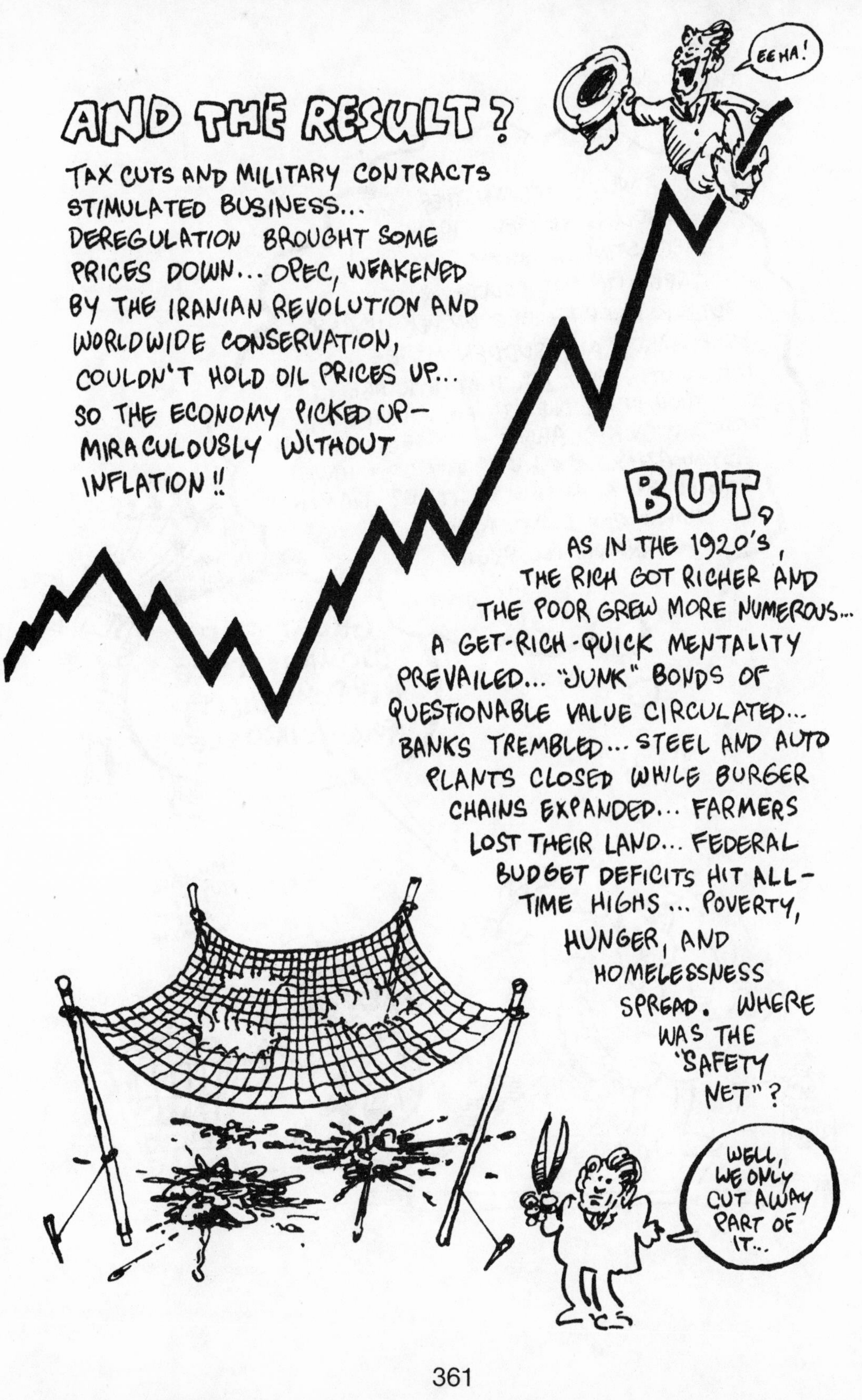

AND THE RESULT?

TAX CUTS AND MILITARY CONTRACTS STIMULATED BUSINESS... DEREGULATION BROUGHT SOME PRICES DOWN... OPEC, WEAKENED BY THE IRANIAN REVOLUTION AND WORLDWIDE CONSERVATION, COULDN'T HOLD OIL PRICES UP... SO THE ECONOMY PICKED UP— MIRACULOUSLY WITHOUT INFLATION!!

EEHA!

BUT,

AS IN THE 1920's, THE RICH GOT RICHER AND THE POOR GREW MORE NUMEROUS... A GET-RICH-QUICK MENTALITY PREVAILED... "JUNK" BONDS OF QUESTIONABLE VALUE CIRCULATED... BANKS TREMBLED... STEEL AND AUTO PLANTS CLOSED WHILE BURGER CHAINS EXPANDED... FARMERS LOST THEIR LAND... FEDERAL BUDGET DEFICITS HIT ALL-TIME HIGHS... POVERTY, HUNGER, AND HOMELESSNESS SPREAD. WHERE WAS THE "SAFETY NET"?

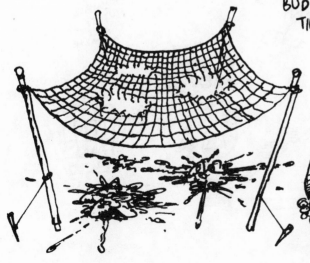

WELL, WE ONLY CUT AWAY PART OF IT...

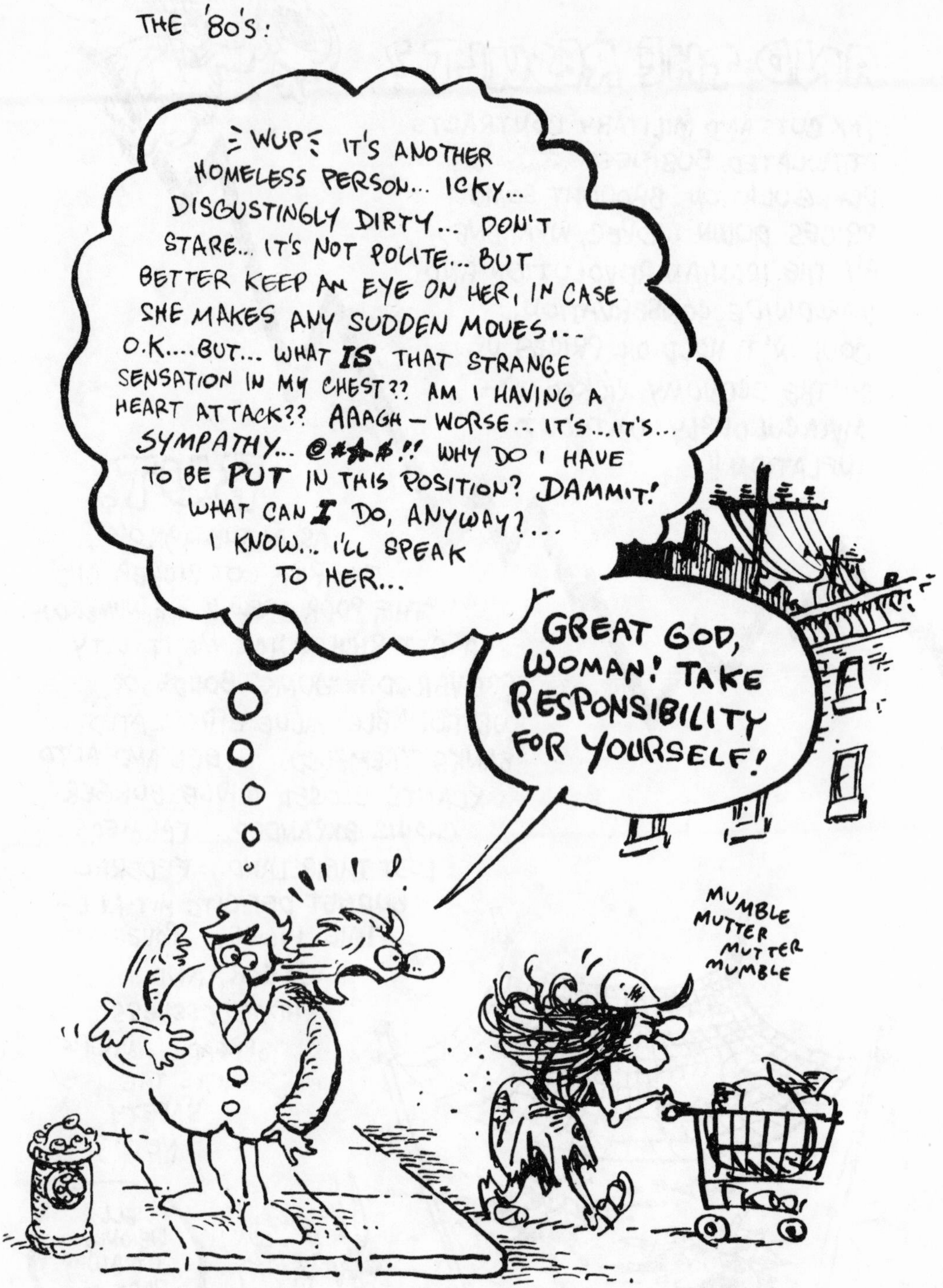
THE '80'S:
≡WUP≡ IT'S ANOTHER HOMELESS PERSON... ICKY... DISGUSTINGLY DIRTY... DON'T STARE... IT'S NOT POLITE... BUT BETTER KEEP AN EYE ON HER, IN CASE SHE MAKES ANY SUDDEN MOVES... O.K.... BUT... WHAT **IS** THAT STRANGE SENSATION IN MY CHEST?? AM I HAVING A HEART ATTACK?? AAAGH — WORSE... IT'S... IT'S... SYMPATHY... @#*$!! WHY DO I HAVE TO BE PUT IN THIS POSITION? DAMMIT! WHAT CAN **I** DO, ANYWAY?... I KNOW... I'LL SPEAK TO HER...
GREAT GOD, WOMAN! TAKE RESPONSIBILITY FOR YOURSELF!
MUMBLE MUTTER MUTTER MUMBLE

BUT NEVER MIND! THE MIGHTY MILITARY MACHINE WAS BACK IN MOTION!! IN 1984, REAGAN ORDERED THE MARINES INTO LEBANON, WITH NO CLEAR MISSION EXCEPT TO BE A PRESENCE.

TWO HUNDRED OF THEM WERE BLOWN UP IN THEIR BEDS... BUT NEVER MIND! REAGAN ORDERED THE NAVY TO OVERTHROW THE MARXIST GOVERNMENT OF GRENADA.

THE ELECTORATE EVIDENTLY PREFERRED REAGAN'S DEAD MARINES TO CARTER'S LIVE HOSTAGES... HE WAS OVERWHELMINGLY RE-ELECTED IN NOVEMBER...

THE POST-VIETNAM SYNDROME STILL RESTRAINED REAGAN FROM INVADING NICARAGUA, SO HE SECRETLY RAISED MONEY FROM FOREIGN GOVERNMENTS TO FUND THE COUNTER-REVOLUTIONARIES.

SEE NO EVIL, HEAR NO EVIL, RECALL NO EVIL..

AID THE CONTRA

THIS THIRD-WORLD TURMOIL, SAID REAGAN, STEMMED FROM THE **SOVIET MENACE.** THE SOVIET MENACE WAS EITHER AN OCTOPUS, A CANCER, OR SOME FALLING DOMINOES.

IT'S A CANCEROUS DOMINO WITH EIGHT LEGS!

AS EVERYONE WHO HADN'T LEARNED ANYTHING SINCE THE '50'S KNEW, THE OCTOPUS LIVED IN MOSCOW...

AND WHEN IT CAME TO MOSCOW THERE WAS ONLY ONE WEAPON' WORTH TALKING ABOUT—

NUKES, GOD BLESS 'EM!

IN THE BEGINNING WAS THE BOMB... IT WAS DROPPED FROM A BOMBER... THEN CAME SPUTNIK, WHICH SHOWED THAT A MISSILE COULD GO ANYWHERE IN HALF AN HOUR... BOMBS BECAME "WARHEADS"... THEN CAME SHORT-, MEDIUM-, AND LONG-RANGE MISSILES... MISSILES WITH MANY INDEPENDENTLY TARGETED WARHEADS ("MIRV'S")... AIR-, GROUND-, AND SEA-LAUNCHED MISSILES... CRUISE MISSILES... NEUTRON BOMBS, BEAM WEAPONS, X-RAY LASERS, ELECTROMAGNETIC PULSE DEVICES... 60,000 WARHEADS IN ALL — ENOUGH TO DESTROY THE WORLD 50 TIMES OVER!

SURELY YOU DON'T THINK THEY ALL WORK?

THE DANGER IS SO OBVIOUS THAT THE SUPERPOWERS HAVE REACHED SEVERAL AGREEMENTS TO MANAGE THE MENACE... THE TEST-BAN TREATY ('63), THE ANTI-BALLISTIC MISSILE TREATY ('72), STRATEGIC ARMS LIMITATION TREATIES I & II ('72 AND '79)... UNDER THE CIRCUMSTANCES, CLOSE COOPERATION WITH THE ADVERSARY IS ESSENTIAL!

GOOD — NOW, LEONID, WOULD YOU PUT ON THE OCTOPUS MASK FOR THE PHOTOGRAPHERS?

AND SO WE LIVE WITH THE PARADOXES OF THE NUCLEAR AGE.

FOR EXAMPLE: YOU CAN'T
ACTUALLY *USE* NUKES, WITHOUT
RISKING PLANETARY
DESTRUCTION... YOU CAN
ONLY *THREATEN* TO
USE THEM!

I'LL BLOW YER BUTT OFF...

ANOTHER PARADOX:
ANTI-MISSILE DEFENSES
CAN DECREASE SECURITY.
WHY? BECAUSE DEFENSES
SEND A SIGNAL TO YOUR
ENEMY THAT YOU THINK
THAT NUCLEAR WAR IS
SURVIVABLE... SO YOU'RE
MORE WILLING TO RISK
A FIRST STRIKE... SO
YOUR ENEMY IS TEMPTED
TO STRIKE FIRST—
IN SELF-DEFENSE!!

IT'S THE PERCEPTION GAP!!

AND THEN CAME REAGAN, WHO ANNOUNCED THAT NUCLEAR WAR WAS "WINNABLE."

HE ABANDONED THE ANTI-BALLISTIC MISSILE LOGIC AND PROPOSED "STAR WARS," DESCRIBED AS A DEFENSIVE SATELLITE SENSOR AND WEAPON SYSTEM, DESIGNED TO DESTROY INCOMING MISSILES AND CONTROLLED BY THE WORLD'S MOST COMPLEX COMPUTER SOFTWARE — WHICH HAS TO WORK PERFECTLY THE FIRST TIME!

THOUSANDS OF SCIENTISTS REFUSED TO WORK ON IT... THEY SAY IT CAN'T WORK... BUT STILL THE RUSSIANS ARE SCARED — AND WHY? BECAUSE STAR WARS HAS **OFFENSIVE** POTENTIAL! WE'RE TALKING DEATH BEAMS FROM SPACE HERE!!

THEN, SUDDENLY, ALONG CAME "GORBY" — MIKHAIL

GORBACHEV."

GESUNDHEIT

(NOT A SNEEZE, BUT A NEW GENERAL SECRETARY OF THE COMMUNIST PARTY OF THE U.S.S.R.)

GORBACHEV AMAZED EVERYONE! IN THE SOVIET UNION HE ANNOUNCED **GLASNOST** (OPENNESS) AND **PERESTROIKA** (ECONOMIC REFORM). DISSIDENTS EMERGED FROM JAIL... EASTERN EUROPE BEGAN TO STIR... AND WHEN GORBACHEV MET REAGAN, THINGS GOT EVEN MORE AMAZING!!

YOU CAN HAVE WHATEVER YOU WANT — THE COLD WAR IS **OVER!**

WHAT?

FOR THE FIRST TIME IN HISTORY, THE SUPERPOWERS AGREED TO **REDUCE** THEIR HEAPS OF NUKES.

WHAT?

SOVIET TROOPS BEGAN LEAVING EASTERN EUROPE. DEMOCRACY ERUPTED UP IN POLAND, CZECHOSLOVAKIA, EAST GERMANY... THE TWO HALVES OF GERMANY REUNITED — IT ALL HAPPENED WITHIN A COUPLE OF YEARS!

AUF WIEDERSEHN!

THERE WAS NO MORE MENTION OF THE "EVIL EMPIRE..." NOW THE CATCH PHRASE WAS

new world order.

IT WOULD ACTUALLY BE RATHER CONFUSING...

...IF I EVER GOT CONFUSED...

IN 1989 REAGAN FINISHED HIS TERM AND WAS SUCCEEDED BY FELLOW-REPUBLICAN GEORGE **BUSH.** BUSH PROMISED "A KINDER, GENTLER AMERICA..."

...WHICH IN NO WAY SHOULD BE TAKEN AS A CRITICISM OF MY PREDECESSOR...

...AND IMMEDIATELY DECLARED A

WAR ON DRUGS.

BUSH

DAMN THE 4TH AMENDMENT! FULL SPEED AHEAD!!

AN ANTI-DRUG CRACKDOWN AT HOME WAS COMBINED WITH THE USE OF U.S. TROOPS IN COLOMBIA, WHERE COCA GREW, AND PANAMA, WHERE COLOMBIANS BANKED.

AND WHO CAN BLAME HIM? DRUGS WERE A REAL PROBLEM! AND SO WERE FALLING REAL WAGES, THE LOSS OF DECENT JOBS, SKYROCKETING HOUSING COSTS, INCREASING POVERTY, DECAYING PUBLIC SCHOOLS, AN EPIDEMIC OF SEXUALLY TRANSMITTED DISEASES, HOMELESSNESS, HOPELESSNESS, AND A NEAR COLLAPSE OF SOCIETY WITHIN THE BURGEONING BLACK UNDERCLASS...

OTHERWISE KNOWN AS "THE UNDERLYING CAUSES!"

BUT AFTER EIGHT YEARS OF TAX-CUTTING AND MILITARY BUILD-UP, THERE "WASN'T ANY MONEY" FOR THESE PROBLEMS.

AND, AS FOR RAISING TAXES, THE PRESIDENT SAID, "READ MY LIPS: NO NEW TAXES."

B·BUT—HE DOESN'T HAVE ANY LIPS...

AH, BUT THERE WAS MONEY FOR THE

SAVINGS & LOAN CRASH/SCANDAL/ CRISIS/MESS

MILLIONS OF AMERICANS HAD PUT THEIR SAVINGS IN SO-CALLED "SAVINGS AND LOAN" OR "THRIFT" INSTITUTIONS. THESE WERE GOVERNMENT-REGULATED BANKS, REQUIRED TO MAKE LOANS PRIMARILY TO BUY AND BUILD HOMES.

BUT REAGAN AND REGULATION WERE LIKE OIL AND WATER! HE THREW OUT THE SAVINGS-AND-LOAN RULEBOOK.

WOW! IS THIS AN INVITATION TO **OUTRIGHT FRAUD**?

PLEASE. CALL IT "ENTERPRISE."

THIS OPENED THE WAY TO "QUESTIONABLE" PRACTICES: SUPER-HIGH RATES PAID ON DEPOSITS, UNSECURED LOANS, RISKY LOANS, LOANS TO THE BANKERS' FRIENDS, ETC ETC ETC....

MA & PA'S LI'L OL' SAVINGS & LOAN

"QUESTIONABLE?" WHAT'S THE QUESTION?

PREDICTABLY, SAVINGS AND LOANS BEGAN TO COLLAPSE — IT SOUNDED JUST LIKE THE 1830's, 1870's, AND 1930's ALL OVER AGAIN!

BOOM

THUD
CRASH FALL

WHAT ABOUT MY LIFE'S SAVINGS?

BUT HEY! THIS TIME, EVERY DEPOSIT WAS INSURED, UP TO $100,000, BY THE FEDERAL GOVERNMENT. NO PROBLEM! WELL, MAYBE ONE PROBLEM: THERE WASN'T ENOUGH CASH IN THE INSURANCE FUND TO COVER THE LOSSES. IN FACT, THERE WOULDN'T HAVE BEEN ENOUGH IN TEN FUNDS...

PRESIDENT BUSH PLEDGED THE GOVERNMENT TO BACK EVERY LAST DOLLAR OF LOST DEPOSIT, NO MATTER IF IT COST

$150 BILLION—

A DRAIN ON THE TREASURY FOR YEARS TO COME.

OOP. MAKE THAT $250 BILLION.

UM... $500 BILLION...

ER—. $800 BILLION?

WE OWE IT TO OURSELVES — LITERALLY!

MEANWHILE, BACK ON THE INTERNATIONAL SCENE, THE "NEW WORLD ORDER" WAS LOOKING MORE DISORDERLY. GORBACHEV'S REFORMS WERE LEADING THE USSR INTO CHAOS, MAYBE EVEN COMPLETE DISINTEGRATION.

BUT DON'T WORRY — WE STILL LIKE YOU...

JUST ONE THING— WHO HAS THE NUKES?

THEN, IN AUGUST, 1990, THE OIL-RICH PERSIAN GULF ERUPTED WHEN **IRAQ** INVADED ITS SMALL BUT INCREDIBLY RICH NEIGHBOR **KUWAIT.**

THE WEST HAS PUSHED THE ARABS AROUND LONG ENOUGH! IT'S TIME WE PUSHED EACH OTHER AROUND!

IN PREVIOUS YEARS, EAST AND WEST HAD COMBINED TO BUILD UP THE IRAQI MILITARY TO STAGGERING PROPORTIONS. A COUNTRY OF 17 MILLION PEOPLE, IRAQ NOW HAD HALF A MILLION IN ARMS, 5000 TANKS, CHEMICAL WEAPONS, A NUCLEAR PROGRAM, HARDENED BUNKERS, UNDERGROUND AIR FIELDS (!) — AND ONE OF THE WORST HUMAN RIGHTS RECORDS ON THE PLANET.

OOPS!

WHY DID THE U.S. MAKE WAR ON IRAQ? WAS IT TO PRESERVE THE IMMENSE KUWAITI INVESTMENT IN THE WESTERN ECONOMY? WAS IT TO IMPOSE THE "NEW WORLD ORDER" ON THE MIDDLE EAST? WAS IT TO PROTECT U.S. ACCESS TO OIL? THE ANSWER STILL ISN'T CLEAR — BUT IT CERTAINLY WASN'T TO PRESERVE KUWAITI DEMOCRACY (IT DIDN'T HAVE ONE!). WITH THE BACKING OF THE UNITED NATIONS, INCLUDING THE USSR, THE UNITED STATES BEGAN BOMBING IRAQ IN JANUARY, 1991 — IT WAS THE HEAVIEST BOMBARDMENT EVER...

FORTY DAYS AND FORTY NIGHTS OF BOMBING, A GROUND ASSAULT LASTING A MERE FIVE DAYS, AND IRAQ WAS VANQUISHED — UNLIKE THE DOMESTIC PROBLEMS....

WELL! THE WORLD HAS CERTAINLY CHANGED SINCE 1776!

WE FACE CHALLENGES UNDREAMED OF THEN: TECHNOLOGICAL THREATS TO LIFE, LIMB, AND PRIVACY; ENVIRONMENTAL PRESERVATION; BUREAUCRACY IN GOVERNMENT AND BUSINESS; SOCIALISM, UNIONS, AND OTHER ASSERTIONS OF WORKERS' RIGHTS; AND THE RIGHTS OF WOMEN.

AND, AT THE SAME TIME, THE FOUNDING FATHERS' ISSUES REMAIN LIVE ONES: RACIAL JUSTICE, RESTRAINTS ON GOVERNMENT POWER, FREE EXPRESSION OF IDEAS, RELIGIOUS TOLERATION, SECURITY OF OUR HOMES AND SELVES, ECONOMIC JUSTICE...

AND MIRACULOUSLY, THE FOUNDERS' CONSTITUTION ALSO REMAINS, TO GUARANTEE EVERY CITIZEN SOME VOICE AND INFLUENCE IN FACING THESE PROBLEMS.

NOW THAT'S EXCITING!

HOW WILL IT ALL TURN OUT, ONE WONDERS...?

IN ONE SENSE, THE HISTORIAN IS THE LUCKIEST OF AUTHORS:
UNLIKE THE NOVELIST, WHO ENDS A BOOK AT THE END, THE
HISTORIAN ALWAYS FINISHES IN THE MIDDLE OF THE
STORY.   NO TIDY, PAT CONCLUSIONS HERE!

IN FACT, I THINK I'LL END THE BOOK IN THE MIDDLE OF A...

END

BIBLIOGRAPHY

BAILEY, T.A., *THE AMERICAN PAGEANT*, 4TH EDITION, LEXINGTON, HEATH, 1971; A FAT, STANDARD, SELF-SATISFIED TEXT

BAYLISS, J.F. *BLACK SLAVE NARRATIVES*, N.Y., MACMILLAN, 1970

BRAILSFORD, H.N., *THE LEVELLERS & THE ENGLISH REVOLUTION*, PALO ALTO, STANFORD, 1961

BILLINGS, WARREN, *THE OLD DOMINION IN THE SEVENTEENTH CENTURY*, CHAPEL HILL, U. OF N. CAROLINA PRESS, 1975; GOOD INSIGHTS INTO OLD VIRGINNY

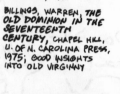

BRODIE, F., *NO MAN KNOWS MY HISTORY*, 2ND EDITION, N.Y., KNOPF, 1972; THE AMAZING STORY OF JOSEPH SMITH, FOUNDER OF MORMONISM

BRODIE, F., *THOMAS JEFFERSON, AN INTIMATE HISTORY*, N.Y., NORTON, 1974; THE LIFE & LOVES OF OUR FUN-LOVING FOUNDING FATHER

CAULFIELD, C., *THE IRON WILL OF JEFFERSON DAVIS*, N.Y., HARCOURT, BRACE, JOVANOVICH, 1978

COLEMAN, R.J., *LIBERTY AND PROPERTY*, N.Y., SCRIBNER'S, 1951; A GOOD, OLD-FASHIONED NARRATIVE OF COLONIAL TIMES

DAVIS, W.C., *THE DEEP WATERS OF THE PROUD* (3 VOLS), N.Y., DOUBLEDAY, 1982, '83; THE COMPLETE CIVIL WAR

DOUGLASS, F., *NARRATIVE OF THE LIFE OF FREDERICK DOUGLASS, AN AMERICAN SLAVE*, CAMBRIDGE, MA, HARVARD, 1960; THE SECTION ON PLANTATION MUSIC IS ESPECIALLY POWERFUL

EDMUNDS, R.D., *TECUMSEH AND THE QUEST FOR INDIAN LEADERSHIP*, BOSTON, LITTLE BROWN, 1984

FONER, P., ED., *LIFE AND WRITINGS OF FREDERICK DOUGLASS*, N.Y., INTERNATIONAL PUBLISHERS, 1950; DO YOURSELF A FAVOR & SAMPLE THIS BRILLIANT PROSE!

GREENE, L.J., *THE NEGRO IN COLONIAL NEW ENGLAND 1620-1776*, PORT WASHINGTON, KENNIKAT PRESS, 1966; A NEGLECTED SUBJECT

HIGGINSON, T.W., *ARMY LIFE IN A BLACK REGIMENT*, MICHIGAN STATE U., 1960; CIVIL WAR CLASSIC

HUGHES, L., MELTZER, M., AND LINCOLN, C.E., *A PICTORIAL HISTORY OF BLACK AMERICANS*, N.Y., CROWN, 1973

HULTON, P., ED., *AMERICA 1585*, CHAPEL HILL, U. OF N. CAROLINA PRESS, 1984; THE STUNNING WATERCOLORS BY JOHN WHITE, GOVERNOR OF THE "LOST COLONY"

JAMES, M., *THE LIFE OF ANDREW JACKSON*, N.Y., BOBBS-MERRILL, 1938; MUST BE READ TO BE BELIEVED!

KETCHAM, R., *BENJAMIN FRANKLIN*, N.Y., WASHINGTON SQ. PRESS, 1966

LONGFORD, EARL OF, *ABRAHAM LINCOLN*, N.Y., PUTNAM, 1975

LYND, S., *CLASS CONFLICT, SLAVERY, & THE UNITED STATES CONSTITUTION*, N.Y., BOBBS-MERRILL, 1967; A PENETRATING ANALYSIS

ROWBOTHAM, S., *HIDDEN FROM HISTORY*, N.Y., PANTHEON, 1974; THE IMPACT OF THE INDUSTRIAL REVOLUTION ON FAMILY LIFE

SCHROEDER, J.H., *MR. POLK'S WAR*, MADISON, U. OF WISCONSIN PRESS, 1973; THE POLITICS BEHIND AMERICA'S LEAST-KNOWN WAR

TROLLOPE, F., *DOMESTIC MANNERS OF THE AMERICANS*, N.Y., OXFORD U. PRESS, 1984; EYEWITNESS ACCOUNT FROM 1832

WILSON, R.R., *LINCOLN IN CARICATURE*, N.Y., HORIZON, 1953; A REMINDER THAT LINCOLN WAS LAMPOONED

WRIGHT, T., *A CARICATURE HISTORY OF THE GEORGES*, LONDON, CHATTO & WINDAM, 1904; 18TH C. ENGLAND THRU THE EYES OF CARTOONISTS—A FORGOTTEN MASTERPIECE!

ZINN, H., *A PEOPLE'S HISTORY OF THE UNITED STATES*, N.Y., HARPER & ROW, 1980; POLEMICAL & ICONOCLASTIC

PART II

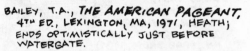

BAILEY, T.A., *THE AMERICAN PAGEANT*, 4TH ED., LEXINGTON, MA, 1971, HEATH; ENDS OPTIMISTICALLY JUST BEFORE WATERGATE.

BERNSTEIN, I., *THE LEAN YEARS*, N.Y., PLENUM, 1960; LABOR IN THE 1920'S.

BOYER, R., + MORAIS, H., *LABOR'S UNTOLD STORY*, N.Y., UE, 1955; UNITED ELECTRICAL WORKERS, 1955; USEFUL BUT BIASED.

CRONON, E.D., *BLACK MOSES: THE STORY OF MARCUS GARVEY*. MADISON, WISC, U. OF WISC., 1969.

DE TOLEDANO, R., *J. EDGAR HOOVER*, NEW ROCHELLE, N.Y., ARLINGTON HOUSE, 1973; UNCRITICAL IF NOT WORSHIPFUL.

BRECHER, J., *STRIKE!*, SAN FRANCISCO, STRAIGHT ARROW BOOKS, 1972; FULL ACCOUNT OF 1877; MAKES A CASE THAT DIRECT ACTION, NOT UNIONS, HELPS WORKERS.

DOYLE, E., + WEISS, S., *THE VIETNAM EXPERIENCE*, IN SEVERAL VOLUMES, BOSTON, BOSTON PUBLISHING CO, 1984; LOADS OF PIX AND INFO.

DU BOIS, W.E.B., *BLACK RECONSTRUCTION IN AMERICA*, N.Y., ATHENEUM, 1979; SCHOLARLY YET IMPASSIONED.

BRODIE, F., *THADDEUS STEVENS, SCOURGE OF THE SOUTH*, N.Y., NORTON, 1959; FINE BIO.

CODY, W.F., *AN AUTOBIOGRAPHY OF BUFFALO BILL*, N.Y., COSMOPOLITAN, 1920; A LIFE OR A LIE?

FRIED, R.M., *MEN AGAINST McCARTHY*, N.Y., COLUMBIA U. PRESS, 1976; THE "MEN" IN QUESTION, MOSTLY DEMOCRATS, INCLUDE SEN. MARGARET CHASE SMITH.

CONNELL, E., *SON OF THE MORNING STAR*, N.Y., HARPER & ROW, 1984; RAMBLING BUT THOROUGH ACCOUNT OF CUSTER, THE SIOUX, AND THEIR MEETING.

GALBRAITH, J.K., *THE AFFLUENT SOCIETY*, 3RD ED., N.Y., NEW AMERICAN LIBRARY, 1978; A CLASSIC.

GALBRAITH, J.K, *THE AGE OF UNCERTAINTY*, BOSTON, HOUGHTON MIFFLIN, 1977; BASED ON A TV SERIES.

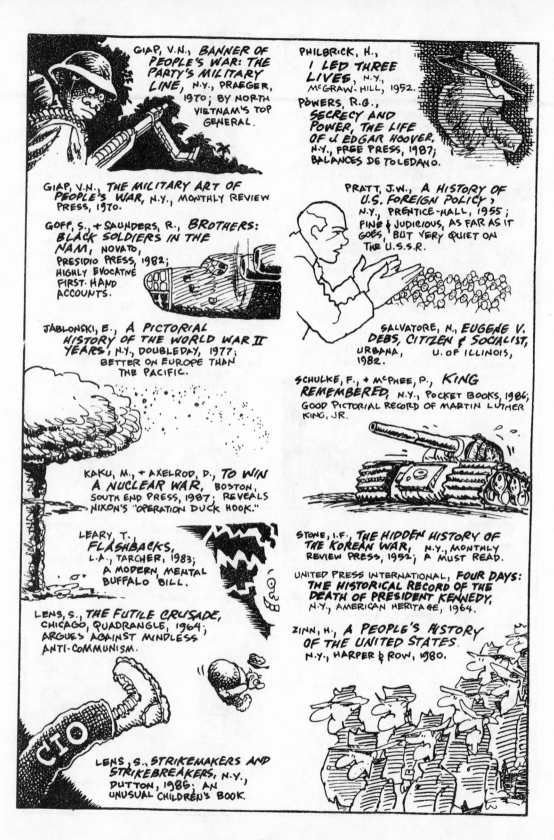

GIAP, V.N., *BANNER OF PEOPLE'S WAR: THE PARTY'S MILITARY LINE*, N.Y., PRAEGER, 1970; BY NORTH VIETNAM'S TOP GENERAL.

GIAP, V.N., *THE MILITARY ART OF PEOPLE'S WAR*, N.Y., MONTHLY REVIEW PRESS, 1970.

GOFF, S., + SAUNDERS, R., *BROTHERS: BLACK SOLDIERS IN THE NAM*, NOVATO, PRESIDIO PRESS, 1982; HIGHLY EVOCATIVE FIRST-HAND ACCOUNTS.

JABLONSKI, E., *A PICTORIAL HISTORY OF THE WORLD WAR II YEARS*, N.Y., DOUBLEDAY, 1977; BETTER ON EUROPE THAN THE PACIFIC.

KAKU, M., + AXELROD, D., *TO WIN A NUCLEAR WAR*, BOSTON, SOUTH END PRESS, 1987; REVEALS NIXON'S "OPERATION DUCK HOOK."

LEARY, T., *FLASHBACKS*, L.A., TARCHER, 1983; A MODERN MENTAL BUFFALO BILL.

LENS, S., *THE FUTILE CRUSADE*, CHICAGO, QUADRANGLE, 1964; ARGUES AGAINST MINDLESS ANTI-COMMUNISM.

LENS, S., *STRIKEMAKERS AND STRIKEBREAKERS*, N.Y., DUTTON, 1985; AN UNUSUAL CHILDREN'S BOOK.

PHILBRICK, H., *I LED THREE LIVES*, N.Y., McGRAW-HILL, 1952.

POWERS, R.G., *SECRECY AND POWER, THE LIFE OF J. EDGAR HOOVER*, N.Y., FREE PRESS, 1987; BALANCES DE TOLEDANO.

PRATT, J.W., *A HISTORY OF U.S. FOREIGN POLICY*, N.Y., PRENTICE-HALL, 1955; FINE & JUDICIOUS, AS FAR AS IT GOES, BUT VERY QUIET ON THE U.S.S.R.

SALVATORE, N., *EUGENE V. DEBS, CITIZEN & SOCIALIST*, URBANA, U. OF ILLINOIS, 1982.

SCHULKE, F., + McPHEE, P., *KING REMEMBERED*, N.Y., POCKET BOOKS, 1986; GOOD PICTORIAL RECORD OF MARTIN LUTHER KING, JR.

STONE, I.F., *THE HIDDEN HISTORY OF THE KOREAN WAR*, N.Y., MONTHLY REVIEW PRESS, 1952; A MUST READ.

UNITED PRESS INTERNATIONAL, *FOUR DAYS: THE HISTORICAL RECORD OF THE DEATH OF PRESIDENT KENNEDY*, N.Y., AMERICAN HERITAGE, 1964.

ZINN, H., *A PEOPLE'S HISTORY OF THE UNITED STATES*, N.Y., HARPER & ROW, 1980.

INDEX

West, American:
  expansion of, 135
  exploration of, 120
Williams, Roger, 24
Wilson, Woodrow, 251, 252, 255,
    259, 260, 261, 262, 263
Witchcraft trials, 33
Women, 247, 265, 268, 284, 295, 313
Women, abolitionists, 152
Women's Liberation, 187, 265, 266,
    350–51
Women's movement, 152–53
Women's Rights Convention, 153
Worker's compensation, 252
Worker's Party, 232
Workers, 187, 229, 240
  black, 184, 288
  Chinese, 284
  in Depression, 286
  wages, of, 185, 230, 233, 240,
    248, 252, 277
  women, 295
  and World War I, 254
  See also Labor; Strikes

Working conditions, 19th century,
  146
World War I, 253–59, 290, 304
World War II, 292–301, 320
  Allied invasion of France in,
    296
  Allied victory in, 296, 297
  invasion of North Africa in, 296
Wounded Knee (S. Dakota), 246
WPA (Works Progress Administra-
  tion), 281
Wright, Martha, 153
Wyoming, 247

Yorktown, Virginia, battle of, 89
Young, Brigham, 139

Zenger, Peter, 36
  and class struggle, 233
  free market, 185–87, 277, 361
  and GNP, 312
  and housing, 312–13, 361
  and New Deal, 280–83
  war, 294